BUSTED! THE BIG CON

How The Media, Politicians, and
Wall Street's Game of Charades
Are Destroying Our Country

Jay D. Glass, Ph.D.
Donington Press, Ltd. Inc. © 2012

BIOGRAPHY: JAY D. GLASS, Ph.D.

Dr. Glass has a BS degree in psychology from Tulane University (1967), a dual Ph.D. in psychology and neurobiology from the Center for Brain Research at the University of Rochester (1972) and a post-doctoral fellowship at New York's Albert Einstein College of Medicine. He spent a decade as a neuroscientist and teacher at the University of Pittsburgh School of Medicine.

In 1981, entrepreneurial interests led Dr. Glass to obtain an MBA degree from the University of Pittsburgh. He spent five years with the venture capital group of Henry Hillman, pioneer of both leveraged buy-outs and venture capital. In 1987, Dr. Glass founded MedCorp Development Fund, the largest single-person venture capital fund in the United States. He has served on the board of directors of many public and privately-held companies.

Dr. Glass has written 3 books, *The Animal Within Us: Lessons About Life from Our Animal Ancestors; Soldiers of God; and The Power of Faith, Mother Nature's Gift.* He is active in wildlife and wilderness preservation. He lives in Laguna Beach, CA and Jackson Hole, WY.

DEDICATION

This book is dedicated to my parents who gave me the genes that caused me to think these ideas and to write this book

Copyright ©2012 by Jay D. Glass, Ph.D. All rights reserved. No part of this publication may be reproduced, distributed, or transmitted in any form or by any means, including photocopying, recording, or other electronic or mechanical methods or by an information storage and retrieval system, without prior written permission from the publisher. For permission requests, write to the publisher, to the attention of the Permissions Coordinator at the address below.

Published By:
Donington Press, Ltd., Inc.
P.O. Box 22
Corona del Mar, CA
92625-0022

Library of Congress Cataloging-in-Publication Data

Glass, Jay D.
Busted! the big con : how the media, politicians, and Wall Street's game of charades are destroying our country / Jay D. Glass.
p. cm.
Includes bibliographical references.
ISBN 978-0-9660536-2-3 (ebook) -- ISBN 978-0-9660536-3-0 (pbk.)
1. Fraud--United States--History--21st century. 2. Deception--United States--History--21st century. 3. United States--Economic conditions--2001-2009. 4. United States--Economic conditions--2009- I. Title.
HV6695.G55 2012
364.1'3230973--dc23
2011047378

Table of Contents

I. Welcome to the United States of Charades	5
II. Charades Played By Pros	12
III. War on Drugs Charade: Not In My Backyard	24
IV. Wall Street's Charade Takes Down The Economy	38
V. Student Athlete!!! Oxymoron of Charades	65
VI. A Flim-Flam Charade: Health Care Cost Control	79
VII. A Deadly Game of Charades	109
VIII. Charadelettes: from Art to Nice Guys	116
IX. If it Bleeds It Leads: Talking Head Charades	137
X. Politicians: Charades As a Way of Life	149
XI. The Grand Charade: U.S. is #1	184
XII. The Academy Awards of Charades	205
XIII. Will It Ever Stop, Our Future Hangs in the Balance	208
XIV. Epilogue	218

I. WELCOME TO THE

UNITED STATES OF CHARADES

Something has happened in the United States. It is not working anymore. This claim is not just an old fogy like myself, as seems to occur in every generation, saying "back in the good old days." Instead it is about facts, statistics on this or that parameter by which countries are measured and compared with one another. We are losing our place as the unambiguous #1 in the world. Our standing amongst the community of nations has in the past decade been on a rapid descent.

Why should this be important? It is very important since the quality of our lives, from education to health care, to standard of living is highly dependent upon our ability to make things go our way in a globalized economy. If we are vulnerable, our ability to for example negotiate favorable trade agreements or to get our hands on scarce natural resources is reduced. We can be pushed around in that variety of interactions that occur with other nations. As we begin to lose our ability to make things go our way, we will fall further and further down the "quality of life" list.

There are several measures comparing ourselves with other countries where the facts are stark. Studies on student test scores show the United States is not even in the top ten amongst developed countries. Our health care on many measures is similarly out of the top ten. We are however #1 in amount of money spent per student and per patient. We spend more than any other country yet we accomplish not as much. Something is indeed happening and it is not good. Not good in particular as several of the Asian and European countries pass us by economically.

The day must soon come when our main competitors will decide to overtake us in one area that we are still #1, the percentage of our gross domestic product (GDP) that we spend on our military. Their economic muscle will eventually be transformed into military muscle, then the real fun will begin. How about that competition for rare-earth minerals without which high-tech does not exist, only so much of that stuff around. This will not be the first time that sabers have been rattled over access to crucial natural resources. Our once glistening saber will soon appear dull in comparison to the sabers of other countries and the impact will be felt in our quality of life.

We watch as our elected representatives act at times almost clownish, whether it is setting economic policy, regulatory affairs, or playing around with the laws of the land. Our military forays in the international arena end up as quagmires of fuzzy outcomes, much less not even knowing what the outcome is we want. Most often it seems the politicians are more interested in playing to the idiosyncratic attitudes of a minority segment of their local electorate to insure reelection than doing what is good for the sake of all Americans.

The folks who destroy our economy get bailed out by the government, none are prosecuted and just 2 years later they are making bonuses bigger than before the crisis. Goldman Sachs top 5 compensation in 2010, $70 million, 13 times higher than 2009 even though the owners of the business, the stockholders, have seen the value of their holdings tumble. Thanks to the politicians, those who created our financial meltdown are now more prosperous than before it happened.

Main Street however is suffering terribly. The gap in wealth between the top few percent and everyone else is at record levels and grows every year. A weird example of this is that the fastest growing demographic on "mutually beneficial relationship" websites are young women turning in increasing numbers to the world's oldest profession to finance their college education.

The United States just seems to have lost its mojo. As the tag line from the movie *Network* said: "we are mad as hell and we are not going to take it anymore." Well, I hope through this book to explain why and how all the dismal facts about our downward slide came to be. It is only through understanding the nuts and bolts of how it all went downhill so fast that we can start to make the changes to bring the United States back to its position of leadership.

The theme of this book is that there are three institutions within our country that are the major influences on how well our country and its people are making their way from one day to the next. These institutions that hold our personal fate and the country's fate in their hands are the media, politicians, and Wall Street. It is the changes in these institutions over the past few decades that have sent us downhill. All three are playing a game of charades upon the American people. Out of mutual self-interest they play a game of charades that benefits no one but themselves.

Once upon a time, Wall Street balanced making money for themselves with trying not to lose the money of the people who entrusted their live-savings to them. These days they tout the latest high-tech public offerings with their own research analyst reports that the company is the greatest thing since slice bread. It took the tech-bubble bursting and the destruction of billions in household's wealth for the media to expose that those same companies described by the glowing analyst reports were at the same time described in internal memos as "a piece of s_ _t."

The investment banks sold mortgage backed securities to clients as virtually risk free, yet internally with their own money, they bet that their value would fall. With the media making money from "everyman" watching the financial networks and the politicians reaping massive campaign contributions from these investments banks, the media and governmental watchdogs closed their eyes while these bubbles were inflated, not wanting to compromise their own self-interest. Charades played upon the American public out of a mutual self-interest between politicians, Wall Street, and the media.

The term "muckraking" once upon a time had no red or blue state color to it. The media kept a wary eye on politicians and on Wall Street and raked the muck when those making it deserved to be exposed. The media are supposed to present the people who watch their shows with a certain caliber of truthfulness in the news. Today, all the national media are a part of a conglomerate whose stock is traded on Wall Street. Maximizing ratings maximizes ad revenues which maximizes profit. As publicly traded entities it is hard to argue that maximizing their profits should not be the main goal.

Once upon a time it used to be that the individual owners of these broadcast and print media, although some on the right and others on the left, were responsible to no one but themselves so when push came to shove they did what they felt was in the best interest of the country. Today, the financial statement's bottom line determines what we are told and from what perspective. What is in our or the country's best interest is now a far distant second place to the parent company's self-interest.

The campaign contributions that keep politicians elected, the investment bank's prosperity, and the media's profits are all inextricably linked. It is in each of their best interests to turn a blind eye to the others games of charades: "I won't rain on your parade if you don't rain on mine." The decline in the United States' standing in the world is the result. The country and its citizens suffer financially, educationally, as well as in other ways to be described in the chapters to come while the politicians, Wall Street, and the media prosper. Charades after all have no substance, they are just charades. An economy and its country built on a game of charades is doomed for trouble.

The old line about how you know when a politician is lying, "Whenever his lips are moving" is more true than false. As the financial meltdown showed us, Wall Street is duplicitous beyond even our wildest imagination. The media works behind an all too thin veil about what master they serve, telling and showing us a kernel of truth wrapped in a thick layer of spin designed to maximize their ratings. Ugh! China is licking its lips.

In the past, as Democrats and Republicans swapped control of the Presidency, Supreme Court, and Congress, one decision went a bit left of center and another went bit to the right. In the main, a part of our country's prosperity, no matter what the measure, has come about by our not letting an extreme minority on either side of the middle-ground set the agenda. Filibuster statistics show that it was used once per Congressional session in the 1950s and 30 times per session in the 1990s. Votes for cloture, the ending of a filibuster went up from 160 in the period 1970-1980 to 420 from 2001-2010.

Partisanship has brought the country to its knees, a stagnation while others are rapidly catching up to us. If we ever needed a consensus it is now. Today is absolutely the wrong time for this partisan bickering. Instead of working for the best interests of the country, individual politicians look to placate a small and fringe point of view that in a close election will spell the difference between reelection and their having to find an honest job.

The destructive impact upon the country as a whole of politicians placating small extremist voting groups as is happening today was predicted in 1982 by the Nobel Prize winning economist Mancur Olson in his book, *The Rise and Decline of Nations*. Mr. Olson warned that as elections became closer and closer, special-interest groups would demand action on their behalf in exchange for delivering a solid voting bloc to politicians. Mr. Olson warns that these policies may win the support of this small group and be beneficial to only them, but the cost of these policies would be spread over all Americans, inhibiting the country's growth and producing economic stagnation.

With our elections being decided by a few percentage points, Mr. Olson's warning has come true. A small but coherent voting group can have a significant impact on policies that affect all Americans way out of proportion to the special interest group's size when measured against the country's total population.

In writing this book, I am faced with a big challenge because everything is now so partisan. Do I describe a charade in the regulation of Wall Street that might cast aspersions against the former president George W. Bush and by doing so provoke in about half my readership, the thought about me and my book, "what a pile of crap, screw him"? Or do I risk provoking the other half to the same thoughts if I talk about how the Democratic majority leader in the Senate, Harry Reid of Nevada, is helping the United State flush $15 billion already spent down the toilet by his blocking the opening of the nuclear storage facility in his home state of Nevada?

Maybe I will piss off folks on both sides by asking the question of why the country is so upset and cares so much that over the eight years of the Iraq and Afghanistan wars about 5000 of our soldiers have died. Yet we seem not to give a damn that each and every year more than 30,000 Americans die on our roads. 240,000 killed on our highways during the course of these wars compared with 5000 in battles. Why does the cause behind the 5000 elicit such outrage and the 240,000 not a whimper. To make it even more peculiar, if we spent an amount on automotive safety that would be a rounding error in the amount spent every year on these wars, we could save as many Americans every year that died in Iraq and Afghanistan during all the years of these wars combined.

The answer is that what concerns us is what the media presents to us in a concerning way. They choose to present to us events and issues that will win the best ratings. It is just a big game of charades, and we play along. 5000 dead Americans and 240,000 dead Americans over the same period time, yet we never hear about what is killing 240,000. Think about it.

So I will make every effort to avoid provoking the reader's partisan sensibilities, but sometimes the numbers speak for themselves. Trust me though; there are more games of charades happening on both sides of the political aisles than I have space to mention in this book. Evening it out will not be hard. I am sure however that we all will agree that the tragedy is that most of these charades are played by people who do not seem to give a damn about what happens to the country and its people. They don't give a damn even though they are the ones in whom we put our trust, whether it is the people making choices in Washington, controlling what we hear and read through the media, or on Wall Street looking after our finances.

Here is a brief glimpse of a few additional charades exposed in the coming chapters. For example, over the past several decades, tens of billions have been spent on something called the War on Drugs. In the past the war was mostly fought in Peru, Bolivia, Columbia, whereas now it is focused on Mexico. In spite of all this money and lives lost, there is more drug use in the United States and drugs are more readily available now than when the war began.

Perhaps the most grotesque aspect of this charade is that when someone is murdered with a gun or run over by a car, it is a long standing principle of U.S. law that the manufacturer is not liable, instead it is the consumer/user who pulled the trigger or drove the car that is held liable. Yet somehow, the rampant drug use is here in the U.S., but the war is being fought south of our border. So for drugs, it is the producer that is bearing the main responsibility not the consumer. Why for everything else is it the user that gets the blame, not the manufacturer. Can you imagine if we put that much effort and money into fighting drug use here in the U.S. Any of you out there ever smoked marijuana—striped pajamas for you.

In almost every major college football or basketball game on television, there is a mention of how proud the NCAA is of its student athletes. "You can't be serious." Daily, new allegations appear in the press of cheating by the schools to recruit great athletes who are grotesquely unqualified academically. We now have a whole new group of "Joe Colleges" distinguished by their rap sheets as much as their high school transcripts. Stop the charade, let's just pay the players and call them a minor league as has served baseball so well. Can you imagine the Dallas Cowboy's farm team, SMU, playing the Houston Texans' farm team, University of Texas or the Dolphins farm team, U. Miami, playing the Tampa Bay Bucs farm team, Florida State. If they so desire, let the minor league players earn a few credits toward a degree cost-free each semester. Everyone wins, big bucks all around for everyone involved, in particular those who have been the main promoters of the charade from its inception, the TV networks.

The whole hullabaloo over cutting our health care spending has been about private versus public insurance, who pays for workers premiums, and other issues that are simply about shifting the burden for paying these bills from one person to another. It is clear that we pay over twice as much for health care than any other developed country and get in comparison second tier service. The only issue that will change this outrage is looking into the health care equivalent of the thousand dollar hammer from the defense industry exposé. As long as the makers of the products used in health care and the providers of the services can charge whatever they want and the private insurers simply raise premiums or the government ups reimbursement to cover these costs without asking hard questions, nothing will change.

Here is how the Congress works. The oil spills in the gulf due to falsification of inspection records and complete failure by regulatory agencies with which the oil companies have a very cozy meant in its most literal way relationship. People die in coal mining accidents due to the government regulators grotesque incompetence. Safety records and inspections are few and far between and government inspections are announced long before they happen.

So people die on the oil rigs and in the coal mines as well as the SEC fails to spot billions of dollars in fraud in spite of people screaming at them that it is going on. Following such events, the curtains open upon the Broadway of the game of charades, Congressional hearings. The House and the Senate each hold their own hearings. The committees in each under whose jurisdiction the industry falls also hold hearings. Hearings about the same stuff with the same people in the witness chair. Instead of focusing on questioning those responsible, the representatives give speeches of outrage and desire "to protect the citizens of these great United States from this ever happening again."

After the hearings are held, Congress's ladies and gentlemen announce widespread new regulations so that this will never happen again. Several years later it always seems that the final language is still to be written and what will be written is a greatly watered down version. It is all simply elaborately staged theater to provide sound bites for the voracious appetite of the 24 hour new cycle. A well-choreographed game of charades.

There is one charade that is a thread woven through the fabric of this book. It is an easy one to point out. I am certainly not the first. Dwight Eisenhower warned about it and Ross Perot spent a fortune running for the Presidency by trying to alert America to its dangers. We think of other countries as third-rate because they are run with graft, bribery, and corruption. We are led to believe these countries will never make it to the top because of the inefficiencies brought about to their governments and to their industry by these evil deeds.

Yet if the truth be told, the United States is no different, no different at all, glaringly no different. In fact, bribery, graft and corruption are so much a part of the relationship between business and government here in the United States that we have institutionalized them by giving them a collective name, lobbying. Read on.

II. CHARADES PLAYED BY THE PROS

As a way to begin our understanding of how this mutuality of self-interest between the media, Wall Street, and politicians can let things go so terribly wrong, let us take a look at two specific case studies. One is the collapse of one of America's greatest investment banks, Lehman Brothers, and the other is the BP oil spill which had several games of charades ongoing at the same time and both resulted in the grandest charade of all, Congressional hearings followed by "regulations."

CASE #1

There are three types of banks. One are the banks that built themselves by serving business and individual customers with the types of services that most us of think of banks as offering, such as checking and saving accounts as well as making loans for a variety of purposes. A second are the banks known as investment banks that grew up providing expert financial advice to large companies both on their internal finances as well as assisting in growing through providing advice on mergers, acquisitions, selling parts of their business, and raising money through both debt and equity offerings. The third type are a blend of the two, combining investment banking with the traditional retail banking services. Most local banks, known as community banks are the first type whereas almost all national and international banks are the third type.

In the great banking crisis of 2008 several of the national and international banks neared collapse. The community banks suffered but mostly not from their own actions but as part of the fall-out from the troubles of the larger banks. Thanks to a government bailout or just a major restructuring most of the major banks survived. Others were on their way to filing bankruptcy but before they did so, they were acquired at fire-sale prices by other banks. One major bank did enter bankruptcy, Lehman Brothers.

Lehman Brothers was not just any bank. It had a revered place in the history of American investment banking. Its origin goes back to 1844 when a 23 year old Henry Lehman left a prosperous family of cattle merchants in Bavaria and moved to Montgomery, Alabama. Over the next few years two of his brothers came and joined him and the dry goods store Henry started became Lehman Brothers. Due to its location in cotton country, many customers would pay with raw baled cotton. By 1858 trading in cotton had become such a big part of their business that they opened an office in New York solely as cotton traders.

Over time, they prospered and moved into trading other commodities. As entrepreneurial sorts they found themselves starting to serve as what we know of today as an investment bank. They raised money for private company expansion and then began to do so for public companies as well. Lehman Brothers became one of the great names on the international banking scene. How could it happen that such a legendary business, with long-term banking relationships around the world would be the only bank not to survive. There must have been a lot of charades being played at the time. When times get tough is when the lack of substance under a charade, its pure superficiality becomes exposed, and the people playing the game are just sitting ducks ready to be shot by the competition.

Businesses that have public shareholders are required to file certain reports on a regular basis with the federal government. The purpose of these reports is two-fold. First, is for the people in the various agencies of the federal government that are responsible for regulating the financial industry to be able to keep an eye on them to make sure that they are not breaking the laws that govern their industry's behavior. Secondly, to provide reliable information so the public that does business with these companies as well as investing their money in their securities offerings, can judge their long-term staying power based on reliable information about how well they are doing.

In Lehman's case this system broke down, both the validity of their financial reports and the governments watchdog role, which led to their downfall. The financial information they put out in their quarterly reports was bogus. Yet the government agencies responsible for keeping an eye on them raised no alarm, even though a "whistleblower" did his best to alert them. One of the most troubling aspects of this story is that the accounting firm, Ernst & Young, which for now I will call "independent" of Lehman Brothers joined Lehman's management in fabricating their quarterly financial statements.. We will soon learn that the independent accounting and law firms that we rely on for their judgments such as providing their *imprimateur* as to the accuracy of financial reports and legality of the company's activities, are rarely as independent as represented.

As someone whose very nature is scientific minded, data and logic oriented, most of my writing tends to be heavy on the facts and light on the literary flourishes. Now onto my fourth book, I try hard to be literary, but I am who I am. So here goes an attempt at the soft and fuzzies of writing and story-telling: The fellow who ran Lehman Brothers, Richard Fuld, was simply not liked as a person. His nickname in the industry was "The Gorilla." He was given this name only in part from the shape of his head and his general physical appearance but also he was a very forceful kind of guy. People did not like him.

He was a tough negotiator and just not a likeable personality. Any interaction with him was bound to be annoying. When I first joined an industry that was closely allied to investment banking, a wag told me the joke: "What's the first thing you have to be able to do to become an investment banker?" Answer: "sell your mother." So he was a tough, competitive, aggressive, personality amongst tough, competitive, aggressive personalities.

As the situation at Lehman became desperate, investment banks came-a-calling to save Lehman from bankruptcy by some form of acquiring the troubled bank. Fuld said no, "screw you," I've saved companies from disaster before and I will do it again. He was playing brinksmanship, looking for the best deal he could get. Eventually, Hank Paulson, Secretary of Treasury, formerly president of one of Lehman's rivals Goldman Sachs, said enough is enough, it is over. So Lehman filed for bankruptcy and its stockholders lost everything. If Fuld had handled matters in the final weeks differently and welcomed the offers with just normal tough negotiating, or had put a deal together that might need just a little help from the feds, perhaps Lehman would not have failed but probably merged with another bank.

Another factor in why Lehman may have been the only bank to fail were the rumors that the firm's books had been cooked. Cooked not just "rare" as would probably be true of any bank run by folks of the conniving spirit that it takes to reach senior management in the first place, but in Lehman's case, they were all the way to "well done."

So what lies did Lehman's financial statements tell that when combined with their leader's reputation as someone about whom it certainly must have been said: "He stepped on people on the way up, they will kick the s__t out of him on his way down" that led to its collapse. It mainly had to do with one of the three parts of the financial statement that companies must file with the government and distribute to shareholders, the balance sheet. The balance sheet takes a look at the substance behind a company. Essentially how much stuff does a company own, how much is this stuff worth, and how much do they owe other people. For example, your own personal balance sheet would list the equity in your house and/or car, cash in a checking account, investments in stocks and CDs or maybe some art, furniture, jewelry, or other objects that had value worth mentioning. All those things that you own and could convert into money are your assets. On the other side are your obligations, money you owe on a mortgage, car, student loan, and other debts. If we take the realistic value of your assets and subtract your debts, that is your net worth, your true value in the marketplace.

The balance sheet is supposed to be an accurate representation of your ability to function as a going concern as of the date you show them to someone. For example if you were applying for a loan and your assets were 1 million dollars and your debts 100 million, it would be hard to have optimism in getting the loan. However, if the reverse were the case, 100 million in assets and 1 million in debts the chances for the loan would be great. Thus sprang the famous saying "that banks loan money to people who don't really need it."

Lehman Brothers balance sheet misrepresented their financial condition. They were hiding debts through doing something called a repo 105 transaction that by itself was a perfectly acceptable transaction. However, Lehman Brothers did this transaction just days before the end of the quarter so it would show-up in their financial statements, and then reversed the transaction right after the end of the quarter. The repo 105 transactions were charades, used to hide debt and purposely mislead their investors and the government. This is what a whistleblower had warned both the government and Ernst & Young, the independent auditing firm about. Neither bothered to do anything.

Oh, yeah, by the way, the whistle blew at board meetings as well. Still, the people whose main job is protect the interest of the shareholders, the members of its board played deaf. I mean this is not a joke. Lehman stock was held by individuals, pension plans, college tuition accounts, and people's life savings. Yet the independent auditors, government regulators, and the board of directors, chose to ignore the detailed warning coming from someone whose position makes him someone who knows what is going on.

The repo 105 transaction was a way of simultaneously reducing the amount of debt on the balance sheet while at the same time increasing the amount of assets. With this transaction the all-important debt-to-asset ratio, the measure of both a company's financial health would be biased significantly to the favor of the company. If the transaction were a real transaction and once done was not reversed two days later it is a perfectly legitimate way of accounting. However in Lehman's case, the transaction was a pseudo transaction by itself and furthermore it was done the day before the end of the quarter and reversed the day after. A clear charade.

Sure enough, just before the end of the quarter, Lehman Brothers unloaded a variety of assets, oh about 50 billion dollars worth as collateral for loans, the proceeds from which were booked as sales. The day after the transaction was reversed. Only to repeat as needed at the end of the next quarter. That senior management knew it was a questionable transaction is reflected in the fact that they needed their lawyers to sign-off on the booking of the pseudo transaction and used the lawyers in their London office because they knew that these lawyers looked more favorably upon such transactions than did the lawyers in New York.

Now there are a select few, perhaps 4 depending upon the exact time you choose to count, accounting firms that are considered large enough and with the requisite expertise to be an arms- length judge of a publicly traded company's financial statements. A more thorough discussion of the great charade of all this in terms of just how long or short is the arm will come in another chapter. Ernst and Young is one of the very oldest and venerable firms qualifying for the honor and massive fees that such auditing brings. A bright fellow named Mathew Lee had put in his time counting beans for E & Y, much of which was spent keeping an eye on the financial reporting of Lehman Brothers. He then decided the grass was greener, as in stock options, salary, and year-end bonus, at an investment bank so he joined Lehman Brothers and eventually became a senior Vice President.

Now that he was part of the inside he got a much better view of the goings on, in particular repo 105. After 14 years of working for Lehman, he circulated a letter, May, 16, 2008, to Lehman's senior management, people like Erin Callan, the Chief Financial Officer, in which he questioned the propriety of masking Lehman's true asset and debt levels through use of repo 105. He thought this was a "material" fact that was distorting the quarterly financial reporting. The term "material" is critical since not each and every transaction involving a company can show up on their financial statement. The key to both how lawyers and accounting auditors give their seal of approval to business activities is a decision about whether or not an event is "material." In the sense of accountants and lawyers passing judgment, "material" refers to the importance of an event to someone being able to understand the financial and legal condition of a company. If a transaction is relevant then it is material and must be reported, if it is deemed "not material" then it can be omitted.

The old saying "beauty is in the eye of the beholder" is very germane to the decision on materiality especially when the fees collected by the accountants and lawyers from serving such large clients is a major part of their firms yearly income.

Mr. Lee felt hiding 50 billion was material in contrast to senior management, the board, and Ernst & Young who felt, "Oh, well what's 50 billion between friends" not material, no need to report it. It turns out that large investors and financial analysts had already been noticing strange goings on with Lehman's quarterly financial reports and had raised questions about these very same repo 105 transactions. Mr. Lee sent a letter to his former employer E & Y, "What's up with the $50 billion repo 105 you left off the balance sheet?"

Ernst and Young it turns out was very troubled by the letter, in an internal memo, the E & Y partner in charge of the Lehman account said: "We are also dealing with a whistle-blower letter, that is on its face pretty ugly and will take us a significant amount of time to get through." (WSJ, 3/13/10). However, after the bankruptcy, that did not stop one E & Y auditor telling the bankruptcy examiner that he did not recall Mr. Lee ever raising the Repo 105 issue—I feel sorry for the poor guys mother. The left hand seemingly ignorant of the right hand, another E & Y employee had in her notes from an internal meeting that were reviewed by the bankruptcy examiner, comments all about the Lehman 105 repo transactions. Equally troubling was that the bankruptcy examiner uncovered that the board of directors knew about Mr. Lee's charges and directed E & Y to investigate. After E & Y reviewed Mr. Lees claims, they told Lehman's board, "the allegations were unfounded and there were no material issues identified" (WSJ, 3/16/10).

No reason for the board to worry since Lehman's management had reported to the a committee of the board charged specifically with keeping an eye on financial reporting that there were no material issues of concern. I think you are probably getting a sense of why this term "material" is so critical to accountants and lawyers signing off on a businesses' public statements.—not just beauty but materiality as well is indeed in the eye of the beholder. Oh, just in case you thought the SEC was a backstop of protection on these shenanigans, the bankruptcy examiner also uncovered that the SEC identified these repo 105 transactions as improper but did nothing.

Well, for his troubles, Mathew Lee was fired a few months after he wrote his letter. Litigation about his firing is ongoing.

This example raises any one of a number of very troubling questions. Maybe at the top of the list is that the investors in Lehman Bros., to use an investment banking term for the general public, "widows and orphans" were being misled not just by Lehman Brothers but by the folks at E &Y as well. Come on now, it is these A+ accounting firms that all investors rely on to insure that the financial statements that are the basis for investing are an accurate representation of the company's condition. If these statements are a charade than the whole damn concept behind a stock market is a charade. Well in the case of Lehman there can be no question that they were fraudulent. A one in a million or just another case of the only thing Lehman did different from others was to get caught? How's that 401K working for ya?

So Lehman Brothers is cooking the books at the same time it is trying to sell itself to another bank or getting the government to bail it out. As mentioned previously, that really wonderful guy Richard Fuld, just maligned because people didn't like his looks and personality as some were saying, had cooked the books of his company. There were other shenanigans discovered in addition to the repo 105. Lehman was a doomed company, doomed to filing for bankruptcy in short order, no government bailout for Mr. Fuld and his merry gang of pranksters. Chalk up one for Hank Paulson.

Oh by the way, the questioning of Fuld's lawyers at the various investigations by the various government committees took on all the aspects of theater that one might expect. The lawyers repeatedly made the claim that Mr. Fuld was completely unaware of the repo 105 shenanigans as well as other financial statement missteps. Now as the Chief Executive Officer, what is worse, that he knew about these transactions and approved them or that even though he was known for his intimate involvement with every detail, he really did not know about 50 plus billions of dollars improperly accounted for on its financial statement.

Into bankruptcy went Lehman and the vultures picked at the bones.

So there you have it, an unambiguous display of how one of the world's great investment banks went bankrupt, making its shareholders investment zero. From the most savvy of professional investors at mutual funds, to the amateur at home who thought a legendary investment bank was as good as gold it was all a charade. It happened because the accounting and law firms whose *imprimateur* of the company's financial statements was also a charade. The lawyers and accountants violated the public trust because in both cases it was more important not to piss off and risk losing a very profitable client. An arms-length review by one of the country's top law firms and accounting firm, another charade, worthless.

At these levels, with so much money and ego at stake amongst folks for whom these things are as important as life itself, there is little that goes on that is not a charade. To work for the SEC is considered by most who work there, simply the minor leagues where you get to show your stuff in front of the guys and gals in the big leagues, the major investment banking houses. It is a revolving door between the door leading out of the SEC and the one into the investment banking house. To expect an SEC official to do anything other than moving the papers around is unrealistic. When that job comes up at Goldman Sachs, just the one you have been preparing yourself for your whole life, how would it look if you were the one who got the ball rolling on an SEC investigation or if you went the extra mile to tie down the critical loose end. I mean, chapter and verse was presented to them about Lehman, not to mention Madoff, not to mention….out to infinity.

In Washington, these investment banking firms and their senior employees are at the top of corporate and personal donors. They give the money that politicians use to get themselves elected. Of course the *quid pro quo* is to "get the government off the back of American business" and let the free enterprise system trickle down its prosperity to all Americans. A charade, how about another million for my next run for office. In fact, a mutuality of self-interest amongst the lawyers, accountants, Lehman's board and senior management and politicians cost the country and its citizens dearly. Your retirement plan and your child's education savings lost because from lawyers through the accountants to the SEC and politicians they simply put their own self-interest ahead of their responsibilities to the public.

CASE #2

Next let us do another case study of mutual self-interest, this time focusing our attention on how the Congress and the various federal agencies that establish regulations keep us safe from harm. Safe as employees of an industry such as drilling for oil that has a fair amount of danger in much of its goings on, especially when that drilling occurs in the ocean. Safe as a country when its product is at the heart of much of our commerce and when spilled can have an economic snowball effect on a variety of industries other than oil. Safe as a country when it's product is toxic to the land and waters and the critters, humans included, that live upon and within it.

After all, we do understand that a company's job is to make profits for its shareholders. As a former venture capitalist it would be hypocritical if I believed anything else. It is the government's job to make sure that they do so in ways that do not do "material" harm. At least sort of the governments job, as we shall see.

The explosion, fire, and oil spill in the Gulf of Mexico that occurred April 20th, 2010 on a deep water drilling platform for which British Petroleum (BP) had responsibility is a sadly typical example of the charade of government regulations. Toothless regulations that allow politicians to represent to the people that they are watching over potentially dangerous and toxic industries but also not to irritate the donors whose money is most of the funds that pay for their campaigns.

The oil industry and the investment banking industry would easily occupy the top two spots in importance for our country's continuing prosperity. As should be the case, the oil folk try to maximize profits while trying not to run afoul of the regulatory agencies. However, as we shall see, it is sometimes hard to tell where the line is that separates one institution, the business, and the other, government regulations, from each other.

Now we all know any inspection, whether it is about how tidy you kept your bedroom at home or how sloppy is the record keeping on an offshore platform will be a different event where it is a surprise inspection or one that that is announced well ahead of time. Sort of like a pop-quiz versus an exam announced days in advance. Keeping that in mind, the folks who wrote the initial regulations for deep-water drilling platforms require a certain number of unannounced inspections each year. Surprise surprise, federal authorities have not made an unannounced inspection of a deep-water well since October of 2006. In fact even though the number of offshore wells increased from 2005 to 2009, the number of announced or unannounced inspections dropped in that period from 1,292 to 760.

What I am sure will be even more shocking is that the U.S. agency responsible for collecting royalties for drilling on government land and is judged by how much they collect is the same agency that is responsible for regulating the drilling activity, making sure it is safe. The revenue generated by this agency from collecting royalties is the second largest source of government revenue, behind only income taxes. So the same folk whose performance is measured by the amount of royalties collected is the same group of folks who ought to shut down the flow of oil and its royalties if its safety rules are violated. The agency is called the Minerals Management Services (MMS).

MMS is a very interesting agency. A great group of people, with nothing but the country's interest at heart and one that we hope is atypical of government agencies in general. I say that since as a result of a scandal at the agency, the

Interior Department released its report to Congress in September of 2008, which summarized the agency as "a culture of substance abuse and promiscuity."

At least eight people at the agency were found to have repeatedly violated the ethics rules that govern the relationship between regulators and the companies and its employees that they regulated. The report is full of the usual golf outings, freebie vacations, concert tickets, and tickets to major sporting events that seem to be the norm in such business-regulatory relationships. However, not so typical, or maybe the others just have not been caught yet, are the reports detailing officials "frequently consumed alcohol at industry functions, had consumed cocaine and marijuana, and had sexual relationships with oil and gas company representatives."

Dear reader, I wish I were making this stuff up.

To add insult to injury, one of the higher-ups at the agency, just before retiring, drafted an order to hire a consultant to perform specific types of work which sounded like a job description of his former position. Guess who received that consulting contract, the same guy who just before retiring put in the order for the consulting work. Yes, another servant of the public interest.

Well, now I can understand several very troubling things about MMS that I came across in my research. One is the MMS actually writes few of its rules itself. Instead it just sets general guidelines and lets the industry write the actual rules and approves the rules. These are the rules that say that the industry does most of the inspections and writes the reports of the inspections itself, even to the extent of reporting its own violations. Another is that in 2000 MMS did begin a conversation with the drilling companies about setting standards for the now legendary cement that is so critical in preventing a well blow-out, as in the BP disaster. Now a decade later, at the time of the big spill, they still had no formal rules in place.

A similar sequence occurred regarding regulation of the blowout preventers. In 1998 industry was asked to write guidelines on improving blowout preventers. They did, they wrote their own regulations, but as of the time of the spill, MMS had taken no action in putting regulations in place. It should come as no surprise that in congressional hearings after the spill, an MMS official testified that the agency requires as part of the application for approval to drill that the driller submit proof of the adequacy of the blowout preventer to do just that, prevent a blowout. However, the official at MMS who approved the application for the BP well said he was not aware of such a rule and he did not check for such proof as part of his approval process. And the rest as they say is now history. However, I do now understand at least in the MMS case why "trust me, we are from the government and we are here to help you" has become such a catch phrase for expected government incompetence. In the party-hardy culture of MMS how could they ever find time for excellence?

So let's see, buying, selling, and using cocaine and marijuana and sexual relationships between the folks working for the government to regulate an industry and the people who work for the industry. Of course the environmental damage done by this industry's oil spill was horrific, but let us not forget often lost in the constant images of oiled birds that the real tragedy was the loss of eleven oil workers lives. Oh and by the way, in a 2009 letter, the Offshore Operators Committee of the American Petroleum Institute and other trade groups argued against proposed new stricter rules, saying they "quickly become paperwork exercises" not genuine improvements. Eleven people died.

Now the land under the water in which these drilling platforms work and in which the oil is located is owned by the federal government, thus firmly establishing their right to regulate that activity in the best interests of the people of the United States. Remember the same folk who are judged by how much royalties they collect are also in charge of regulating this production. A balancing act with an inherent conflict of interest if there ever were one.

As described by Senator Bob Graham from Florida during hearings about the spill, "This is not government regulating a private enterprise. This is government regulating land that the people of the United States own." Other countries are in the same situation. One organization, the International Association of Drilling Contractors that represents the industry showed that a US worker is more than four times as likely to be killed than a worker in European waters. Another group, The International Regulators Forum, representing specifically the regulatory agencies of offshore oil producing countries, the UK, Norway, Australia, Canada, Netherlands, in a study showed that from 2007 through 2008 the US had five major loss-of-control incidents, while the members of their organization had none.

We are number one at something.

As a result of the BP disaster, of course the usual sequence of events happened that happens after every major headline catastrophe. As described more fully in the first Chapter it begins with everyone who can hold hearings doing so and it ends with wonderful "sound bites" created for the next reelection campaign. Years later maybe some new regulations written by the industry themselves are in place, maybe not. If they are, you can bet they have no teeth and numerous backdoors for flaunting their intent. At least, their intent as described in the campaign ads.

At the time of the BP spill there were several thousands of wells out there in the Gulf of Mexico, built before any standards were in place and left to operate with little regulation. About 2000 are at least 20 years old and at least half are now in operation longer than their expected lifetimes based upon the engineering and materials used in their designs. There is minimal inspection of these platforms and problems due to age happen. Fortunately none so far that cannot be corrected. Oil has certainly been spilled but not enough to make the national news so no hearings and no regulation—party hardy.

In September of 2010, the government did put new rules in place to deal with this problem of aging oil rigs, sort of. In their own wisdom however, it applies to wells that are now plugged, no longer in use. Wells still operating, no matter how many decades back they go and no matter how many "accidents" have happened are exempt from these rules. Also ignored by new regulations are the 25,000 miles of underwater pipelines that allow for the harvesting of the oil pumped by the rigs. So the rules created to try to prevent accidents from older wells that are still producing, only apply to wells that have been plugged. Huh?

Of equal concern is the central issue of the competing agendas of MMS. On the one hand they are charged with maximizing the royalties that are collected by the U.S. government from the leases that allow the oil companies to take oil from land owned by the government, supposedly in trust for its citizens. On the other hand, MMS is also in charge of regulating the oil industry, making sure it drills and collects the oil in a way that is safe for both people and the environment. In Senate hearings during May of 2010, the Interior Department announced it was looking into separating these two functions. Do not hold your breath or bother "googling" to see if anything has happened. "Never overestimate an underachiever."

III. WAR ON DRUGS CHARADE:

NOT IN MY BACKYARD

It is called the "War on Drugs" (WOD). Lots of people have been killed and a great deal of money spent so in that sense it is a war, people dead and money spent. In many ways it is one of the great charades the American government has ever perpetrated. That it is a useless and pointless charade makes the loss of all those lives and all that money wasted, not just in the U.S. but for our coalition partners as well, even more tragic.

Perhaps the most important factor that makes a charade of this effort is the underlying rational of the war, its most fundamental premise. In American law, time and time again, a person who purchases a "product" and uses it to do harm to another's life or property is the one held liable for that harm. The perpetrator may be sent to prison for their crime and may be sued by the victim in civil court for financial compensation. It is clear that the manufacturer of the product, be it a gun used to commit robbery or murder, a car that kills or injures someone or the poison that someone puts in a drink to kill someone cannot be held liable. It is the consumer, the person who buys and uses the product that is at fault.

Yet in the case of the WOD, our main focus has been on the producer of the drugs, not on the consumer who commits the illegal act by purchasing and using the product/drug. A complete break in the U.S. tradition of holding the user of the product accountable for the crime.

We fight the WOD in Mexico and Central and South America where the drugs are grown, harvested, and turned into the final product. Of course we make a gesture to arrest drug users here in the U.S., but really the big money is spent and most of the lives are lost holding the producer accountable for the illegal acts instead of the consumer.

The WOD began unofficially through a resolution passed by the United Nations in 1961 focusing on the growing and production of cocaine from the leaf of the coca plant. The resolution gave countries where the coca plant was grown 25 years to stop it. In many such countries chewing the coca leaves and drinking the tea brewed from the leaves is a "pep-me-up" tradition well woven into the cultural fabric of the country. It is also administered medicinally for such things as high-altitude sickness, common in many of the high-altitude regions where it was grown. Even today, bizarrely enough, the U.S.'s own State Department recommends its use for fighting high-altitude sickness for visitors to these South American countries.

The WOD as an American enterprise began about forty years ago. We were going after the production of cocaine, marijuana, and heroin in Central and South America. Initially the war was fought in Bolivia and Peru where most of the cocaine and heroin consumed in the U.S. was grown and manufactured. With our BFF coalition partners, Peru and Bolivia, the war fought by the U.S. was fairly successful. Successful enough that growing at least cocaine and marijuana shifted to Columbia; so off we went to fight the war with our newest BFF member of the coalition.

When one traces our efforts to eliminate the growing of these drugs, it is interesting to note how factors other than military have played an even more important role in changing their growth and production. Sort of like how although our best military efforts against the communist countries, including the many dead in Vietnam, may have played some role in the eventual defeat of communism in many countries, other factors were more important. It was these other factors, cultural and economic, that drove countries such as Russia, China, and Vietnam to now be well on their way to full-fledged capitalist economies. The ever-present fear of war with them has receded over a fantasized far distant horizon of struggles for natural resources to fuel each of our capitalist machines of production. Who'd have ever thunk it?

Cocaine for example, as a drug of use in the Western countries has a fascinating history prior to our launch of the WOD. A history that shows how as Robert Burns in *To a Mouse on Turning Her Nest with the Plough,* put it poetically and some other knave paraphrased as: "Man's best plans to get laid, sometimes get all screwed up." Weirdly enough, another potent drug, but a legal one, may have played as important a role, perhaps even more important a role in stopping the production of cocaine and heroin in some countries than did the WOD. It turns out that drug is caffeine. Caffeine is as totally legal today as the perhaps equally poisonous drug nicotine was not that many years ago. Caffeine is used in the United States by hundreds of millions of Americans everyday, just as was nicotine in its heyday.

Why is caffeine used so heavily today, because its effect on the user is very similar to the now illegal cocaine. It is a "pep-me-up" drug, allowing one to stay awake and avoid feelings of sluggish drowsiness; less potent than cocaine, but still very similar in its effect. They both also have many of the same potentially lethal side effects upon the body.

A history not often discussed is that prior to 1970, although regulated, cocaine was legal in the United States. In fact, it was used in drinks sold throughout the United States. Drinks that were every bit as popular as today's variety of colas and energy drinks. The name of one of today's most popular drinks, Coca Cola, is no accident; it was initially full of cocaine. No wonder the original formula is such a carefully guarded secret.

None other than Sigmund Freud was responsible really for introducing cocaine into Western culture. In the late nineteenth century he was to medicine, and deservedly so, what Einstein came to be in Physics. He not only invented the underlying basis for pretty much all theories of human behavior, the id, ego, and superego, but also made truly groundbreaking discoveries in childhood paralysis, the loss of speech following brain injuries such as stroke, known as aphasia, and showed that cocaine was useful as an anesthetic for the eye, allowing all the various surgeries done to the eye that followed. He was so busy with his other discoveries that another fellow, Dr. Koller, took Freud's discovery of cocaine as an anesthetic and ran with it himself all the way to multiple nominations for a Nobel Prize.

Freud was so enamored with his own cocaine experiences that he turned all his pals on to it and even got some medical buddies in the U.S. to give it a whirl. All of this was done in the interest of Freud's work in trying to uncover the fundamental operating principles of the human mind. The first cocaine addicts in European and American society were Freud and his buds. He was able to kick the habit on his own, some of his friends and the many billions thereafter not so lucky. Thanks Siggy.

So caffeine, an extract of the coffee bean, and cocaine, an extract of the coca leaf have a very intertwined history. Today's energy drinks, just packed with vast amounts of caffeine are really nothing new. Just a replay of all the drinks laced with cocaine prior to its becoming illegal. Anyone care to speculate on the direction all this will take as we begin to gather data about the long term effects of the excessive consumption of caffeine through daily glugging of the energy drinks.

It turns out that the coca plant which gives us cocaine, the poppy which gives us heroin, and the coffee plant which gives us caffeine, require many of the same growing conditions. In Bolivia and Peru, most of the cocaine and heroin growers had started out as coffee growers and only began to dedicate part of the fields to cocaine and heroin once the demand in the United States began to expand in the 1960s. Since the U.N. resolution was being taken only semiseriously, there was limited pressure on the growers to eliminate coca plants and poppies from their fields. It was pretty much ignored. Why grow the relatively cheap product coffee when with the same effort one could grow the much more valuable product, coca leaves and heroin poppies.

At least some of the success in the WOD since the mid-1990s has certainly been driven by the significant rise in prices for the coffee bean that led to a shift in just which crop the farmer grows. A shift that was also in part motivated by the pressure on growers by the military campaign. However, a victory that certainly would not have occurred other than for the dramatic rise in the price paid for coffee beans, making it a much preferred crop than the opium poppy and coca plant. Even though growing these plants may have still have been a bit more profitable than coffee, the difference was certainly not worth the personal stress and logistical efforts of evasion in growing an illegal crop versus a legal one.

In the beginning, the WOD was thought by many to simply be a cover for funneling money, arms, and occasional boots on the ground assistance to other countries in the Americas that were under pressure from communist guerila groups. To some extent this was undoubtedly true, especially in Peru, Bolivia and Columbia. It turns out that many of these guerila groups were in addition to direct support from the Soviet Union also self-funding through their own growing of these illegal crops.

Efforts to stop the growing of these plants along with taking down the manufacturing facilities that turned the natural product into a consumable drug were of value to the WOD's overt purpose, but also helped to damage the guerila's ability to fund their own activities. In this case the WOD could be considered a double charade. The main one being that instead of the United States going after the users of the product, it was also a way of funding its political agenda in these countries as well. Primarily it allowed for the U.S., the ability of the executive branch to take military action in another country without declaring its intent and obtaining approval from Congress. So the WOD was truly, literally and figuratively, killing two birds with one stone.

Certainly the WOD efforts did show some progress. Peru and Bolivia were in 1995 the world's number one in production of cocaine. In the several years that followed, the WOD's effort seemed to have at least played some role in shutting down its production. In terms of the goal however, the amount of cocaine coming onto the market was never really affected, production simply shifted to Columbia.

The whole charade is really a pretty sad story, much like the "whack-a-mole" game where one has to whack a mallet on the mole that pops up from the board and then another pops up somewhere else on the board and on and on. After a big U.S. effort then worked its "magic" on Columbia and that mole was whacked, the mole popped up again back in Peru and Bolivia, which saw an increase in both countries by about 50% from recent lows. The customers still wanted the product. We were whacking the wrong moles. It the people who buy and use the stuff—duh, how hard is that.

Since the fall of Communism as a credible threat, the guerilla movements in countries such as Bolivia and Peru in terms of the international scene are little more than regional curiosities. In fact, any politician wishing to get elected must in a sense pay some homage to them since the fantasy of a workers paradise still holds some sway in these poverty ridden countries. In fact the president of Bolivia, Evo Morales is also the head of the coca growers union. To show you just how much of an irrelevant cultural artifact some of these guerilla movements have become, in Peru they still show their allegiance to Chairman Mao and his teachings (who and what? Oh yeah, I read about him and communism in a history book, but I can't find his blog, the hell with him.).

So these governments, our former BFFs no longer respond to the pressure from the United States to play along in the game of charades known as the WODs. The recent emergence of politic power amongst the groups championing the rights of indigenous peoples, especially within the U.N., has pretty much eliminated any local efforts to stop the "traditional" uses of drugs.

All of these activities, cultural shifts, the waxing and waning of crop prices and the disruption of the distribution channels by boat and airplanes, have significantly shifted the focus of the WOD to our neighbor with which we share our southern border, Mexico. It is a long border that historically in the best of times has been loosely policed and in the worst of times pretty much wide open.

About ten years ago I read a book, *God's Middle Finger: Into the Lawless Heart of the Sierra Madre,* that described an Americans attempt to travel on land from the Northern extent of Mexico's "spine," the Sierra Madre Mountains, and come out at its Southern tip. It seems that this large percentage of Mexico's area was legendary for its lawlessness, where local feuds and those who ran the drug growing and producing were the law, the only law of the land. I mean this was not limited to just one little area, but encompassed much of the center of Mexico from its north to the south. No law, just whoever had the biggest guns and had the resources to buy the loyalties of the meanest hombres was the law of the land.

It seems legend had it that no single gringo had ever made the trip and come out alive.

The author, Richard Grant wanted to be the first to do so. He was cheating a bit, having lined up "letters of reference" from connected people he knew that were supposedly going to grease his path. In fact, these references did indeed save his life which seemingly was threatened on a daily basis. Occasionally a bit of dumb luck came in handy as the folks who were out to kill him were distracted by other events usually involving booze, women, and orders from higher up to go kill more important targets.

Something that I have often found stunning, and truly upsetting, is the disparity in some countries between the haves and have nots. I mean here in the U.S. it can seem at times perhaps unfair. But I am talking about the Indias of the world where the major cities are just as modern and with all the conveniences of any modern city. However just go even a few miles outside these places and it is not just a few steps down, but these folks have no sewers, clean water, electricity, zippo, nothing, poverty that makes our worst seem like fat city. Intellectually I can sort of understand the dynamics, but emotionally I simply do not know how the folks in the cities can emotionally deal with the deprivation just a stones throw away. Growing up along the gulf coast of Texas, my first trip to Mexico was about 1954 and that was my first view of this injustice. I then came to learn it was more the typical around the world than the atypical.

Reading that travel book about the spine of Mexico made me realize that it was far more than just the traditional notion of food, shelter, and hygiene that was a disparity, but this disparity also extended to the rule of law. In much of Mexico, just across our border, law did not and still in some places does not exist. The rule of law that allows us to get up everyday and go about the pursuit of our pleasures and then go to sleep at night secure in the knowledge that we can get up the next day and we get to do it again much as we did the day before does not exist. In fact, on that trip in 1954 we were shaken down by the police in Mexico City for some phony traffic violation that my father had to pay a bribe so that we could be on our way. I mean a car with Texas plates, mom, dad, kids and dog. We had the fare for a bottle of high-quality tequila written all over us.

Those who did not understand just how primitive or perhaps more importantly nonexistent was the rule of law in Mexico are by now fully aware of it, but when the narcoterrorism battle in Mexico first started making headlines, I expect there was a lot of surprise. Having read that book, no surprise here. No surprise either to read in the summer of 2011 an article about how the drug cartels have now added stealing oil, $250 millions worth in the first four months of the year, from the pipelines in Mexico to their bag of tricks. Pemex, the state owned Mexican oil company has said, "The increase in theft…is due to the fact that the pipeline system has been virtually taken over by groups associated with organized crime." No surprises left.

Our involvement with Mexico in the WOD took a significant turn with the Meridia Initiative begun in 2008 with a commitment of $1.3 billion to assist our newest BFF coalition partner in the WOD. From the U.S. perspective we were going to replicate the successes in South America.

One thing that seemed to be overlooked with the Merida Initiative is that in contrast to South America, there was nowhere else for the narco-folk to run. We turned up the heat in Peru and Bolivia and they moved to Columbia. We turned up the heat in Columbia so they moved North, to Mexico. However, if we turned up the heat in Mexico there was nowhere else to go; it created a stand and fight to the death situation. And indeed, that is what it became. The game whack-a-mole had run of new places for the mole to pop up.

Whacking the mole in Mexico seemed to start out with killing limited to high profile narco locales and gun battles held discreetly only between gangs. In the last few years the violence has spread, bringing with it much collateral damage, as in the towns on both sides of the border.

McAllen, Texas was a small farming community. Then came the new trade and open border agreements which led to the establishment of the maquiladoras, the manufacturing plants just across the border where the inexpensive Mexican labor pool would produce products for U.S. based companies.

Just across the border from McAllen is the town of Reynosa, about 130 miles a bit to the south but mostly west of Reynosa is the major industrial city of Monterey. The highway between Monterey and Reynosa/McAllen became dotted with factories and McAllen grew from a small farm town to a major commercial center of over 700,000. Folks in the U.S. worked in the factories just across the border while those in Mexico who worked in the factories as well as the people from Monterey would make shopping pilgrimages to the malls in McAllen. It was prosperity on both sides of the border.

The economic boom has begun to wither as the narco-cartel warfare has spread up and down the highway from Monterey to McAllen. That highway it turns out had a dual use. It became the scene of the stories of beheadings and discoveries of mass graves as the various cartels battled for control of the highway, one of the major distribution routes to the U.S. for their products. As a result of the instability brought on by the lawlessness, investment from U.S. companies dried up, the shopping at the mall dried up, and the area is under a grave financial pinch because of the WOD, collateral damage. The situation is a lesser known story parallel to the mayhem in Ciudad Juarez just across the border from El Paso where a new mass grave and mutilation stories are carried on the national news every night.

Until 2011 the "word" was that the main tourist areas of Mexico, such as Cancun, San Miguel Allende, and Acapulco were still safe for some fun in the sun. In the summer of 2011, that changed dramatically at least for Acapulco. The drug cartels are now fighting it out in Acapulco. They are fighting it out for control of drug transportation and distribution in and through city. Cab drivers pay extortion money to this or that cartel depending upon which routes they work. In one weekend alone in August, 11 people were shot and killed.

Much of what is discussed in the media certainly seems to suggest that this violence is crossing the border. It is true, but so far actually minimal compared to the general impression of hearing the politicians do what politicians do, put on dramatic theater in the halls of Congress for the sake of the American public. More of those well-orchestrated hearings combining the dual themes of immigration with the WOD.

In fact, although just one death is a tragedy, very few border patrol officers on the U.S. side of the border have indeed been shot and killed. In fact, El Paso just across the border from the killing fields of Ciudad Juarez is ranked as one of the safest cities in the U.S.

The impact on the United States of this mayhem in Mexico is really dominated by two issues. One is the smuggling of guns from the United States into Mexico. In Mexico, gun ownership except under very special circumstances is against the law. The supply of guns into Mexico comes from many countries, yet without a doubt, the guns smuggled into Mexico from the U.S. are a mainstay of the cartels.

The cartels have carriers to bring the drugs across the border and sophisticated distribution networks to spread the product around the U.S. These same folk acquire guns and the carriers instead of crossing back empty handed simply use the routes and techniques to avoid detection in order to bring these guns into Mexico. Seventy percent of firearms found in Mexico come from the U.S.

The Mexican authorities are now raising hell about the lawlessness and criminal activities in the United States that then leads to all these shootings in Mexico. They are with a very noticeable tone of sarcasm in the voice making the same demands on the U.S. authorities to stop the gun smuggling into Mexico that we make to them about the drug smuggling from Mexico into the U.S.

Throwing our own insults about Mexico back at us really came home to roost when the head of the ATF had to resign over the ineptness of his team in trying to capture a group of drug smugglers. It was the biggest operation to date, called "Fast and Furious" and ended up accomplishing nothing but allowing as many as 2,500 weapons to be smuggled into Mexico. Another part of the fiasco was one part of the U.S. effort not knowing that some of the people they were targeting were really under-cover agents from another part of the U.S. effort.

The extent of the "fact is sometimes stranger than fiction" and that the chickens have indeed come home to roost is that the mayor and police chief of a border town in New Mexico are amongst the 11 people recently arrested under an 84 count indictment for smuggling guns into Mexico. Something about pots calling kettles black as well as stones and people who live in glass houses.

The mole is more brazen than anyone had expected and being whacked in Mexico, it has taken the dramatic step of moving its operations to the United States. Some years ago when I was in business school we did a case study about a company that made a certain product that was used in a variety of different types of factories on a daily basis. The point of the study was that eventually this company decentralized its own production and built mini-plants near their largest customers to more efficiently provide them with its products. Sometimes building a plant within their customers own factory. The cartels maybe read the same study, why not just set up our own production and distribution within the United States itself, to heck with the whole smuggling hassle.

National parks and national forests in California are known areas where the local folk have been growing marijuana to the extent that it is now the largest agricultural product in the state. Everyone knows this, there is an existing infrastructure to support the marijuana growing, it is not secret. A county in northern California has a marijuana crop grown each year with an estimated value of $1 billion. The total U.S. production is estimated at $40 billion. All the while the WOD, especially targeting marijuana, rages in Mexico. Once again, sad to say, I am not making this up.

The cartels from Mexico are joining in and taking advantage of the lawlessness in the United States (LOL). Kentucky, Tennessee and Michigan have similarly become "outsourcing" locales for the Mexican cartels. Local officials, as in park rangers, are poorly trained as one might expect for the job of interdicting murderous drug cartels from Mexico. It is estimated that over a million acres in the United States are currently under cultivation run by the Mexican cartels. Perhaps this is the answer, for marijuana at least, for where the mole pops up next and last. I mean, there is a certain humor in the U.S. ranting and raving about outsourcing of U.S. jobs to other countries whereas Mexico is outsourcing the growing of marijuana to the U.S., the leader of the WOD. Charade!!!!!!!!

The problem is now so bad that according to the U.S. Secretary of State for Mexico and Canada, the Mexican drug cartels have set up operations in 230 American cities. An investigation just sent the head of the Mexican Sinaloa cartel's operation in South Carolina to jail for 20 years. The investigative work uncovered similar rings in Seattle, Anchorage, and Minneapolis. Much of this activity uses a variety of gangs initially formed in U.S. prisons where they sign-up for loyalty to one or another Mexican cartel and take up the cause upon release.

Since the WOD came to Mexico, about 40,000 people in Mexico have been killed in drug related murders, 15,000 people have been killed in the last year alone. Relations with our neighbor south of the border have been devastated. The free trade agreement, NAFTA, spurred the whole *maquilodora* movement that gave tremendous economic expansion to both sides of the border. The drug stuff however has brought all that to a screeching halt, both the economic development and any feelings of good will between neighbors.

Our Ambassador to Mexico recently resigned. It seems that Wikileaks had released some private State Department cables that made a mockery of the Mexican government's efforts to fight the drug cartels. The official cables described an enforcement apparatus rife with corruption and ineptitude and a bureaucracy of chaos. Let us not lose sight of the fact that as a result of the importing of illegal drugs from Mexico to the U.S. it brings a return cash flow to Mexico of $10 billion dollars. Hmmm, maybe they ain't so dumb after all.

Where is all this going, who knows? Shakespeare was fond of structuring his plays in a way that showed that what is begun in immorality, chaos, and where "fair is foul and foul is fair" (Act I, Macbeth) rarely ends well. Recent studies indicate that about 5% of drugs that are sent into the U.S. actually get stopped at the border. To quote a Mexican official: "Until legalization, all you can do is make it someone else's problem." Perhaps the moles that can pop-up on the board are diminishing. We seem done in South America. Mexico is sooner or later going to have to give up the madness that is killing so many of its people for no gain.

Or perhaps the gain is that the cartels will follow the concept of that case study and begin in earnest to shift production and distribution where it really belonged in the first place, in the lap of the country where the consumer lives. Sometimes the chickens indeed come home to roost.

In spite of ourselves, the U.S. may have to truly confront that the problem is not the producing of these drugs but lies with the consumer. If it is truly a heinous act to use these substances, deserving of punishment, then put your money where your mouth is. Stop sending the money to Mexico, Columbia, anywhere except here at home, and start putting all that time, effort, money, and boots on the ground, into arresting and punishing all the producers, distributors, and users right here at home.

Nothing can demonstrate the charade of the WOD better than a review of the scene in Miami in the 1970s. Similar scenes were played out also in Hollywood, Wall Street, professional athletes, and anywhere the entertainment industry stopped for the weekend. The agent and road manager as drug pimp is well documented.

Miami has always been a fun in the sun town, for many years primarily a tourist destination, its economy mostly dependent on tourism. However, things began to change when it became in the 1970s the main stop-over for cocaine trafficking between its production in South America and its distribution throughout the United States.

The relatively sleepy resort town of Miami exploded with money. New restaurants, hotels, jewelry stores, condo towers, McMansions, yacht and luxury car dealers, clothing boutiques, night clubs, you name it. If it were glitzy and glamorous and cost a lot of money it was suddenly all around. The growth in the part of Miami where it was all happening was sufficient that it took on a name of its own, South Beach. Rock stars, professional athletes, and everyone with big bucks looking for the greatest Sodom and Gomorrah since the Bible, flocked to Miami.

The only thing that exploded faster than the above commercial activities were the local banks. The South American cocaine traffickers picked Miami as the watering hole on their travels from the production plants to the South on their way to the customers to the North. As a result, billions of dollars of drug revenue were mostly laundered through the banks. A little was kept and used to fuel a life style that had never been seen before on these shores and probably will never be seen again.

In one year alone, $6 billion dollars in new cash found its way into Miami banks. This was in the 1970s before anyone with a good scheme to be played on Wall Street got a couple of billion of their own from IPOs of pointless internet companies to Ponzi schemers—meaning when a billion bucks was still a very big number. Banks opened that specialized in taking care of the new inflow of cash. Even the local Federal Reserve branch saw its flow of cash increase from the standard $12 million per year to $600 million. It had an annual surplus of $5 billion a year, more than the combined surplus of all other Federal Reserve branches combined.

Have no doubts that there was no secret about what was happening in Miami. The cops were in on it, even using their patrol cars to make deliveries of the money and the white powder. The airline pilots and stewardesses, a group back then known for their fondness for a good time, seemed willing to help move the goods out and the cash in. Gosh mom, all the kids are doing it.

The local politicians were certainly not going to bite the hand that feeds the real estate developers, bankers, and other local prominent citizens whose car and yacht dealerships, and other high-end consumables were creating a boom town. Given the amount of money the cartels were passing through town, bribes that could not be resisted were rounding errors to the traffickers.

The federal drug enforcement agencies did what they could. In some of the heyday years, seizures of many tons of cocaine occurred. It was being smuggled through South Florida using freshly scraped runways that were here one day and gone the next. Fast boats zipped up and down the coast picking up shipments out of the water left by freighters plying their normal trade routes along the coast. The typical yearly import of cocaine into S. Florida was estimated to have a value of $20 billion.

What brought it all down was when the cartels starting fighting amongst themselves, and just plain folk started to become collateral damage. It seems that Miami drug dealers and distributors had traditionally been Cubans, mostly dealing marijuana. Now that cocaine was the drug of choice, the Columbian cartel wanted to run the show. The Cubans and Columbians went after each other. The blood on the streets merited in 1981 the cover of Time magazine with an article about how the bad guys were now ruling the streets of Miami. Gosh, just like in Mexico. There is very little that is new, the Mexico of today was S. Florida in the late 1970s and early 1980s. Shootouts in the streets in broad daylight in the "nicest" of neighborhoods.

In the mid 1980s, the feds came in to take the war over from the local police and this was one WOD that they won. Without a doubt the Miami of today, one of the Eurotrash glamour capitals of the world, would never have existed if it were not for the cocaine fueled decade. For those who have an interest in this period and this town, there is an excellent documentary film, *Cocaine Cowboys*, that shows up on TV occasionally and provides chapter and verse on the subject.

If ever there was a microcosm of the entire WOD charade fought over many decades and many countries, the example of Miami is it. Once the federal government decided to fight the WOD on the soil of the consumer of the drugs it won. The defeat of the cocaine cowboys had nothing to do with going after the growers and those who manufactured cocaine from the coca leaves, but everything to do with taking down the local distributors and users.

The demand for the product is here in the U.S. and it grows larger every year. How many people will have to die in Mexico because of our never-ending desire for these drugs? When will Mexico develop a long overdue and completely justified "screw you" attitude toward the U.S. and its drug-users and give its growers, manufactures, and distributors free-run to produce all the product the U.S. wants to consume. They can point to the language and philosophy of NAFTA, the free –trade agreement, for justification of this policy. Why should their people die making a product for the U.S. market. Gee, do we stand for free market capitalism or not. A charade if there ever were one.

The dirty not so little secret of this whole business is that amongst those 60 years old or younger, the percentage of those who have at least tried marijuana I expect is at least 75% if not higher. Within certain groups, such as the entertainment industry, professional athletes, and Wall Street, those who have at least tried cocaine is certainly less than marijuana but significantly above zero. The very leaders and even pillars of our community have used these illegal substances. What would happen if the WOD would go full-out in the United States? Perhaps we need not go much further in our thinking to understand why we have chosen to fight the WOD elsewhere.

Or, perhaps the issue is if there really needs to be a WOD in the first place? As discussed in detail in the chapter about comparing alcohol with marijuana, how can you have a war on certain drugs that take a far distant second place in their perniciousness measured in any imaginable way to alcohol which is legal, consumed, and heavily advertised in every corner of the United States.

IV. WALL STREET'S CHARADE
TAKES DOWN THE ECONOMY

The answer to why year after year there is one scandal after another on Wall Street must include an understanding of the types of people that are Wall Street. We speak of Wall Street as some vast entity. Yet as with any other business activity it really just comes down to an individual or maybe a couple of them sitting around a table making decisions about how to make money primarily for themselves and if their investors also make some well so much the better, sort of. Understanding who these people are that create the bubbles and scams that lead to Main Street's woes is essential if one is to understand the game of charades that they play upon John Q. Public.

Make no mistake about it, money and the power and status it brings them is an obsession for them, trumping everything else. They are people who always seem to be pushing the limits of legality and often exceeding the limit in a drive to enrich themselves at the expense of the clients they are supposed to be serving. At the time of their decision making that led to the economic collapse, to them it was the right thing to do, a gamble with John Q. Public's future well worth taking. For as you will come to find out, "they are doing God's work."

In the Lehman Brothers case study I commented upon the old Wall Street saying that the first hurdle in the career path of becoming an investment banker was to be able to sell your mother. This is not an exaggeration. I worked with them and have known many socially. They are a toxic mix of high intelligence, competitiveness, and aggression. Throw in a desire for fame and fortune and that mix of personality traits produces people who because of their high intelligence believe they can take risks and be able to figure out a way to defeat those risks and thereby they can become the top dog. The bats and balls with which they play their competitive games are Main Street's money. They key to all this is the fundamental fact that they get paid to play regardless of whether they make or lose Main Street's money. The stock goes up or the stock goes down and your stockbroker still makes a commission. The investment banking shenanigans behind the financial collapse of 2008 were at their core about the banks making commissions by selling securities related to mortgages. Even though it has now become clear the banks knew these securities were worthless, the commissions were in the many hundreds of billions of dollars.

Investment bankers give new meaning to ambition and competitiveness. Recall the term "big swinging dick" made famous in *Liars Poker*, all about the competitive games of the bond traders at the investment bank, Solomon Brothers. These folks are really a breed apart. They just do not want to win, but want to pound their opponent into the ground. As in why Lehman Brothers was the only bank that went under in 2008, remember how despised was its CEO Richard Fuld by his fellow bankers.

The 10,000 square foot and up houses with gyms, movie theaters, double-every-appliance kitchens, and pool houses alone that would trump most folks even dreams of a regular house are in the main a creation of the incredible sums of money that the investment banking community makes (by this I mean the name banks as well as the variety of folk involved in hedge funds, private equity, and the variety of other financial-engineering activities). For their houses, prices in the range of $10-$50 million are not uncommon. As an old car hobbyist I have been fascinated how during this same period of megahomes, car builders have responded similarly in a way that harkens back to the glory days of Pierce Arrows, Deusenbergs, Bugattis and such. Today, $150,000 seems the starting place and over $250,000 is where the air begins to get rarified for cars that fill these houses garages. The next time a new record for a Picasso, Van Gogh, etc. selling somewhere north of $100 million at an auction makes the news, no doubt you will know the occupation of its purchaser.

So if you sweat competition out of every pore of your body, and want to play with the big dogs, and "winning isn't everything, it is the only thing" rings true, investment banking is the place for you. As the intensely competitive former racing driver well known for his take-no- prisoners driving style, even at 180 mph, A.J.Foyt once said, "I don't go out there to finish second." Not everyone who wants to be top dog will make it, there is only so much money to go around. If running on the edge of the law and at times going over the edge is called for, it is worth the risk. After all, they don't give all those campaign contributions for no purpose as we shall come to see.

So, how do all these games get played, well let's start with the recent shenanigans of the tech bubble of the 1990s. The promise of the computer revolution seemed to be ushering in a new age of prosperity and quality of life and creating opportunities for those so inclined to amass great wealth. Venture capitalists were putting up high-risk money to fund a few folks with an idea on the proverbial "napkin' about the next great electronic gizmo or way to use existing gizmos with brilliant software to help us buy, sell, interact socially, and learn about this, that, or the other thing.

First, let me make sure you understand that in the old days, a new company would raise money from certain "private equity" sources and then turn to its own profits to fuel its growth. Then and only then, when it has proven its ability to make a profits, a company would be listed on the stock exchange for the public to buy and sell its shares. Today, the way venture capitalists make their money is for them to take the big risks of betting money on the idea. As the company progresses they place additional bets, adding money as needed to grow the company to the size that it is ready for a last round of financing so it can make it to the stage where its own profits will fuel future growth.

Instead of doing that last round of financing from venture capitalists who are tough guys with whom to deal, thanks to the publics falling in love with initial public offerings (IPOs), a company could now raise a large sum of new money through having it shares listed on the stock exchange even before it has made any profits. Since the public is willing to invest at a higher stock price and in ways that have far fewer strings attached than the venture capitalist, why not just sell stock to John Q. Public.

The IPO occurs through the company hiring an investment bank to manage the process of converting the private company into a public one. This initial offering of new shares is usually presold before the listing on the stock exchange primarily to institutional investors and the investment bank takes a part of the proceeds as a commission for having raised the money. After the IPO occurs the shares are now listed on a stock exchange and are available for anyone to buy and sell.

With that summary of how a company that begins with a private equity investment from venture capital ends up as a company listed on the stock exchange, let us take a bit more detailed look at the earlier stages of the process as it is critical to understanding one of the great charades of Wall Street. The venture capitalists at the beginning of the company probably bought the company's stock for around $0.50 per share. Over the next few years, through a succession of rounds of financing, as the company made progress the price of the stock would rise to about $3.00 per share. As the company developed, it became less risky, so the owners of the company could demand a higher stock price. If all went well, at each successive fundraising, the higher the price then the fewer the number of new shares had to be created for a given amount of investment. Each time the company raises money, the new stock given to the investors dilutes the percentage ownership held by the company's founders so it was in the founders interest to get as high a price as possible, creating as few new shares as possible and thus diluting their own ownership percentage less. (Raising

$1,000,000 dollars at $10.00/share creates 100,000 new shares, doing so at $100/share creates only 10,000 new shares; therefore the shares the founders own will be a higher percentage of the total number of shares the higher the stock price when the money is raised).

Eventually the company needs a large sum of money to bring their product to at least the national, if not international market. Given the demands of private equity investors for a low share price, raising money at this stage from the venture capitalists would mean unacceptable dilution to the founders and early stockholders ownership. Thank God for the public's willingness to invest at a stock price ten times higher than would have been acceptable to a private equity investor. Now is the time for the IPO.

Thanks to the publics willingness to pay such a high price to get in "early" on the next great internet winner, the venture capitalist would make at least 10X their money in just a few years, and if lo and behold the stock should zoom up after it became public, well then the return was just extraordinary. The investment bank responsible for managing the IPO not only made money as a fee for executing the public offering, but usually would also get stock in the form of options to purchase shares at a price that was at least the public offering price and often times much lower. A public offering is the Holy Grail; everyone gets rich, very rich. The public is left holding the bag, stock in a company that has yet proven it can earn a penny. The earlier investors sell as soon as it is public at the price well above what they had previously paid. Please, to be fair, remember when these initial investment rounds were done, the proof of principle for the product was still very risky.

The very rich happens because you, the reader, wants to buy the stock through your stockbroker who talked about "getting in on the ground floor" and "this could be the next Microsoft." What he did not tell you was that as part of the deal to manage the IPO, his company's investment banking division made a commitment to move so many shares through their retail (stockbrokers who sell to the public) network. To make sure they met that commitment the bank might offer a free trip to Hawaii to all the brokers who sell X number of shares. Hey, it could be the next Microsoft. Conflict of interest, oh you ain't seen nothing yet.

The charade that created the tech bubble was not about stock purchases at the IPO by the public investor, but by what happens to the stock once it is public. It takes a lot of folk eager to purchase the newly public stock for the venture capitalists and investment banks to be able to unload the large number of shares that they hold and not cause the stock to plunge. This extra volume of stock transactions are done with what are known as institutional investors consisting of pension plans, mutual funds, very wealthy individuals, and other organizations that have hundreds of millions and even billions of dollars to invest.

The bulk of the shares in the IPO are sold to these institutional investors. These sales, as well as promoting the stock after the IPO, involves a group of people who work for the investment banks and are known as research analysts. Their role was little known to the general public until the bursting of the tech bubble caused them to "burst" into plain sight but they were the truly essential cog in the machine that created the tech bubble.

The analysts job is to apply a variety of erudite analytical tools to understanding the prospects of a company and then to issue a report of their findings. The analysts are usually divided up along industry lines, some experts on pharmaceuticals, others steel, and others computers and software. On a regular basis they issue recommendations on specific companies as to whether investors should buy, sell, or hold specific stocks.

In spite of the analysts focus on just that, analysis, these analysts are not neutral observers. They act as if they surveyed the entire universe of companies in a certain industry, picked the best, and write these reports and make the presentations because of all available stocks, their Harvard MBA and years of experience have led them to pick this very stock. One of the grand charades of Wall Street.

The truth is that because investment banks make so much from handling a company's IPO, being able to do so is usually fought over by several banks. When the company's management and the venture capitalists decide the company's progress has made it a candidate for an IPO, several investment banks are called and if they are interested they stop-in and make presentations about why they should get the order to manage the IPO. A central piece of the presentation is a description of how successful and respected is the research analyst who works for them and covers the company's industry. A commitment is made for the analyst to publish a certain number of research reports touting the company not just for the sales of shares at the IPO but also over a certain period of time such as the next two years. This commitment is made before anyone has any idea how the company will perform, neutral analysis indeed.

So the research analysts who advise the institutional money managers, as in the pension funds managing your pension and the mutual fund managing your savings, send out their reports and make in-office presentations to investment managers about why this dot-com is the next big winner. CNBC and other financial news shows feature these analysts and in days gone by, before the bubble burst and exposed the whole charade, presented them in a completely neutral way to the viewing public.

Without a doubt the talking heads of all these shows know full well the inherent conflict of interest of an analyst who works for the bank that took the company public. That he would write a certain number of glowing reports was part of the deal that won the right to manage the IPO for the bank for which he worked. This commitment was made long before the company had actually done the business that he would be writing about.

CNBC and other financial networks exist and prosper through selling advertising. The higher the rating the more advertising is sold at higher prices. It is of course in these shows best interest to keep as much of the public involved and excited about the potential to make vast riches through investing in the markets. The high-tech bubble, fueled by hokum analyst's reports created the frenzy of day-traders and other market players that created household names out of CNBC's talking heads. Anyone even sort of close to the world of investment banking knows the role of the research analyst, to tout the stocks that that investment bank for which they work have as clients. CNBCs silence over this issue was deafening. It is that mutuality of self-interest, in this case Wall Street and the media that keeps the charades going, at least until it bursts of its own insincerity. The analysts coated with conflicts of interest were presented to the viewing audience without disclosure of their conflict of interest!!!!!!

In the 1990s, at the height of the technology bubble, the ratio of "buy" recommendations from these neutral research analysts to "sell" recommendations was 100:1. A University of California finance professor studied the performance of stocks after an analyst issued his research reports. The stocks given a strong buy recommendation underperformed the market by 3% per month whereas those stocks they recommended be sold actually outperformed the market by 3.8% per month.

The conflict of interest when a research report comes from the investment bank that did a company's IPO is directly shown by the finding from Investor.com that when a recommendation by an analyst at the same investment bank that did a company's IPO was followed, investors lost over 50%. Professors at Dartmouth and Cornell published a study that showed investors following the recommendations of analysts who worked for firms <u>without</u> an investment banking division did better than those whose employers had an investment banking division.

It was this very activity, the charade of the investment analyst running up a stock, that launched Elliot Spitzer on his road to fame when he was the Attorney General of New York state. He took to trial an analyst at Merrill Lynch who was a very high-profile analyst for high-tech companies, one of the go-to-guys for guru-like pronouncements. He even was ranked #1 technology analyst by the gold standard list published in *Institutional Investor*. It seems that when the guru was publishing Merrill Lynch reports to buy certain stocks, privately in emails within Merrill Lynch, they were being described as "junk" and "dogs." As so often happens, before the trial against Merrill began, Merrill settled for a $100 million fine.

However, thou shall have some pity upon the poor research analysts just trying to earn a living by applying their God-given analytical skills to companies on the stock exchange. You see, analysts who dare to put out sell recommendations or speak ill of companies are dealt with harshly and swiftly. Donald Trump's charismatic way of uttering "fired" is not just for his television show. An analyst who spoke ill of bonds backing trump's casino, Taj Mahal, and gave them a less than flattering treatment in his research report was fired by his investment banking firm after The Donald made threatening legal noise. Oh, and by the way, the bonds eventually went into default.

A similar fate was met by an analyst who issued a sell recommendation on none other than that glamorous high-flyer, Enron. Forest Laboratories, a pharmaceutical company has recently taken a more subtle approach with two analysts at an investment bank, Oppenheimer & Co. Two of Oppenheimer's analysts recently issued a negative report on Forest. In retaliation, Forest cut-off the analysts from participating in conference calls where management updates analysts on company progress as well as sending them threatening letters and refusing to communicate in any way which makes it kind of hard for the analysts to do their job.

So it is you the garden-variety investing public that are the cannon fodder for the venture capitalist to be able to cash-in on the next hot dot-com opportunity. The venture capitalist makes 10X his money and your stockbroker gets a free trip to Hawaii. So you lost a part of your savings for your kids college tuition, hey dude, no risk, no reward. You see I know of that which I speak, I was one of them. From 1981 until the mid 1990s I took all my knowledge from 10 years of teaching and research in academic medicine and ventured out with a recent

Executive MBA into the world of venture capital, focusing on health-care companies. I took the money given to me for my fund and invested in people with ideas to start the next big thing in the field of medicine. Diabetes, Alzheimers, cancer, you name it, we had a company that cured it.

I sat through the board meetings as new investors for the companies we started, were brought in along the way to take the company to the next stage. And God willing and the creek don't rise, I sat in the meetings when investment banks came by for the privilege of taking our humble companies public and heard the promises of positive analyst reports once the company went public.

Now investment bankers being the clever people that they are, sometime in the mid to late 1980s, it occurred to them: "Hey, why don't we raise a venture capital fund ourselves, then we can become investors in these companies, and when it comes time to take the company public, we will certainly have our feet in the door." So, after many rounds of still risky financings, nothing was better than to have an investment bank come in to the last round of venture investment prior to the IPO. Eager to get involved, they would pay a much higher price for stock, and as described previously, resulting in less dilution of the previous investors ownership.

Some of you may have read or heard about Goldman Sach's involvement with investing in Facebook at a very high stock price that made some question how could they eventually make money. Well, now you know part of the motivation. By becoming a part of the investor group, they would get their foot in the door for managing the upcoming IPO. Even if the venture-level investment broke even or lost some money, they would more than make it up through managing the IPO of stock to you, John Q. Public.

If indeed Facebook does go public, someday Goldman's analysts will be writing reports touting the wonders of Facebook. Perhaps they will say that even though Facebook has achieved near 100% market penetration, not to worry since it is rumored that a new planet has been discovered with people just like us and Facebook is gearing up for that market. Trust us, we are neutral research analysts with MBAs from Harvard and experts in social networking companies. Right up there with "trust us we are from the government and we are here to help you."

Venture capital is pretty straight forward investing. Money invested directly with a start-up company to build the company into a profitable enterprise. Once it is an ongoing company it does an IPO and is traded in the public markets which allows the venture capital investors to sell their stock for a very large profit. The charade wrinkle is that the public price is driven artificially high by the less than honest glowing reports written by the research analysts. If the company has very little true substance eventually it goes bankrupt and the public loses all its money, but the venture capitalists get to keep theirs (nice work if you can get it).

Before going directly into the charade of the mortgage backed securities that took down not just the United States economy but damaged economies worldwide there is one more type of investment to consider, the leveraged buy-out (LBO). The point of this sequence is to prepare those without much investing experience to understand the grand charade of the very complex investment structures that took down the economy.

The LBO is a method of acquiring all the shares of a public company, what is known as taking it private. Since there are no more public shareholders, the investors can do whatever they wish. The first thing to be done is to loot the company of most of its cash by the new shareholders voting to pay themselves a dividend. First they create cash by borrowing money on the company's assets and then raiding the company's bank account. They own all the shares and can do whatever they want.

The term "financial engineering" which was taken to the extreme in the 2008 collapse has been used to describe this type of investing. Nothing new has been created. Same old company stripped of everything that can be turned into cash. If it can still survive as an operating company for at least a few years, it is sold to the public at a higher price than the LBO group initially paid to take it private. That profit added to the very large dividend makes for a windfall.

Once upon a time the way to get really rich was to make things that you could sell in great quantities for more than it cost you to produce, such as refrigerators or shoes. Another way was to supply things already made but that needed a great deal of effort to dig them out of the ground and distribute to consumers, such as lumber, coal, and oil. Venture capital although dependent mostly on the research analyst, was not that far from this old school method. A company was built that had a product or service to sell. The LBO, very different, nothing really "industrial" happened, just financial engineering. However, both venture capital and LBO investing were highly dependent on the affluence of the baby boomers that gave them sufficient money to invest in "stories" charades instead of companies that made real profits from making refrigerators or digging coal out of the ground.

To understand how the LBO ushered in the era of financial engineering that destroyed the economy in 2008 here are a few examples. In the early days of intercity bus transportation, companies like Greyhound and Trailways built depots in every major city in America. As the decades passed, this real estate in downtown grew tremendously in value. The value of a company on the stock exchange is primarily based on the price to earnings ratio (PE). For the bus companies, their earnings had nothing to do with the asset value of all this real estate, but only the profit from the operating business of moving people around the country.

Soooo, why not take a publicly traded bus company private, raising money by leveraging the value of all that real estate. Off to an investment bank goes our financial engineer and makes the case that if one takes a look at the assets on the balance sheet of the bus company, the land it owns across the U.S. alone is worth 75% of the amount it would take to buy up all the shares of the bus company. So how about if the investment bank raises the 75% from public investors through bonds and the other 25% would be in cash from the financial engineer and his partners. With the proceeds from selling the bonds to investors and the cash, all the stock is bought and the bus company has now been "taken private."

The real estate is sold and its new owners lease it back to the bus company. The cash from the sale of the real estate will now be distributed as a dividend to the financial engineers as is the cash in the companies till built up over the years from the operating profits. Next, the new owners bring in an outside hot-shot manager to take a hard look at the company and streamline its operations. Companies do have operating momentum, "well this is the way it was always done" and in fact, a fresh look can produce significant improvement in its operating results. And last, but not least, firing 20% or so of the employees as part of the new more lean-and-mean company capable of generating greater profits even when downsized.

Now, through this financial engineering, the dividends usually in large part allow the investors to get the money they put in out, and still own 100% of the equity in the bus company. As long as the company makes enough profit to pay the interest on the bonds and keep the buses rolling another payday looms a few years out, selling the shares back to the public through an IPO.

There is a great truism written on the heavens, just look up at the sky and it is there: "Where thou haveth great reward thou also haveth great risk." There are no exceptions. If it were properly designed, the bus company's initial offering of bonds is done so that the operating profit of the company is just enough to pay the interest and keep the company running. Any downturn in business is big trouble. Since the original group behind the LBO took all the excess cash out, there is no fallback from deteriorating profits. Similarly, if the streamlining of the company's business fails to produce results that allow for raising additional cash through an IPO, the company will probably eventually descend into bankruptcy with the bondholders receiving whatever comes out of a sale of the remaining assets. The public stockholders would see their shares become worthless. Oh and by the way there are also the employees who were fired during the initial restricting as well as the workers with now no place to work as the financial engineering melts down to bankruptcy.

As the 1980s came into full bloom, everyone had at least one car and airplane travel was becoming affordable to more and more people and the small town ridership decreased as folks moved to the big city. Intercity buses became the mode of travel of last resort. Although this was a fictitious story, I wonder, Greyhound did acquire Trailways at fire sale prices, hmmm.

Not fictitious are the many examples where the critics of LBOs would say, the original investors raped the company of its cash and assets, fired a lot of employees, and then hyped up an IPO for a company that eventually went bankrupt leaving its equity holders with nothing and bond holders with pennies. Examples of companies known to the general public that were bankrupted by their overwhelming debt load incurred by the geniuses of LBO financial engineering are Federated Department Stores (owners of the major department stores in many of the U.S. biggest cities), Macys, Revco Drugs, Tribune Company, Harrah's Entertainment, Station Casinos, Regal Cinemas, Sbarro, and Owens Corning.

As I am writing this book (March, 2011), the largest hospital chain in the United States, Hospital Corporation of America (HCA) is currently at the end stage of the LBO process. The IPO of the transformed company occurred two days before I write this paragraph. It started in 2006, when a group of banks and LBO fund investors put up $4.9 billion in cash and borrowed $28 billion in order to purchase the company from existing shareholders at a 30% premium over the share price for HCA stock in the public markets.

True to form, the new group streamlined the company to enhance profits. In just three years the company had accumulated sufficient cash for the investors to declare themselves a $4.3 billion dollar dividend, recouping just about all of their initial investment. Meaning that they still held all the stock and a future sale of that stock once the company would become publicly traded again would provide a staggering profit.

In fact the just occurring IPO provided the investors with a 250% return in 4 years. HCA, so far at least, is a true shining example of what the pro LBO folks claim is the "unlocking" of value from a company badly in need of a new approach toward running its business. It can be argued that the current debt of just under 30 billion dollars which matches current annual revenue is very high. However, since the IPO, the changes made in streamlining the company have both increased the number of patients as well as the profitability of HCA. Of course with health-care reimbursement in a state of flux and the heavy debt load making the company very cash-flow sensitive perhaps should add a note of caution. Still though, quite an achievement of financial engineering.

An example of the other side of the LBO story is the still evolving LBO of a Texas based electricity generator, TXU, which is now pitting a hedge fund that invested in the debt behind the buyout with the LBO group that financially engineered the buy out and put up 8 billion of the cash side of the transaction. Since as is frequently the case in LBOs, the debt side of deal was not collateralized so the bonds had to pay a comparatively high rate of interest to get the investors to buy the bonds. It was such transactions that created the term "junk bonds," the same as described in more polite society as "high yield," the words used in ads and prospectuses sent out to investors.

TXU is currently struggling to makes its payments on the bonds, with negotiations currently underway as of this writing to change the terms of the bonds in order to avoid default. What happens to the high yield bonds is really important because exposure to TXU is not limited to the gunslingers of Wall Street. The dollar value of all the unsecured bonds represent 1% of all such bonds traded on the stock exchange. They are probably a part of the holdings of all such junk-bond funds in the United States (oops I meant to say "high-yield bond funds"—I mean after all just look at what it says in the prospectus your mutual fund sent you). If you do not own them personally, how about that "professionally" managed 401K or pension plan. Most probably, in a restructuring these bonds will see their value drop to zero. The LBO fund behind this deal has written their EQUITY investment down by 80%.

Once again, if all else fails, dress it up and take it to the IPO ball. Have some analysts write glowing reports and let John Q. Public's stockbrokers work the phones, and voila, new funds are raised.

In the old days if you bought stock in Ford, you owned a certain percentage, no matter how tiny it might be. If the company were to be liquidated, you could lay claim to a set of wheels in a Ford factory somewhere that represented the percentage of total value held through your 25 shares. In the world of financial engineering, nothing is left for the stockholder, and just crumbs for the bondholders.

Once the meltdown of 2008 occurred, it came to light that the financial engineers had pushed the envelope and created investment structures that made LBOs seem positively substantive. Known as synthetic derivatives these structures were created out of thin air. They were a pure charade in ways that most in the investment community would never even have imagined were possible, much less legal, financial engineering taken to the extreme. When exposed, they took down the world economy. Here is how they worked and what happened. Charade, scam, and con, fail to describe the scene.

A credit default swap (CDS) is really complicated and they were at the heart of the financial meltdown of 2008. As many of the talking heads on the media were apt to describe, some of the folks on Wall Street did not even understand what was behind the instruments they were buying and selling for your pension plans and mutual funds that held your life savings. After much work to get myself up to speed, here is one way of presenting it that might help explain what is a synthetic derivative. It is borrowed in part from the website of Richard Isacoff, a lawyer specializing in financial matters.

Here we go: A fantasy sports team is constructed of players from many different teams and people bet on the fantasy teams performance which is then measured by the performance of the real players in real games. This new league is a derivative of the actual league. So let us now change the names of the players on the fantasy teams and let people then make up a second-order fantasy team based upon the first fantasy teams. This new league would now constitute a synthetic derivative league on which people could also bet. Synthetic in the sense that teams from which it is derived are fictitious themselves and do not actually play baseball. Last but not quite least, lets create a company that offers insurance on the performance of the players. Then on top of that let us create a market where people can buy and sell these insurance contracts. No joke this really happened. A stock market like system allowed people to buy and sell the insurance policies on the second level fantasy-team players performance. This is what happened to your 401K and pension plan money.

Okay now we have the model set in ways most of us I hope can understand or at least get a sense of how "derived" and "synthetic" these financial instruments were. Let us substitute a group of loans for the individual players who actually played the game. It started out with just mortgages bundled together into financial instruments called CMOs, collateralized mortgage obligations. The collateral being the houses underlying the mortgage debts. These instruments had such a great reception, that banks started adding every loan imaginable such as credit card debts, car loans, and even student loans and called these collateralized debt obligations, CDOs. Investors could purchase the CDOS and expect to receive the loan payments as dividends on their investments. So what if houses and student loans were being considered as equally valuable and risk-free collateral.

Now we need to go one step further. Banks are supposed to follow rules on the ratio between the amount of cash the bank has and the amount of loans they can make, this rule therefore sets a limit to how many loans and commissions on those loans they can make. If they could find a way to "lay off" some loans, at least as it would appear on the balance sheet (yes, same deal as in Lehman and its repo 105s) as if they had made fewer loans so then they could start making more loans. So investment banks created something called a credit default swap (CDS) that allows the bank to lay-off to another person the risk for the loan. Sort of like swapping the risk of a loan onto an insurance company. For a certain fee, the insurance company will give the bank a guarantee of repayment in case the person who took out the loan enters default. If the player on your fantasy team strikes out, you would get paid as if they had hit a home run.

Where we are now in the chain of transactions is that a variety of loans are packed together into instruments, CDOs, in which investors put their money. These instruments are then offered up to insurers who for a fee (the insurance premium) paid by the bank will assume responsibility for the principal behind the loan, such as a house behind a mortgage. This insurance for the risk of the loan is the Credit Default Swap (CDS). The investment bank J.P. Morgan came up with the bright idea of creating the equivalent of the New York Stock Exchange for Credit Default Swaps, it was called BISTRO for Broad Index Secured Trust Offering.

The folks who were acting as insurers could offer up their Credit Default Swap as if it were a financial instrument and investors would buy and sell them with one another. The value of the houses, cars, etc., the collateral that is behind the loans that were at the beginning of the process is long ago detached, and thus the use of the term Synthetic Derivatives. All of this was done in the beginning as a way to make the number of loans on the balance sheet look smaller. A way of hiding the true financial vulnerability of the bank from investors (as in your 401K) and bank regulators.

The trading of the CDSs took off like wildfire. Trillions of dollars were involved worldwide, not in the underlying loans, but in the amount of money spent trading the derived synthetic derivatives and the contracts on the insurance of these derivatives. When the mortgage market went soft and people started to actually default on their loans, all the players went on the disabled list, and the house of cards (synthetic derivatives) collapsed. The banks holding the actual mortgages in the first level instrument, the Collateralized Mortgage Obligation (CMO) could at least retrieve the fire sale value of the house, but the folks actively trading the synthetic Credit Default Swaps (CDS) had nothing but air underlying their investment and lost everything. In fact, not even the folks at the beginning of the chain, having a right to the house as collateral could collect, because the level of panic selling meant the insurance companies were on the hook for an amount they did not have and just declared bankruptcy.

Trillions of dollars were involved and played a major if not the trigger role in the ensuing meltdown of the investment banks. Remember the whole idea for this in the beginning is the investment banks looking for a transaction from which they would earn commissions. Every time any one of these instruments was created and then bought or sold the investment bank made a commission. Also remember that in the beginning of this chapter I mentioned understanding the personalities of an investment banker is important to understanding the financial collapse. We are like Gods, no not actually, not "like" Gods, we are Gods was their self-image as will be substantiated in their own words later in the chapter.

To show you just how bizarre all this is, General Motors of course went through bankruptcy and most of its bondholders were wiped out. The new General Motors emerged with very little debt and has been aggressively paying off what remained. However, dear reader, and you may find this hard to believe, there is still an actively traded market of CDSs (the insurance on the debt instruments) for General Motors. General Motors has no debt so it has no collateralized debt obligations that can be insured. The very basis for Credit Default Swaps does not exist, yet people are buying and selling CDSs on General Motors through BISTRO. Perhaps it is no longer even right to use the term "air" for the lack of collateral underlying the loans upon which CDSs are based, maybe in this case it should be "vacuum." However, as the current GM evolves and releases its reports on car sales and quarterly financial statements, those who are addicted to trading CDSs dive in and place bets on GMs ability to pay off its debts if and when they ever have any. Feeling better about your 401K, well do ya, John Q Public.

So with all the geniuses of financial engineering enjoying themselves trying to outdo each other and push the limits of creativity up against that rather thin veil of regulatory and legal boundaries, what is the average investor to do. After all, from the stockbroker who takes clients orders for 25 shares of this or that stock or the investment bankers who create the acronym financial instruments and sell them to their hedge fund and institutional money manager clients, they all get rich on the sales commission whether the stocks and acronyms go up or down. They have no skin in the action.

But wait, all is not lost. There are law firms and accounting firms who base their reputations on providing a stamp of approval on the legality of the company's transactions and validity of the numbers presented in their financial statements. Moreover, when it comes to things such as debt instruments, as in all those bonds investors from individuals to professionally managed funds like to own, there are these famous ratings agencies, Moodys, Fitch, and Standard & Poor's looking out for us. Now I feel safe.

Not so fast there bucko. There is an organization call FASB, the Financial Accounting Standards Board, FASB sets the standards for how the day-day to financial life of a business is gathered together into a manageable group of transactions that can then be displayed on the three financial statements, Income, Balance Sheet, and Cash Flow. That a company has followed these standards is left up to accounting firms that will audit the financial statements and put their stamp of approval that FASB standards are met, thus giving the investor or anyone else who is curious about a company's financial health and prospects for the future their stamp of approval. For publicly traded companies on a major stock exchange there are a select group of companies that do their financial audits. In the Lehman Brothers story you met one, Ernst & Young.

After all the deception at Lehman Brothers and loss of investor value from its bankruptcy, there are no legal actions being taken by the government against Lehman Brothers. The only action underway is against their auditor Ernst & Young. The whistle blower, Mr. Lee, sent Ernst & Young a letter detailing the repo 105 and other fraudulent activities. Lehman's Board of Directors received a similar letter about repo 105 from Mr. Lee and the board asked Ernst & Young to look into his claims on their behalf. Ernst & Young reported back to the board a clean bill of health. That is why the government is going after Ernst & Young.

Another very practical reason is that they are the deepest pocket around, Lehman Brothers is no longer.

Why you may ask would Ernst & Young have acted that way, knowing full well that the repo 105 transaction was used purely to present a fraudulent balance sheet for the quarterly reports. Well, the biggest billing event for an accounting firm is these audits of public companies. Audits for private companies and doing people and small business tax returns are small potatoes. In addition, there are only three accounting firms that are considered qualified to audit public companies. The competition is fierce.

Remember the issue of materiality, whether one or another events in a company's financial life is of sufficient size and/or importance to merit it being displayed in the audited statements. As discussed previously, materiality is in the eye of the beholder. If Ernst & Young had decided that the use of repo 105 timed for the end of the quarter was a "material" event and needed to be described as such on the quarterly report, no doubt it would have triggered within Lehman the practice of "opinion shopping."

Opinion shopping happens for both accounting issues and legal as well. I have been in meetings where opinion shopping was on the agenda. Needless to say, not on a piece of paper or other form of permanent record. There are other law and accounting firms that would be hungry for the business. If for example one firm says that a certain piece of information is material and must be described in the company's public disclosure, but from the company's perspective would be considered less than favorable, there is always the chance that another firm might view it otherwise. One of the other big three firms would probably love that new piece of business, it is certainly worth shopping around for a different perspective on "materiality." So let's hear it for the guarantee of propriety given to us by the law firms and accounting firms. It is considered "not material" and therefore does not have to be disclosed that the accounting firm signing off on the financial statements received the business after "opinion shopping."

Well, maybe the answer is to stick to bonds, after all those credit-rating agencies are lifting the rug and giving us a good look see. Bonds are the mainstay of the risk-averse, no stocks for them, just collect the dividends and get your principle back when the bond matures. After all what more could one want than the *imprimateur* of Moodys, Fitch, and Standard & Poor's. The guru of bond investing is Bill Gross who manages the largest bond fund in the world and when Mr. Gross speaks on CNBC it is preceded with trumpets blaring and rose petals scattered, he commented on the rating agencies: "Like vampires in the dead of the night (*rating agencies*) will outlast us all."

You see, many of those mortgage backed securities instruments as well as the instruments derived from them that destroyed the banking system had been rated by these agencies as AAA, the highest rating, at the time they were issued. A year or two later they were all considered "junk," oops "high yield." Just as with the accountants and lawyers, the rating firms derive their income from the fees paid by their clients, the issuers of the bonds. Shopping around is the standard. For example, in 2009 Deutsche Bank AG put together a debt instrument containing a number of loans the bank had made to U.S. companies. Fitch gave the rating of AAA whereas both Moodys and Standard and Poor's turned down the business out of concern for the quality of the loans. From the mortgage backed securities at the basis of the financial meltdown to the variety of other bonds that are out there, their trustworthiness is based upon the ratings of a credit rating agency firm. All of whom are in a dog-eat-dog business for market share. The California state pension fund is currently suing all three agencies, alleging "wildly inaccurate ratings."

Weirdly enough, this system of outsourcing bond ratings was put in place by Congress right after the depression to make sure that banks did not put themselves at risk by investing their own money (also known as their depositor's money) in bonds that were risky. Good ol' Yogi Berra, in his infinite wisdom got it right, "It's *déjà vu* all over again." As a part of the new financial regulation in Congress is one proposal of setting up a special group within the SEC that would assign to each bond offering a credit rating agency on a random basis. The group would keep track of the bonds and over time create a data base that would be used based upon the accuracy of their ratings to then favor one agency over the other.

So the research analysts are shills for stock offerings being peddled by their investment banking employers, the accountants and lawyers make their living telling their clients what they want to hear, and the ratings agencies compete with each for business by fudging the rating system that is supposed to tell us their opinion of the creditworthiness of the debt instrument they are rating.

DO YOU KNOW WHERE YOUR MUTUAL FUND OR PENSION PLAN IS INVESTING YOUR MONEY? REMEMBER, MOST OF THESE CMO AND CDO INSTRUMENTS WERE RATED AAA BY THE RATINGS AGENCIES EVEN THOUGH THE AGENCIES HAD NO KNOWLEDGE OF THE

INDIVIDUAL LOANS PACKAGED TOGETHER INTO THE INSTRUMENTS.

With all these shenanigans, cons, and charades being perpetrated on mainstream America whose money is used to prop-up the whole system through the stocks and bonds bought by their pension plans and mutual funds, where can one turn to try to learn a fair assessment about a company. I say this sort of as a joke to segue into a new subject: How about senior management of the company?

It is the CEO who sets the tone, the corporate culture in which all these activities take place. The buck stops with the CEO. Can they be trusted to tell us the truth? Recent history helps us out on this one. Enron, an energy trading company, is one of the emblematic names as an example of the charade Wall Street plays on the investment public. Its shares peaked in early 2001 at $84/share on January 2, 2001 (thanks in no small part to analysts' recommendations). By the end of the month Enron senior managers unloaded their options to purchase shares and made $82 million in profit.

In August, the CEO, announced via a press release that he would be leaving the company for "family reasons." He certainly was going to enjoy a nice retirement since his combined take-home from a variety of sources for that year would be $184 million. Eventually Andrew Fastow, the CFO, would earn a little over $60 million before also announcing his retirement. A bright lawyer read these traditional reasons for retirement along with the also perhaps a bit on the high-side, but not out of bounds, last year pay packages and thought it would be worthwhile lifting the carpet. The rest as they say is history, Enron is no more and the stockholders were left with nothing. That same lawyer that got the ball rolling on exposing the Enron charade eventually ended up doing time for his own shenanigans, as Kurt Vonnegut said so often: "and so it goes," as in, what else would you expect.

The traditional comment when a senior manager quits their job and the company issues a press release about why they quit, says something along the lines of: leaving for "personal" or "family" reasons. This is rarely true. These press releases are approved by the company's legal counsel. I have never seen a study so I am simply eye-balling the statistics but it is a very fair bet that these reasons that are always without comment on the goings on of the company are at least 75% of the time false.

The issue of CEO resignations had always been on my mind as another example of the charade played by corporations on their shareholders, but was nowhere near the top of my list for inclusion. It was researching other prime subjects such as research analysts and opinion shopping amongst accounting and law firms, and the credit ration agencies, that I just came across such egregious examples I simply could not resist, it so helped me make my case. Writing this in March 2011, it came to light that Clearwire Corporation's CEO resigned for "personal reasons." Goshum-golly-gee, never heard that before. However its Chairman of the Board I can only presume did not receive a copy of the script since he made a comment to the press about how now that the CEO was gone the company could pursue a merger that would lead to a focus on cost cutting and enhanced profitability.

So it does not take years of experience on corporate boards to read between the lines that the board was unhappy with the direction given the company by the CEO. The board wanted a change in focus and a merger, a strategy that the CEO did not share, so he quit. Back to my finger-in-the-air guess on how often the reason given for CEO resignations is true. Most of the time it is probably over a disagreement in company strategy and business plan going forward between the CEO and the board. Some of the time, and troublingly more often than it ought to be, the CEO quits because the books have been cooked in the past and/or the company's future looks grave and CEO wants out before this stuff becomes public. Of course the truth cannot be told because of its impact on the stock price, so the ubiquitous "personal" or "family" reasons are trotted out.

On the subject of management trustworthiness; although not about resignations but about something more important for the investing public is the "conference call" when a company announces its at least annual, if not quarterly results. The research analysts, prominent members of the financial media, and managers of institutional investment funds are a part of the conference call emanating from corporate headquarters. On the call senior management announces their financial results, discusses their general feelings for the future, and takes questions from the callers.

A group of professors from Stanford decided to record these calls. They then analyzed them for characteristics that would predict whether or not there was evasion going on as measured by things that management would have known at the time but did not disclose and subsequently became public such as oh minor issues like having to restate earnings.

After analyzing 30,000 transcripts of these calls over a four year period the researchers found some striking results. Remember these are CEOs and CFOs, folks who are supposedly bound by law not to gild the lily and only report the truth in public information about their companies. Lo and behold the Stanford folk found they could predict 50%-65% of the times which companies would end-up later qualifying the numbers used in the conference call by specific words that were used, suggesting that management knew all along they were not being truthful and preferred to deceive and then later issue revised numbers.

I was tempted to wind-up this chapter about here with just a few concluding comments. However, in the context that although this book is about a group of separate charades, maybe none is more important, even the one about how Washington works, than this chapter about Wall Street. These days there are few who do not have a direct investment with stocks and bonds either by yourself or through a pension, 401K, or other professionally managed fund. Your ability to make your way through life is very much a function of how these investments turn out. I expect that you probably have as little an understanding of how Wall Street works than with any other institution you interact with. So let me wind up with a few more pages that I hope will slam-dunk for you just what kind of people they are who are making the decisions on your financial future.

I first came across the term "corporate culture" back when I was getting my Executive MBA to make a transition from being a neuroscientist to another career. I have to admit that at the time, still wearing my science hat which infected my brain totally, I was skeptical of such a concept. After all, decisions are all logical, data analyzed, and the one and only conclusion reached. Everyone sees things the same logical way, after all didn't Spock say "It's only logical captain." Corporate culture, how can that have an effect and make one company different from another, after all two plus two always equals four. Hah! pride does indeed goeth before the fall.

Nothing could be more emblematic of the true existence of corporate culture than the Goldman Sachs affair known as "Abacus." Abacus came to light in the hearings following the banking meltdown and really does nail down just how "charadey" is Wall Street. Let us go back to a variation of the IPO process. In the Abacus case there was no actual company to take public. However, since an investment bank makes a great deal from managing a public offering, why not create a security on their own that they can sell to the public. What would really be a winner is if the bank can even then make more money from its own involvement through betting on what it knew would be the future direction of the stock that would never be disclosed to John Q. Public. Thus was created a deal known as Abacus.

The Abacus deal got started when an investment manager, John Paulson, went to Goldman Sachs to help him find a way to make money by betting against all these subprime mortgages that Paulson felt were worth not much more than the paper they were printed on. So the investment bank working with Paulson bundled together mortgages they knew were suspect and created CDOs for Goldman to sell to their clients. The ratings firms Moodys and Standard Poor's gave these CDOs their top rating, AAA. Moreover, ACA Capital Holdings, Ltd. was willing to have its mortgage insurance division write insurance on these CDOs. The bank's brokers called their clients and gave these CDOs their highest recommendations, quoting the glowing reports of its own analysts.

Knowing full well the poor quality of the mortgages underlying the CDOS, both Paulson and Goldman took a "short" position, a bet that the value of the CDOs would fall. The deal was put together and sold in Spring of 2007. By November of 2007 the mortgages in the Abacus deal had been downgraded by both Moodys and Standard and Poor's reflecting the dramatic lowering of housing prices. So let's tally up the score. According to the SEC, Goldman's clients, the investors who bet positively on the CDOs lost more than a billion dollars while Paulson who bet negatively profited by a billion and Goldman made a billion in fees and profits from its short position.

A cute vignette from the whole episode involves a Paulson senior manager and his wife while on vacation in Anguilla in late 2007. She put her card in an ATM and was astonished to see on the printed receipt a recent deposit of 45 million. In fact it was just a part of the 175 million bonus he received that year.

As is the pattern, after things go bad the SEC pays attention and holds hearings. At issue was that Goldman and Paulson had prior knowledge that the CDOs would go bad and that they were recommending securities to clients as a "buy" while at the same time taking the other side of the trade, betting they would go down. As time lines and who said what to whom were presented in evidence at the hearing, an expert in such matters and professor at Duke Law School described Goldman's defense, "That strikes me as plain and simple laundering of the deal,...To me it goes directly to the materiality of the omission (leaving out Paulson's role in choosing dicey mortgages to insure his bet that they would go down would win)."

The SEC did file a lawsuit in April, 2010 against Goldman Sachs focusing on the lack of full disclosure in its sales documents to its clients. Goldman responded to the filing of the lawsuit with: "The SECs charges are completely unfounded in law and fact." In July of 2010, the SEC and Goldman reached a settlement of $550 million and Goldman admitted to no wrong doing. What was that about "unfounded in law in fact?"

A variety of investors in the Abacus CDOs have filed lawsuits on their own which are still in process. Goldman was not alone in being in on "both sides" of the trade. J.P. Morgan did the same with its own CDO deal and ended up paying a $153 million dollar fine with of course not admitting guilt being a part of the plea deal. By the way J.P. Morgan also kept encouraging its clients to invest in Bernie Madoff's fund, earning themselves a nice commission, long after they had made the decision something smelled in the house of Madoff and stopped investing their own money with him.

Kudos however go to the investment bank Bear Stearns, well sort of. John Paulson had initially contacted not only Goldman with his idea of finding a way to place a big bet on mortgage based CDOs tanking, but also Bear Stearns, as well. Bear turned the deal down thinking it was wrong to take both sides of the trade—selling securities to investors as great investments while at the same time betting they would go down. Bear Stearns no longer exists, taken down by the financial meltdown. Who knows how a billion dollars in fees might have helped? Perhaps "good guys do finish last" (see discussion of "nice guys finish last in a later Chapter).

Corporate culture is very real. It is more than accounting and legal opinions on financial statements that are "shopped." Shady deals are shopped as well by shady people.

So Goldman paid the SEC about 50% of what they made from doing the activity that was the basis for the SEC litigation. Some writers have discussed the additional downside to Goldman of the damage to their reputation from having "allegedly" sold their clients a security that that they knew the guy behind creating the security as well as themselves were betting its value would go down. Well, one would think so, but when big money and world-wide stuff is on the line, and Goldman is the 800 pound gorilla in the room of investment banking, it just does not matter. Enter the fray, Facebook.

Facebook is an incredible story, mentioned daily in every media channel on the planet. Investors are making the lemmings look like rational thinkers as they scramble to get a piece of the action. Facebook's Board of Directors has decided it wants to stay private and build more value before going public, but to build that value a few more bucks in the bank would be helpful. So they turn to Goldman Sachs for help and got exactly what they should have expected.

Goldman had great success selling Facebook stock to well-heeled private investors, $500,000 million worth in fact; but done in a way that put Goldman once again on the wrong side of the law. Although the deal got done, it was clearly embarrassing to everyone involved. There is a law in the United States, that in an offering of private stock to investors, the investors must show a certain level of wealth to qualify and only a certain number of investors can own any one class of stock. Goldman clearly violated several of these points, the central one being the number of investors. To get around the law, Goldman attempted to create an investment vehicle we will call "X" which would have all the different investors in it and then X would be the only investor making the investment directly in Facebook. The SEC notified Goldman it had a dim view and Goldman backed away.

Goldman took the hottest company on the planet, created an investment vehicle, solicited its favored U.S. investors, then took the deal away from them when the SEC got wind of it. So Goldman went outside the U.S. where such laws did not exist and easily got the deal done. When it comes time, probably in about a year, for Facebook to be taken public, wanna bet who will be the lead investment banker, yup, Goldman Sachs, "they get the deal done." Selling their mother is a no brainer for these types of folk.

Right now, the hottest story on Wall Street is the developing case of insider trading that involves a hedge fund, Galleon Group, that received insider information from a person who at that time served on the board of guess who, Goldman Sachs. Goldman's CEO, Lloyd Blankfein will testify against this now former member of Goldman's board. In an attempt to block the discrediting of Mr. Blankfein's testimony due to Goldman's many legal problems, the prosecutors in a letter to the U.S. District Judge said: "Rajaratnam (hedge fund manager) might suggest for example, that because Goldman Sachs is tied up in many different legal proceedings, the firm-- and by extension its CEO, Mr. Blankfein—is not to be trusted."

Anyway, prior to actually digging into the research for this book, I never intended to spend so much time on Goldman, but from Abacus, then Facebook, then the blockbuster insider trading scandal, everywhere I looked Goldman was on the wrong side of the law. Even the European debt crisis, who pops up with a deceptive con but Goldman Sachs. Its name was Titlos, created by Goldman in 2001 as way for Greece to make real debt disappear and then resurrected during the ECB bailout for reasons according to a Stanford University finance professor: "The ECB [European Central Bank] knew this was happening and decided that they wanted to play along in order to get liquidity out of there. The details were mind-bogglingly complex, but clearly another shadowy structure to get around the laws and make something appear as if it were different from what it really was. I guess that is the definition of a charade. Just like Abacus was not created by someone betting against it and the Facebook investment entity was not to get around U.S. private placement laws.

Twenty four hours a day, a world of shadows and charades, nothing is at it appears. Some investors win and others lose, and on both sides, Goldman Sachs and the others that aspire to their greatness are the puppet masters raking in fees from both sides. As its CEO Lloyd Blankfein said in late 2009 when interviewed by a reporter that he was just a banker "doing God's work." The government is always a few new tricks, moments, and I.Q. points behind.

One thing, however remains the same whether Goldman gets in trouble with regulators, its share price falls, it pays a $550 million settlement for misleading customers, or it loses money for its clients, its partners come out smelling like roses. That is at least if the smell of money is the most important thing in the world to you. In 2009 Goldman's top five executives made $5.3 million. In 2010 Goldman's net revenue fell 13% and profits fell 37% yet the top five made $69.6 million.

The only heartening thing about Goldman is that it took in $1.3 billion from the Libyan government for investment purposes and not much more than a year later, 98% of that money had been lost. The Libyans were not happy and made threatening noises. Well, something tells me the folks at Goldman are well trained in sleeping with one eye open, but one never knows, as the old Libyan saying goes, "don't get mad, get even."

A very discouraging story for the general investor. How do you put your family's life savings into play with these guys? If your timing is when markets are going up for solid reasons you may have a clean 10 year period of a reasonable appreciation in your money. Throw darts at the newspaper stock listing page as a way to pick stocks and you should at least do as well as the Dow Jones Industrial average. However, if it is the money for your kid's college and your timing is bad, and you hit a bubble which of course is not called a bubble until it blows up, it could spell catastrophe as your reward for 20 plus years of working hard and saving.

Sometimes a figure does stand out as seeming a decent, forthright individual. All in all, if one is going to place their bet with a money manager, he seems like as good a choice as any and perhaps better than most. If there were ever such a figure it is Warren Buffett. A seeming fine fellow with a heck of a good track record over many decades of ups and downs. However, even Mr. Buffett can get snookered, and it happened recently by one of his own employees. A Mr. Sokol had been identified by the octogenarian Buffett as a likely successor, at least until recently.

It seems that an investment bank had prepared a "book" as it is called in the biz, offering a very large chemical company Lubrizol for sale. Mr. Sokol received the book on behalf of Berkshire Hathaway, Mr. Buffett's investment vehicle, and thought it looked pretty good and was going to forward it on to Mr. Buffett with his recommendation that it was a good buy for $6 billion. However, before doing that he purchased shares in Lubrizol on his own behalf.

Now if there were ever an example of someone trading on nonpublic information, known only to him, and perhaps at most half-a-dozen people, this would be an example. Just the information becoming public that the "Mr Buffett, the sage of Nebraska," one of the most respected investors ever was considering, much less made a decision, to purchase Lubrizol would have an immediate dramatic impact on the stock price.

Mr. Buffett agreed with Mr. Sokol and began the process of a detailed investigation of Lubrizol and Berkshire approached the investment banker to begin the negotiation for its purchase. Now, at the time Mr. Sokol first talked to Mr. Buffet, he did mention to Mr. Buffett that he owned some shares. Neither the number of shares or when it was purchased was a part of the conversation. As the deal progressed with teams of lawyers involved, the sizeable purchase of shares and the timing of their purchase became known.

Mr. Sokol was soon to resign from Berkshire Hathaway. A series of statements from Berkshire Hathaway and Mr. Buffett personally, at first were relatively mild, but as the furor built, the company and Mr. Buffett became more damning about the action. Mr. Buffets mostly silent partner even took his company to task for not condemning Mr. Sokol's actions sooner. Finally, about a month after this all broke, Mr. Buffett stated that Mr. Sokol's action were inexcusable, that they violated all Berkshire's policy in how to handle such matters and that Berkshire had turned over to investigators "some very damning evidence" about Mr. Sokol's stock purchase.

It seems that ten years ago, early in his career Mr. Sokol was to receive a $12.5 million incentive bonus, but told Mr. Buffett that it should really be awarded to Mr. Sokol's assistant. The profit to Mr. Sokol for his early purchase of shares in Lubrizol, a blatant career-damaging move as well as resulting in possible criminal charges was $3million. As the head of Mr. Buffett's enterprise, $3million would be a rounding error on the wealth Mr. Sokol would have accumulated. Another, "go figure," perhaps just being a part of a slime-bucket industry tests your integrity no matter who you are.

So here we have the one person in this entire industry that had a gold-plated reputation, now tarnished. It is really almost Shakespearian. The wise old king is beloved throughout his kingdom and has a son. The son is anointed as successor to the throne and is year after year presented with the temptations of power. Eventually he gives in to temptation and commits a dastardly act that tarnishes his reputation as well as that of his father earned over a lifetime.

V. STUDENT ATHLETE !!!

OXYMORON OF CHARADES

It is hard to watch a college basketball or football game on a major channel without hearing the term "student athlete." As my favorite broadcaster of the human-life game once wrote, well it is not exactly what he wrote in Hamlet, but this is sort of like horseshoes so close is good enough, "Me thinks thou doth protest too much." Never has Shakespeare been more correct about the incessant braying by the National Collegiate Athletic Association (NCAA) and the talking heads of sports broadcast over the term "student athlete." It is one of the truly great charades of our modern American culture.

The evidence will be described below to "slam dunk" this contention. For those with little time on their hands to read on, just take the word of those who have been at the center of the cyclone. Scott Kennedy is the director of scouting for scout.com, a service affiliated with Fox Sports that provides in depth analysis of up and coming high school prospects, he said, "Ninety-nine percent of people gave up the farce of the student-athlete long, long, ago…no one is paying to watch them debate. They're watching them play football." How about taking the word of the President (1988-1996) of the University of Michigan, James Duderstadt, "Basketball is the cesspool of college sports." Or even one of their own, Barry Switzer, the legendary former coach of Oklahoma commenting on the earlier revelations of what turned out to be a major scandal involving Ohio State coach, Jim Tressel, "that's jaywalking to me, these things don't surprise me. This stuff has gone on forever."

Student athletes are truly one of the great charades. University sports teams serve for football and basketball the same function as the minor league does for baseball. Oh, and why does it really matter, as described in the Chapter about the U.S. slipping as a world leader, our educational system is not doing just so super-duper in keeping up with our global competition—really, why should we care. "We're number one," on the football field and basketball court at least.

The networks whose fees paid to the Universities for broadcast rights to their games and season ending tournaments fund the athletic departments, million dollar coach's salaries, and all the necessary infrastructure to train, house, and feed these world-class athletes. Success on the playing field also dramatically increases alumni donations. Everyone is making a big buck, our country be damned. The evidence described below could not be clearer, student athlete is a farce, an ugly charade. At a time when our country is challenged globally like never before, it is our educational system upon which we will rise or fall, nothing but a singular focus is acceptable.

To "kick-off" the chapter and verse, "get the ball rolling," so to speak, let us take a look at Southern Methodist University (SMU) and its football program. SMU has long been known as a decent enough football team. Yours truly remembers as a kid, just about sixty years ago going to see SMU play Rice, pride of my hometown and in those days a pretty darn good football school itself. Who can forget the legendary play by an Alabama football player who got so wrought-up as Dick Moegle of Rice was making a touchdown run along the sidelines, that an Alabama player who was on the bench at the time, ran onto the field and tackled Moegle (LOL).

Well, after that little trip down my nostalgia lane, back to SMU. I can still see in my mind's eye as if it were yesterday, the great player for SMU who became a Dallas Cowboy legend and then a founding member and stalwart of Monday night football, Don Meredith, putting on an astounding passing display against Rice, a game I was fortunate enough to attend.

It was a different time. Rice noted for its world-class engineering school, and back then free tuition thanks to a generous endowment, was also a football team of national renown. SMU was a lesser football power and let us be polite, not exactly known for academic prowess. Yet at some point, SMU decided to put itself on the football map. The decision was driven by a group of boosters who were going to fund the whole program through donations for athletic scholarships and more, the more not being so publically acknowledged, at least not then.

So a first class coach, Ron Meyers, was hired. Scholarships dangled to the best high school football players money could buy. Meyers built a team that becomes a national powerhouse. SMU is soon on national TV primetime and everyone knows its name. From 1980-1985 SMU won 55 games and lost 14, winning three Southwest Conference titles along the way. However, one of their players runs into trouble with drugs and gets thrown off the team. He gets into rehab, comes out cleaned-up and wants back onto the team. SMU refuses and the player goes public with a series of accusations. Accusations are made about SMU violating every imaginable rule of the NCAA in terms of how he was recruited to play for SMU. Most of these accusations involve payments to his family to entice him to SMU as well as payments to himself and his family during his playing years. It turns out this was a pattern for SMU and its well-heeled booster club. Boosters putting various members of the player's family on their company's payroll as a hidden way to grease their son coming to play for SMU

This one player's accusations came at a time when the two main newspapers in Dallas were duking it out for survival. A perfect storm for an exposé. Each one tried to outdo the other with the latest greatest revelations of SMU violations of NCAA rules. It seems that this one player was just the tip of the iceberg. The entire program was rank with hidden payments to the players and their families to get the players to come to SMU.

The real bombshell was the role of the Governor of Texas, Bill Clements, who also served as head of the Board of Governors of SMU, as well as several prominent Texans who were members of the SMU booster club, all complicit in these activities and also taking part in covering it up and lying to investigatory boards. One of the saddest chapters was the Governor trying to keep his nose clean by throwing various boosters under the bus. It turns out that after the scandal broke it was the Governor who was instrumental in pressuring boosters who wanted out to keep paying players and their families to keep them quiet and not putting the Governors role on the front page.

Once it all came out, a new Governor had been elected, and SMUs Board of Governors had some new members. The board made it a policy that only academically qualified people would be admitted to the football program. One board member was quoted as saying in effect that only football players who couldn't play elsewhere would now come to SMU.

In 1986, the NCAA handed SMU its "death penalty," for its consistent and egregious violations of NCAA rules even after repeated warnings. The death penalty was a cancellation of the entire 1987 season. The first and still only time the "death penalty" has ever been given out. To make a statement, SMU's new Board of Governors cancelled the 1988 season as well. It had only one winning season in the subsequent twenty years. ESPN made an excellent documentary on the whole affair and at the end of the show one of the major participants in the rule breaking said, "Everyone does it, we just got caught."

Another sad, perhaps even pathetic story, of a University creating its own downfall through an attempt to make money by creating a first-class athletic program is the State University of New York at Binghamton. Binghamton had been well regarded as being amongst the state system one of the academically higher quality schools. The folks who ran the school decided it was time to make some TV money by building a nationally-ranked basketball team. It gave the athletic director not just financial carte blanche to recruit high school players, but also great academic leeway as well.

Their plan worked. Binghamton made it for the first time to the end-of-the-season tournament that crowns the best college team in the country. Once. You see, after the tournament things went haywire. Players had been recruited that fell well below the usual academic admission standards and a variety of "fudging" of credentials had occurred to get them admitted. Not to be sneezed at were the long rap sheets of the some of the recruits, you know, felonies such as theft and assault, just your typical "Joe College" shenanigans. After the usual months of denials and cover-ups, the schools own students started to protest and the campus newspaper published article after article. It seems that basketball in New York did not quite have the same iconic status as football in Texas, especially around Dallas, SMU's home.

The decision to create this money-making enterprise in the first place was done at the local level by the president of the school at Binghamton without the knowledge of the higher-ups in the state-wide system. So the President of SUNY at Binghamton along with its athletic director were fired. The state of New York created a special commission to oversee athletics at all its campuses. Even though they achieved great success at basketball, the presence of felons and academically unqualified students on campus was clearly viewed in Binghamton as a black mark upon the University.

Historically, college football from its beginnings over a century ago with the Harvard vs. Yale rivalry has always had an avid following. In the 1950s, just as for my hometown team of Rice University, college sports was mostly just about hometown and alumni fans. At the end of the year, a few bowl games such as the Rose, Sugar, and Cotton bowls received national attention. The dominating place of college football in the media really did not come about until the 1970s, and for basketball, even then it was still small potatoes. However, the folks who run the TV networks saw first through football just how much money could be made through college athletics. It was the media that in its own self-interest began to hype college basketball.

An emerging station, ESPN, saw college basketball as a lever to pry open the hold of ABC, NBC, and CBS on broadcasting sports into the nation's homes. ESPN rode college athletics, in particular through its efforts in raising college basketballs presence in the American consciousness, to its own place as a competitor amongst the networks. So if you want to understand the real answer to the exaggerated place of sports played by "student athletes" in our American culture just follow the money.

The money involved in college sports is huge. The televising of the top college regular season football and basketball games brings in hundreds of millions of dollars to the networks through the sales of ads. The season ending tournaments (the now vast multitude of bowl games for football and the "March Madness" tournament for basketball) add another several hundred million a year. In just 2008, the March Madness basketball tournament brought the network over a half a billion in ad revenues. Of course some of this money is then paid on to the schools and athletics conferences for the rights to televise the games. CBS and Turner Sports in 2010 did a fourteen year deal worth 11 billion dollars for rights to the March Madness tournaments.

THE UNDERLYING CORRUPTION IN THE CHARADE OF COLLEGE SPORTS: IN 2009, ILLEGAL GAMBLING ESTIMATES ARE $70 BILLION ON FOOTBALL, $50 BILLION ON BASKETBALL AND THE MARCH MADNESS TOURNAMENT ALONE $6-$12 BILLION. WITH THAT MUCH ILLEGAL MONEY ON THE LINE, ANYONE WANT TO MAKE A GUESS AT HOW OFTEN SERIOUS MONEY CHANGES HANDS TO SHAVE A POINT NOW AND THEN.

It is this money that in part funds college sports, from the athletic scholarships to the outrageous salaries paid to the coaches. The coaches in the major sports at the major colleges make millions of dollars a year. An income that is in the vicinity of 10-30 times what even the most highly paid professors make. A University's main task is to educate its students, yet coaches, whose job involves what has no relationship to the University's primary mission of education are paid salaries in another universe from the professors. In China, the colleges have no sports teams.

The money from television is not the only source of funds for the coach's pay, but through private deals with manufacturers of athletic clothing, they receive other payments as well. These payments are for guarantees that their players will use only that manufacturer's brand of gear with terms describing how the logos will be displayed for maximum impact on the television audience.

An additional source of income to the University that finds its way to the athletic department is targeted donations from alumni. When a University is trying to lure a top coach to its athletic department, it does a special fund-raising campaign specifically to fund the multimillion dollar pay package these coaches attract. Studies have shown that when donations go up for the athletic programs, donations for academic purposes go down.

An interesting aspect of this whole relationship between television and the University athletic programs is the involvement of our favorite defenders of truth, justice, and the American way, the Congressman of the United States. It seems that the money paid to the universities for the commercial rights to broadcast their football games was being treated by the Universities as tax-exempt income; after all they are not-for-profit educational institutions. At least the IRS recognized this for the charade that it is and demanded that the Universities pay taxes on what is most clearly a commercial transaction.

Now since there is big money involved in college athletics, Universities have lobbyists who keep an eye on things in Washington and protect the University's interests. None other than the former Congressman and football player from Oklahoma, J.C. Watts is paid about a half-million dollars a year for his services in this regard. Through lobbyist efforts, Congress passed a law that made the payments to the Universities tax exempt income. In a similar vein that athletics and the University mission of education are one and the same, if a donor's gift is specifically for a coach's salary, since it is given through the University, the donors still get to deduct it from their taxes. Now ain't that just upstanding and 'Merican as apple pie, hot diggety dog, go Longhorns!

In a circle of money, the schools began to compete for the large sums of money that now could be paid by the media to bring their games to the stoked audience. In turn the schools used this money to lure the players and coaches that would create the winning teams the networks wanted to broadcast. Along the way, that these were Universities with the responsibility for educating our nations young people got lost. The big money was now coming in from lucrative TV contracts and going out to the players, their families and coaches that could produce a winning team.

The pressure to win created a type of coach who brought Vince Lombardi's ethos, appropriate in professional football, that winning isn't everything, it is the only thing, to the college game. A fellow named Lane Kiffin was the head football coach at Tennessee. Thanks to whistle blowers, the NCAA was forced to investigate his recruiting practices and they found violation after violation. Finally Mr. Kiffin could not take the heat and in 2010 bailed out for another top football school with its own long history of penalties for violating NCAA recruiting rules, USC. In June of 2011, the NCAA finally got around to stripping USC of its 2004 National Championship for its own recruiting violations involving hundreds of thousands of dollars in gifts to players it was recruiting. Previously USC had to forfeit all its 2005 season victories, also for recruiting violations. USC clutched Mr. Kiffin to its conniving breast.

This pattern of repeated offenders, for both schools and coaches is actually common. An Oklahoma coach, Kevin Sampson, was found guilty of NCAA violations and then went on to coach at Indiana where his illegal acts led to his being banned from coaching for five years. University of Tennessee, not only holds convictions for football, but basketball as well. After having previously been fined $1.5 million and received an eight game suspension for recruiting violations and then lying about it, Tennessee's basketball coach Bruce Pearl was in August of 2011 cited for more recruiting violations, his punishment has yet to be decided. Something about birds of a feather comes to mind.

The craziness that descends on a school once the decision has been made to try to turn a low-profile school into a prime-time athletic powerhouse has befallen none other than Boise State in Idaho. Except for their recent football prowess, how many of you have ever heard of Boise State? Well, not to bring up Shakespeare again, or perhaps this time Dante is more appropriate, but once one delves into the world of evil, the infection seems to spread. Poor Boise State, because of the seemingly hand-in-glove between major sports success and NCAA violations, the NCAA uncovered about two-dozen violations in other sports from tennis to track-and-field. The school has now received numerous penalties and is on probation by the NCAA. Was making a pact with the devil of athletic success worth it Boise State, well was it?

All of these recruiting violations, essentially the paying of great high school athletes to attend a college so they can give that college a shot at fame and fortune as an athletic powerhouse has to, I mean has to, run up against a brick wall eventually. How about the first time one of these athletes has to sit in a classroom with a student who got into that college based upon their grades and entrance exam scores and the jock tries to pass the same test as does the rest of the students. I mean in spite of the few true athlete scholars the media and the university drag out time after time, these true student athletes fail miserably as students far more than they succeed.

The University of Kansas has hit upon a truly peculiar system to make sure their student athletes at least play the game of charades by showing up for classes. The University hires people to follow the students around and make sure they attend class. Mostly these are retired senior citizens who could use a few bucks but sometimes they also use other students with the same motivation.

These "minders" as they are called even hang-out in the hallway to make sure their athlete target does not just stay for a few minutes and then leave to do whatever they would rather be doing with their time than play student-athlete charades. In full keeping with the recent scandals of student athletes using various memorabilia and free tickets to trade for car rentals, paying off gambling debts, buy drinks and women, etc, some of the student athletes try to bribe their minders with free tickets. Kansas is not alone amongst schools using this system to try to at least remove some of the shame from having admitted these grotesquely unqualified students in the first place.

Other efforts to try to find some way to put a brave face on all this sham are funded by the lucrative TV deals that athletic prowess brings to the schools. The major schools build "learning centers" specifically for the use of the student athletes. Tutors are available on an "on call" basis, learning laboratories with books, taped lectures, and every other imaginable learning aids are available. Even at schools with only pretentions of making it to the big time money, they provide athlete-only dining and residence halls. University money being spent on noneducational activities has taken a page from Hollywood and the Oscars. Just as a studio will mount a multimillion dollar advertising campaign to try to win "best picture," Oregon spent $250,000 on a billboard in Manhattan touting one of its players for the best college player of the year, the Heisman Trophy.

How does the rest of the University feel about all this, from faculty to students many are pretty unhappy. However, over the years, protests from both groups have led to zip. In Minnesota, a former helper for the basketball players who had written over four hundred papers for twenty student athletes went public with the information. Four players were suspended. The University of Georgia which has a one million dollar per year budget for educational aid to student athletes, fired a remedial tutor who refused to change grades so certain athletes could retain their eligibility to play. She won a $2.5million lawsuit against the University. I must admit, just about fifty years ago I helped my school quarterback write a term paper.

I mean, really, this is very sad stuff. Playing a game of charades of this magnitude that is so obvious a charade, eventually has to come to grief in a big way. One amongst many examples is the case of Derrick Rose. He was a brilliant basketball talent in high school and for every good reason dreamed of a career in professional basketball Due to the lack of a minor league path to professional teams, as is so successful in baseball, he was forced to find his way through a college to showcase his talents to the professional teams.

Mr. Rose attended the University of Memphis and got them into the '08 final four of March Madness. Memphis, on the back of Mr. Rose, set an NCAA record that year for wins in a season. They lost in the title game, but he was able to showcase his talents. The next year he stopped playing the game of charades and jumped right to professional basketball and became the rookie of the year in the NBA.

Good for him and shame on Memphis. The smell of his brief attendance at Memphis was so bad it forced the NCAA to look into things and lo-and-behold it was found that Mr. Rose had failed his SATs three times but finally made a grade sufficient for admission on the fourth time. Unfortunately, on that fourth time, the evidence showed that someone else had taken his test for him. The NCAA vacated all of Memphis's wins that '07-'08 season and forced them to pay back the money it had received. Similarly the coach was forced to return his bonus for the year. A bonus paid to a University coach? I wonder how many professors get a bonus for their students acing tests?

Not surprisingly, both Memphis and the coach had previously been found guilty of NCAA violations. For the coach it began when he had coached for the University of Massachusetts. Twice convicted of serious NCAA violations, he is now the coach at Kentucky with the highest pay of any college coach, $31.5 million over eight years. Don't you ever say our educational system doesn't have it priorities right, Kentucky graduates 31% of student-athlete basketball players.

Professional sports is just that, professional. Adults make a free choice to accept pay in exchange for a business owner to exploit their talents in order to make money for himself. A sort-of free market exists which allows the athlete to sell his services to the highest bidders. The fans make their own choices and hand over money for a ticket to see a game in person. A source of major revenue to the owner are the fees paid to the owner by the media for the right to broadcast the games. In addition, the tentacles of the money involved in professional sports reaches out in many ancillary directions. The makers of sports apparel pay individual athletes and whole teams for the right to promote the individual athletes and the teams use of the company's products. All sorts of stuff gets sold by vendors at the stadium and it even costs money to park. Professional sports is a vast business run by adults for the sole purpose of making money.

College sports grew out of friendly rivalries between different schools. Students who enjoyed sports could play them while also getting their college education. Some could play in "sandlot" games, teams being formed around fraternities, dorms, or even leagues with no basis for the teams other than just a bunch of pals who enjoy playing. Others could commit to playing for officially sanctioned teams that would represent the schools in what started out as regional leagues. Of course out of this grew an industry. College sports became a business, athletes could get free room and board as well as facilities and coaching to improve their skills by attending a college. Most importantly, these "student-athletes" had a place to showcase their talents in front of the scouts from the professional teams, the end game for most.

As the rivalries between schools began to heat-up and the money paid to winning teams for broadcast rights skyrocketed, the competition for the high-quality athletes coming out of high school intensified. Athletic scholarships along with special booster clubs that focused on athletic recruitment began to offer additional financial incentives to try to convince the best of the best to attend their schools. Money was paid to the athlete's family to help them along with a little parental direction and offers of jobs and apartments to family members who wanted to be near their student-athlete children were used to help the recruiting process along. Given the age of the kids, money for women, booze, and cars was also forthcoming, usually laundered through a "booster" club.

As all of this was evolving, the governing body over college athletics, the NCAA, began to increasingly impose more stringent rules on what was permissible as incentives for the recruitment of players out of high school. In addition, rules were put in place to maintain the "amateur" status of the athletes during the college years. College scholarships were permissible for tuition, room, and board, but other payments were not. Over the past several decades, this back and forth process between the colleges finding innovative ways to motivate high school stars to attend their schools and the NCAA trying to keep college sports amateur and not professional became just another whack-a-mole game between regulators and those they regulate.

As just described, the situation is well out of hand. The top-quality athletes are aggressively recruited by the big-time college athletic programs. Booster clubs are constantly finding new ways to hide payments to the athletes and their families as recruitment incentives. Any pretense that for teams at this level of college sports that the players are there for one reason and one reason only, to showcase their talents for eventual selection by the professional teams and not to get an education has long since dissolved into the mist of money.

Little known to most fans is just how sick this process has become. High school athletics is now seeing the beginnings of the same process. High School coaches receive payments to steer their players toward certain colleges. Athletic apparel companies are now reaching into the high schools to sign teams as well as individual players to contracts for the exclusive use of their products. Summer leagues are now the main showplace for these teenagers to showcase their talents so they will be recruited by the top rank sports Universities. The showcasing of talent for the next run up the ladder has now moved down to high school. Thirteen year olds will spend the next six years or so devoting their lives to nothing but honing their skills for their shot at the Holy Grail, a lucrative contract with a professional sports teams. Education plays little role in not just their college years, but their high school years as well.

There is an organization, the Amateur Athletic Union (AAU) that was founded in 1888 as a governing body over a variety of amateur sports. Its goal is to create opportunities for athletes to play their games independent of receiving pay for their participation. As such it has over its many years been more or less affiliated with the United States Olympic community. Believe it or not, this "amateur" organization is the sponsor organization of the high school summer leagues in basketball that are the most corrupted by money.

The University of Texas, a well-known sports powerhouse, in particular in football and baseball, but never a national presence at the college level in basketball felt it was time to change their failure in basketball to match their successes in football and baseball. It seems that the school had a rule against recruiting players from the unseemly summer leagues run by the AAU. The rule was dropped and that is what has recently propelled Texas to be competitive at a national level.

There is a well-researched book by George Dohrmann, *Play Their Hearts Out*, that chronicles the lives of a few of the young men caught up in the business of high school basketball. It chronicles in depressing detail the destructive effect upon these boys and their family as they move from city to city, chasing the dream of a professional sports contract still some six-eight years out into the future. They move around looking for the right high school with the right coach with the right connections that can maximize their chances of obtaining the Holy Grail. The parallels with the college sports money-game are frightening, even to the point of finding jobs for the parents so a coach at a high school can get a high-quality prospect's family to move to his school's neighborhood in his city. The money trail goes up the chain to the boosters of the University with which this high school coach has a sweetheart deal to guide his players to their school.

Is it worth it to the parents to disrupt their lives for the sake of getting their car loan and house mortgage paid off by the grateful son when he gets his multimillion dollar signing bonus from a professional basketball team? They are taking a big gamble. The odds are really pretty poor. Of all high school basketball players, only 3% get a scholarship from a Division I University. Of those 3%, only 2% go on to have a productive NBA career, which means of the high school pool of basketball players, only 0.06% make it in the NBA. A lousy high-school education, a lousy college education if any at all, and a probability of the big NBA check functionally zero. Then what?

An issue that is occasionally discussed in the "student athlete" troubles that beset football and basketball is that of race. In the colleges that compete for the national titles and are the same ones most frequently cited for NCAA rules violations, most of the top-level players are black. Some writers have used words such as "exploitation" and evoke memories of slavery as the otherwise white schools recruit the black potential stars out of high school, use under the table payments to get them to attend, and fail to provide them with an education all for the purpose of making money for the school.

Even the animated show *South Park* has an episode, "Crack Baby Athletic Association," where the most scheming of the shows stars, Cartman, has created a scam whereby through a not-for-profit foundation to raise money for crack-babies he hopes to get rich through their exploitation. He faces some tricky tax questions and in hope of getting help he masquerades as a Southern plantation owner and visits the President of a major sports school. Cartman talks to the President as a fellow slave-owner and asks how the University retains a tax exempt status for the money it makes off its slaves. The President responds with a "what are you talking about comment?" and Cartman points to a photo on the wall of a sports team of all black players. Enough said.

The three major sports in the U.S. are football, basketball, and baseball. Mostly left out of this discussion of the student athlete is baseball. There are no under the table payments and recruiting scandals in college baseball. There are no scandals about graduation rates and cheating involving college baseball. Professional baseball has an affiliated business called the minor leagues. It serves the purpose that college sports performs in football and basketball. The minor leagues in baseball are where talented athletes fine-tune their skills with the hope of making it to the major leagues.

Colleges do have baseball teams. There is a college world series. Baseball players do receive athletic scholarships. However, the existence of the minor leagues keeps college baseball clear of the skull-duggery of football and basketball. The best of the college baseball players are recruited by teams in the majors and sent into their minor league organizations for their final seasoning and tests if they are worthy for promotion to the majors.

So, would not a minor league system that has worked just fine for colleges and professional teams in baseball also work for football and basketball? I certainly think it would, but there is a problem. How do you make a transition from the multi-billion dollar industry surrounding college basketball and football to a different system? What happens to the avid fan base for this or that specific college team?

There is a way to clean up the system, preserving most of the economics involved in the broadcasting and reporting on college athletics as well as affiliating a team with a University. It would be a new way of organizing college sports into a *de facto* minor league system that would put the money, the business of college sports up on the table for everyone to see. It would also get rid of the charade of the student athlete. No more athletes pretending to be students. No misery in these athletes lives of pretending to be students with all the stresses that brings. No more schism between the jocks, students, and faculty.

In the new system, the team would be branded with the name of the University. The athletes would be paid just as in minor-league baseball. The team would be owned by a professional team just as in baseball or be independent, owned by investors, a group of alumni for example. After a certain period of playing for the team, the student could switch his status from athlete to full-time student with a guaranteed admission to the university. He could even be a hybrid, opting to take a limited class load while still playing for the team. However, he would be judged on his class performance just the same as any other student, with any tutorial assistance provided similarly just as for any other student.

To the fan there would be very little difference; they could still root for their favorite team. To the broadcasters, they would continue to televise the games and make money. From the standpoint of a national championship, such a system would solve many of the problems associated with the current national championship in college football, the often maligned BCS. The new minor league system would be organized just as in baseball into three separate levels, AAA, AA, and A, as appropriate for the teams financial circumstances. A national championship would be decided for each of the three levels.

MOST IMPORTANTLY IS THE STUDENT! No more charade, no more phony student athlete. No more annoyance at having to sit through boring classes. The athlete is there for one and only on purpose, and everyone acknowledges it and treats them accordingly, to improve their skills and display them in front of the scouts for the major leagues. And last but certainly not least, if at some point along the way, either a realization that a professional career is not likely, or simply a loss of motivation, they will be sitting pretty for a start on getting a college education, even being able to put their toe in the water by taking a class or two and earning some credits while also being a true-blue athlete. No more having every year an increasing number of players bail-out on their college career waving the flag of charade by leaving before their senior year to enter the draft for selection by a professional team.

Jerry Jones, are you listening. How about SMU as a AAA farm team for the Dallas Cowboys, University of Miami with the Miami Dolphins, Ohio State with the Browns or Bengals and on and on. I would expect that the money would be even more than in baseball. The problem with a charade is that the game is never clean, there is always the overhang of deception. The honest thing is always better. In this case making more money for the players, the school, and the host big-league team. An additional benefit is the lives of the athletes. No more secret payments and the stress of at least making an attempt at passing exams as well as true preparation to be all that you can be in the profession of your choice.

VI. A FLIM-FLAM CHARADE:

HEALTH CARE COST CONTROL

There can be no question that medical costs are out of control; they are far outpacing inflation year after year. Their costs have reached the point that for those with no insurance at all or even private insurance, they are the leading the cause of personal bankruptcy. Those with Medicare and Medicaid get these inflated bills paid, but they are now so large, they are a main component of the government's budget-deficit crisis.

Some of the most damning aspects to the problem of health care costs are fundamental to the underlying structure of the way the medical profession itself works. So far, the conversation about controlling health care costs avoids that issue but instead simply talks about the shifting of costs around by changing who pays for what, when and where, as if that can solve the problem. It cannot and will not. It is a charade, acceptable to politicians since addressing the real issue means taking on some of their top campaign donors.

There are several parts of this fundamental structure that must be understood before evaluating any attempt to deal with the problem. First is the greed of some doctors and hospitals with their over-the-top disregard for the financial impact upon those who pay for the services they provide and the medications they prescribe. Much of what they do is driven by the income expectations of those who choose to enter the profession and profit expectations of those who make the various products and deliver the services used in medicine.

Second, the medical profession is probably the worst example of professional collegiality, amongst all professions. Professional courtesy causes many a blind eye to some pretty grotesque incompetence and waste. It is usually after someone dies and it hits the newspaper that a state medical board will do anything at all, and that is rarely the suspension of a license. Even if it does suspend a license, what happens in the state of Texas will be unknown to the state of New York. The examples of docs simply moving to a new state and getting a new license are commonplace.

Third is the willingness of third party payers, whether the government through Medicare and Medicaid or private insurers to not lift the rug to see the financial fraud and abuse in the profession. After all, why should they care about what they pay out? As medical costs go up, the private insurers just raise premiums and the government just prints more money to pay for these outrageous costs.

No one has an incentive to lower costs, no one, not the doctors, nor the hospitals and certainly not the companies who make medical products and provide medical services.

This is another of the book's Chapters that have within it a great deal that will seem bizarre and shocking. The behind-the-scenes of the practice of medicine is kept well-hidden from those who have not had direct contact with the business behind medicine. So let me begin with two fairly detailed examples that display many of the major problems in today's medical costs.

Most readers I expect are familiar with the problem of when fatty deposits, plaque, clog-up the inside of blood vessels and restrict blood flow. This restriction deprives the organ that is fed by the vessel of the oxygen its cells need to function properly. In some cases, the disruption of blood flow by these deposits can cause a clot to form at the constriction which then plugs the vessel completely. When the blockage occurs in vessels that provide the heart muscle with oxygen, the oxygen starvation causes the pain of a heart attack and in most cases also the death of heart muscle.

Over the past several decades a variety of useful methods have been developed to open up the restriction in the blood vessel. A deflated balloon, more in the shape of a tiny condom than just a round balloon, can be inserted inside the vessel and when blown-up it will compress the plaque against the vessel wall. After some years however, the vessel will reconstrict.

A better method was then developed that after the vessel is opened, a small device called a "stent," a tube which has walls made of a mesh is installed at the site. Recall from your childhood those tubes made out of a straw mesh that you could stick a finger in each end and as you tried to pull your fingers out, the mesh walls of the tube would constrict and grab onto your finger. The only way to get your fingers out was to push them together, the mesh would expand the opening in the tube and all was well.

A stent is similar; the mesh can be made of fine wires or a plastic. When pulled from each end it constricts into a small-enough tube to be slid into an artery, and then when expanded it pushes the plaque and vessel wall outward and creates its own inner opening through which normal blood flow occurs. Stents are left in place and function usually quite well for rest of the patient's life

When introduced these were very "hot" products, a superior solution to a very serious problem and several of the major medical companies came out with their own versions of this product. Stents became a highly competitive medical product; even a small percentage of market share given the amount of the Medicare and private insurance reimbursement, was significant. The various companies competed intensively, a war was on. Big money was at stake, for the years 2003-2009 Medicare paid out 25.7 billion in payments for stent surgeries.

In early 2010, The Baltimore Sun reported about the alleged misuse of stents by a local Dr. Midei at St. Joseph Medical Center in Towson, Maryland. All his work used stents made by Abbott Laboratories. The article claimed that hundreds of stents had been implanted that were unnecessary. This cardiovascular surgeon did up to 30 stent surgeries a day, thought to be the most ever by one of Abbott's surgeons. It is almost inconceivable under a normal surgical timetable to imagine how that feat could be accomplished.

Thanks to the newspaper's investigation, the Senate took up the issue and ordered an investigation since most stent surgeries are paid for by Medicare. As a result of the investigation and the newspaper's story, Dr. Medei was barred from practicing at St. Josephs. The hospital sent out notification letters to notify 585 patients that they might have received an unnecessary stent. The federal government was planning a suit against St. Josephs for abuse of Medicare. St. Joseph settled out of court for a $22 million dollar fine.

Abbott was none to happy about this turn of events. In an internal email one Abbot executive sent out, in referring to the reporter for the Baltimore Sun, "Somebody needs to take this writer outside and kick his ass. Do I need to send in the Philly mob?" Dr. Medei however; although barred from the hospital and sanctioned by Maryland's State Board of Physicians for putting patients in needless danger by unnecessary surgeries, was too valuable to be let go by Abbott. He was too much of a cash cow. Abbott had the bright idea of sending him to Asia to promote their stents. In Japan, his background caught up with him and the publicity led Abbott to recall their Ambassador of Greed.

The weirdest part of this whole story was that Senator Max Baucus, in response to reading the report about the Senate ordered investigation, concluded, "This could be a sign of a larger national trend of wasteful medical-device use." Gosh Senator, you think maybe there's fraud in Medicare? Once again, massive fraud and abuse of a government funded program, in this case something as trivial and of little consequence to the country's economic health as Medicare and it took a newspaper reporter to get the governments attention.

I mean in front of some bureaucrat in Washington, or where ever Medicare is located, was the data that Medicare was paying a particular doctor at a particular hospital a nonsensical amount of money for stent implants and it did not set of an alarm bell. I guess in the government the expense line is really of no importance to anyone, they keep their job and the company, U.S. of A, can not go bankrupt so why even notice.

Second example: a "bad back" can of course in its most serious case be completely debilitating. For the vast majority of suffers it is just a daily annoyance making most tasks from sitting in the wrong chair to mild physical activity a real balance between pain and pleasure. The snake-oil salesmen have a long and glorious history of promoting solutions for this all too common ailment. The "legitimate" medical promoters, from the physician and chiropractors themselves to the makers of the FDA approved products used in back remedies, view this as a significant market of opportunity, with yet few truly effective and long term fixes for back pain.

One of the major causes of back pain is the "slipped disc." In between the vertebrae of the back are these discs. They are sort of like hockey pucks made of a gelatinous material with a semi-firm outer shell. When you sit down or say ride a horse, the compression of the vertebrae is not bone against bone but each vertebrae is separated from the one below by one of these discs that cushions the blow.

When a disc begins to deteriorate, typically the outer wrapping loses its firmness and when the disc is compressed between the vertebrae above and below it, the inner material creates a bulge where the discs outer wrapping has become soft. This bulge can then push against one of the many nerves that run out from the spinal cord to various parts of our arms and legs. Sciatica, the sense of pain in the leg, is typically from an out of shape disc pushing up against the nerve for the leg.

Needless to say, dealing with this and the other varieties of the various vertebrae and disc related problems is a main focus of those who wish to find a way to make money within the medical field. A common attempt to cure these back problems is through spinal fusion. In the area of the nerve that is the source of the pain, the disc is removed which relieves the discs irritation of the nerve and the vertebrae that now touch one another are simply fused together so they no longer are independent of each other but now move as one double-long vertebrae.

Let us just hope you did not have a bad back in Portland, Oregon and were referred to a Dr. Makker. It seemed that Dr. Makker had a habit of performing spinal fusions over and over on the same patient. In 2008 and 2009, amongst 3,407 spinal surgeons who performed 20 or more fusions per year, in almost all cases it was one fusion per patient. Dr. Makker distinguished himself however as number one, yes the top of the heap in number of repeat fusions on the same patient. His average rate of repeat fusions was 10 times the national average. Thanks to the article, his hospital took away his surgical privileges and he is under investigation as of Spring 2011 by the Oregon medical board.

As we have all learned from endless watching of the various Law and Order shows, when it turns out that a suspect has never been in trouble before that goes a long way to lowering them on the list of suspects. I guess the same is true for Doctors as well. The reporter discovered that in 2006 the Oregon Medical Board had dealt with Dr. Makker before. His punishment was to do remedial education for performing unnecessary surgeries and billing Medicare for procedures he did not perform. "Remedial Training?" you have got to be kidding. How about striped pajamas?

Oh well, the story gets even more interesting since it seems that Dr. Makker saw to it that the hospital purchased the various spinal fusion products used in his surgeries through a specific distributor. A distributor that had a habit of kicking back money to the docs that used its products. Another spinal fusion surgeon received over $500,000 through such kickbacks for his use of their products over just an 18 month period. Although such kickbacks are not unknown in the medical field, it seems that it was more the norm than the exception in the spinal fusion surgery business. Its effect on Medicare: in 1997 Medicare paid out $343 million for spinal fusion surgeries, in 2009 the number had jumped to $2.24 billion.

Much of what is described above was taken from two articles in the Wall Street Journal (WSJ) in the Spring of 2011. In fact it was the first of these articles that led to the hospital in Portland taking action against Dr. Makker. The data obtained by the WSJ came very reluctantly from Medicare. Medicare is loath to give out any information about how it spends its money. It was only by agreeing to very strict limits on what data it would be shown that anything was disclosed.

In examining the data, the WSJ found a few other interesting tidbits. A surgeon in New Jersey was excluded from Medicare and Medicaid for a period of nine years in the 1990s due to the unusual number of deaths that occurred from elective procedures. However, he moved to Texas and resumed his surgical practice. In 2008 and 2009 his death rate based on a per 100 patients for a specific elective procedure was 18.4 whereas the national average for the exact same procedure was 2.4. Eight times as many people died when this guy did the work than would have died based on the national average. In between the lines there is the suggestion that he was performing this procedure on patients who were quite ill in other ways. The implication being that as long as Medicare is picking up the bill, why not just do a surgery whether it is appropriate or not.

These two patient case histories from the spinal fusion wars really bring home the tragedy of this aspect of the medical profession. Individual doctors by their own choice actively defrauding Medicare. However, there is another part of this abuse that to will seem even larger than its impact on Medicare costs. How about the impact on the lives of the patients who have multiple unneeded surgeries done on their spines? The WSJ article gave the details of several patients and it is just terribly sad.

For example, one patient sued Dr. Makker for operating on the wrong disc of her spine, and then in the second surgery botched that one also. It produced numbness in her leg and foot along with urinary incontinence. She went to a different doctor, having a third surgery to correct Dr. Makker's mess. He settled her case for $500,000. Another patient had three surgeries on her spine within 18 months. He tried to persuade her into a fourth but she said no. She also said about Dr. Makker, "an Academy Award winning actor…It's as if he's charming you to go on a date, except the date is going to involve a surgery." Anyone still wants to argue that patients should be limited in their ability to sue docs? Pretty hard to make that case as long as these kinds of folk are allowed to practice.

At the peak of the publicity about the growth of spinal fusion surgery as the cure-all for back problems and the enrichment of certain individual physicians, one of the two top medical journals, The Journal of the American Medical Association (JAMA) weighed in on the whole controversy. One of its lead authors commented, "Many factors are at play, but I think the finances play an important part," and another, "There are some prominent surgeons who have strong financial connections to device manufacturers." A prominent surgeon at Stanford said in discussing the use of fusion surgery versus a variety of other treatments from bed rest, anti-inflammatory medications, to a much simpler and lower-cost surgery ($20,000 for simpler versus $80,000 and a twice as likely complications rate for fusion), "It has not been shown that the more complex surgery is better but people are willing to have it done, the marketing is relentless."

Lo and behold, about a month after writing this section in June of 2011, 5 U.S. Senators have asked the Inspector General of the Department of Health and Human Services to look into this whole issue of docs owning distributorships. It was prompted by a report on the issue by the Senate Finance Committee which report was prompted by newspaper articles initially in the WSJ about the subject.

The report said, in referring to the ability of docs to own the distributorship that sells the products to the hospital for use in their own surgeries, "financial incentives for physician investors to use those devices that give them the greatest financial return." "Physician investors in PODs [physician owned distributorships] may perform more procedures than are medically necessary…" "300% increase in spinal re-operation rates at one hospital following the creation of a POD."

Spinal fusions seem to just attract all the high-quality physicians. In June of 2011 the Senate Finance Committee announced another investigation in spinal fusions, this time for a product called a bone growth protein used to help along the fusion process between the vertebrae. It seems that as a part of the package of study results submitted to the FDA by the company Medtronic that sells the product, some serious side-effects were noted, most commonly occurring when the product was used in the upper spine. The FDA did approve the product in 2002 for use in only the lower back.

The same surgeons who did the studies and submitted their findings to the FDA, then published their results in a professional journal—the way their colleagues learn what happened. Guess what, in the papers published in the journal they left out all the side effect results so other surgeons felt comfortable using the product for off-label locations such as for the vertebra in the neck. By 2008 the FDA had received a sufficient number of adverse event reports from docs that they issued an alert warning against its use outside of the lower back.

Son-of-a-gun if it does not also turn out that the docs who did the original studies for the FDA and then left out the wicked side effects in the papers published for their colleagues received some large consulting and royalty fees from Medtronic, to the tune of tens of millions of dollars. One surgeon alone had received $19 million.

Oh, the reports coming in to the FDA after approval also included complications occurring in the lower back that had occurred in the original studies for the FDA and were unreported in the journal articles. Although it is of course easy to understand how this could happen, after all you are just a physician who lives by the Hippocratic oath to do no harm, so why bother letting your colleagues know that in your own work, some patients became sterilized from the use of the product.

On a personal note, my dad had his cataracts removed. At a post-op visit to the doc, he commented that my father's eyelids were droopy, perhaps from being stretched by the holder used to spread them for the surgery. My father replied that he did not care and would prefer not to have even the outpatient surgery performed to tighten his lids. The surgeon's response, "But Mr. Glass, it's covered by Medicare."

So there you have it, doctors enriching themselves beyond any excusable level and product manufacturers paying doctors to use their products. These kickbacks must come from somewhere and so the price Medicare pays in its reimbursement is in a part to reimburse the manufacturer for the kickback. And that is just the start of understanding all the various factors that are driving the costs of our health care, no matter what system is used to pay for it, out the roof. Nothing described above that greatly inflates medical costs has ever been mentioned in any of the recent conversations about cutting health care costs. Now let's take a look at some other "stuff" involved in why over 60% of all bankruptcies in the United States are driven primarily by medical costs.

A variety of new surgical techniques have been developed to help people lose weight. These are real surgeries requiring general anesthesia and the full surgical show to have for example their stomach made smaller through stapling a part of it shut, or placing a constricting band around the stomach to accomplish the same purpose. With a smaller stomach the patient gets a feeling of being full after eating a smaller meal. Other surgeries remove some of the intestine that is involved in absorption of nutrients.

All of these surgeries are expensive, in the $20,000 and up range. There is even a growing push to perform them in children as young as six years old with obesity problems. Teenagers are currently a hot market for the procedure. Yet, a program of diet and exercise that costs nothing has the proven potential, if it is followed, to be just as effective as the surgeries. It is of course the doctor's role as the authority figure to lay out for the patient the dangers of obesity and pressure the patient to lose weight through the many diet and exercise programs offered at fitness centers or accessible at no cost through the internet. Although I would expect some gyms have referral kickback-relationships with Docs, it is chump change compared with surgery.

A last resort is the doctor simply telling the patient not to eat so damn much crappy food and get your fat ass off the couch. Oh my, oh my, asking for self-discipline, but what about the patient's emotional needs (our focus on emotional needs also discussed in the chapter about the US as #1). Of course that is really really unreasonable when weight loss can be accomplished through surgeries costing on a yearly basis many billions of dollars.

Once again, the insurers do not care, the weight loss surgeries are paid for through higher insurance premiums as are the fixes for the variety of serious illness such as diabetes and heart disease sure to follow obesity. All of this can be avoided by simply eating less and exercising more.

The latter two illnesses, diabetes and heart disease, impact Medicare dramatically. So far, as shown in the cases previously discussed with more to follow, Medicare seems little concerned with keeping its own costs down. In terms of obesity and really very serious health problems that follow with very high costs, weight gain is one case where a few bucks spent on the prevention side will save truly hundreds of billions later on. I often wish when I see obese people scarfing down food at a restaurant that they could spend a week with a 70 year old living with the physical and psychologically crippling effects of diabetes and heart disease. "Well do ya want to take another bite of that cake punk, well do ya?"

A dirty little secret of the medical profession is the relationship between let us call it, the primary physician and their referral for outside services. The outside service can be an imaging service where a CAT scan or MRI scan is done or a laboratory where tests such as blood tests are done as well as a rehabilitation facility for physical therapy. About thirty-forty years ago, the referral issue for tests came to Congress's attention as playing a role in even then what were seen as rapidly rising medical costs.

There was no regulation against a physician owning an imaging center, laboratory, or rehab provider to which he would then refer patients. Studies have certainly shown that physicians who had a financial interest in such outside services referred their patients to them at a much higher rate than physicians seeing the same type of patients but without a financial interest in these facilities. To those who knew this history, there was nothing new about the ruckus over the spinal surgeons owning distributorships. After all, think of those income expectations that motivated the person to attend medical school in the first place.

As a result of this "discovery" of a conflict of interest, federal legislation was passed outlawing this self-dealing. Known as the Stark legislation it had a momentary chilling impact upon the growing industry of physicians taking a financial interest in such outside referral-based services. However, sophisticated lawyers found ways to create arms-length ownership structures that allowed physicians to still reap some rewards from their directed referrals. It has become another "whack-a-mole" story. In the fifteen years after originally implemented in 1992, the Stark legislation has undergone three revisions trying to keep up. Regulations are passed and then smart people figure out a way around them, needless to say, as is true for most other regulations, the smart people are way out ahead. Why not, they are more motivated. If they figure out a way around it they get rich, the regulators have no financial skin in the game so that extra effort, skin in the game that from sports to business separates the winners from the losers once again prevails.

Sadly there is far more involved here than money. Just as for coal mining regulations (see the chapter about politicians), people's health is at stake. CAT scans for example emit radiation. They are very very lucrative to the imaging centers, the hospitals that have their own imaging devices, and to the docs that get kickbacks for referrals. Fortunately, occasionally in every party there always seems to be a "whistle-blower" or some person who wants to spoil everyone else's fun. Recently several such folks have begun to raise serious questions about the overuse of CAT scans from both a financial and a health standpoint.

Recent studies have shown that CAT scans alone account for 24% of the radiation that people in the U.S. receive on a yearly basis. A radiologist at the Massachusetts General Hospital in Boston recently developed a software program that scores the appropriateness of a scan every time it is going to be used and compares its utility to less expensive and less radiation-intense tests. Prior to its use of this program, the hospitals rate of CAT scans had been growing at about 3% per quarter. After the software programs use began, the increase had dropped to 0.25% per quarter. A study published in 2010 in the main journal for radiologists reported that 27% of CAT scans "were not considered appropriate." CAT scans are real money.

Another "doctor-driven" medical-costs shenanigan is the "pill-mill" that sells hundreds of millions of dollar of prescription drugs in fraudulent ways. The two most often abused prescription drugs are oxycontin and vicodin, both prescribed for pain-relief and also at the top of the list for someone looking to get high in a serious way. The routine is that an unscrupulous doctor sets up typically under the guise of a "pain-management clinic," a place where abusers can come and get a prescription for their drug of choice. The doc writes the prescription which is then taken to a specific pharmacy that will look the other way that this is the 800th prescription written this month for this person and kicks-back money to the prescribing doc.

These scams seem especially prevalent in Florida and have been the subject of repeated media exposés. Yes repeated, because it seems that only the media are able to locate them. Occasionally law-enforcement makes a show of a raid but in another whack-a-mole event they just pop-up somewhere else. I mean how hard can it be to just monitor pharmacy records and orders through drug distributors.

Drug costs are simply out of control, there is no other way to describe them. With inflation the last few years in the 1-3% range, drug prices have been going up in the 8%-10% range. Some major drugs have seen price rises the past year between 20%-30%. The fact is that drug companies are major corporations with revenues in the 30-60 billions of dollars range. They are traded on the stock exchange with valuations in the $100 billion plus range. In order to maintain their stock price they must continue to make the kinds of profits and annual growth rate (the two most important parameters that determine stock price) as they have in the past.

Looking down the road the drug companies see major threats on the horizon. Their own ability to bring new drugs onto the market has for the past decade dropped off the cliff. The hey-day of new drug discovery was in the '70s and '80s. True new discoveries in the pharmaceutical field are now few and far between. Most new drug introductions have simply been variations on past drugs that for example allow instead of taking a pill once a day, it may now be taken once a week. Needless to say, the price of the once a week drug is boosted more than enough to make up for the reduction in number of pills the patient takes. In addition, patents tend to be for about 17 years, so some major blockbuster drugs will be soon be coming off-patent and will be vulnerable to competition from generics.

In response to this threat, the major pharmaceutical companies are doing deals with their potential generic drug competitors. The deal with the generic manufacturer is that in exchange for payments that would equal what they would have received had they come to market, the generic manufacturer will hold back their product. These sorts of activities alone show just how much profit the companies make from their drugs. They are able to charge enough that not only do they cover their research and development plus marketing costs, much less the cost of just making the drugs but also add an additional hefty amount to pay off other companies from entering the market with a competitive product. Imagine Ford being able to price their cars so they can pay GM enough to match whatever GM would make from a competitive car. That is just how profitable is the pharmaceutical industry.

Most importantly for the drug companies is the handwriting on the wall that the politicians may find the voters outrage at high drug costs more important than the campaign contributions from the pharmaceutical company's lobbyists. So to beat the coming possible legislation, drug companies are raising prices now to prepare for tough times down the road. Tough times meaning that the drug companies will now have to make profits in line with most other industries.

There are several issues in plain sight that should be very disturbing to anyone concerned with the seemingly ridiculously high cost of drugs in the United States. One is that the same drug, sold in any other developed country is always less expensive than in the U.S., sometimes significantly so. Even in our neighbor Canada they are much less which has of course spawned the industry of patients using the internet to buy drugs from pharmacies in Canada. Of course lobbyists from the drug industry are working diligently to have legislation passed to prohibit such sales. I came across an interesting comment in *The Economist*, of May 28, 2011, p. 68, "America's propensity to pay has one important benefit: it encourages investment in research. Drug makers recoup their investments in America; other countries take a free ride."

The same system seen in the spinal fusion market of kicking back money to docs also plays a role in drug prescriptions. The unnecessary prescribing of antibiotics for colds and flu (both of which are caused by viruses not bacteria) certainly has kickbacks involved. The U.S. Justice Department recently reached a settlement with Merck Serono of $44.3 million in a case involving the company kicking back money to physicians who prescribed one of their drugs. Direct kickbacks of money is just the tip of the iceberg, rewarding physicians who reach a certain number of prescriptions for specific "reward" drugs receive rewards in the form of high-value tickets to sporting events along with all expenses paid visits to luxury resorts under the guise of "continuing education." The nuanced issue when such kickbacks are involved is whether the physician prescribes the best treatment for the patient. In most cases it is a close call or not even so close a call as to which drug is appropriate. Through rewards programs, the physician is motivated to choose the one from the company with the best "rewards" program, just like which credit card one uses.

Even within the United States, different folks pay significantly different prices depending on whether they have a drug coverage plan or not. Even with a drug coverage plan it depends on whether it is a private insurer's plan or a plan run by their employers. A Medicare plan pays a different cost from someone with a plan from one of the armed forces. A real mess.

What is also troubling is that over the past ten years or so we now have a breed of pharmaceuticals where treatment can cost in the tens of thousands of dollars. A years worth easily running into a hundred thousand dollars. Many of these drugs are what are known as "biologics," and most are produced through genetic engineering and other biotechnology methods.

Many of the new genetically engineered and biologic drugs were discovered by small start-up companies that were financed by venture capitalists. If the company was making progress and had invented a compound that seemed to have promise, it would enter into a joint-venture with a major pharmaceutical company. Final development and then clinical trials is expensive, typically beyond the reach of a small start-up company. The joint-venture provides the small company with not just the money but also the expertise to run the clinical trials. The biotech company would split in a predetermined way with the big company the revenues from drug sales.

As described previously, the way the venture capitalist makes money is through the IPO of the company's stock. The company's stock on the public stock markets is of course related to its revenues and profitability. For a company with only one product on the market and who knows what chance of rolling the drug development dice and hitting gold once again, it takes one heck of big drug price to justify it being a public company in the first place, much less selling at a stock price to give the venture capitalists a solid return when they sell their shares to John Q. Public. Biotech drugs were responsible for 70% of the increase in drug prices last year.

These incredibly expensive high-tech drugs have prices driven more by investor expectations than by the actual recovery of the money spent in developing the drug. Once again, Medicare seems pretty much insensitive to how big a check they have to write and the private insurers simply raise premiums to cover their costs. This subject is currently the source of a heated debate in Congress. It has taken the form of a battle over the pharmaceutical companies wanting a 12 years marketing exclusivity for their "biological" products before generic manufacturers can produce them.

On the one side are Senators making speeches for this exclusive period, "incentives for innovators to research and develop new treatments.," while on the other side, "delay the availability of generic biologic drugs restricting access for many Americans and driving up costs for the federal government." It is as if the private investors would not have made the investment if they could only make ten times their money in a few years instead of twenty or more.

Recently a biotechnology company that is publicly traded with a market value of about six billion dollars, Dendreon, received approval for a "high-tech" drug for prostate cancer. One course of treatment lasts one month and consists of 3 doses, each one costing $31,000, or $93,000 for one course of treatment. Now who could balk at costs if it is the difference between life or death. However in this case, the clinical trials data say that the typical result is a gain of putting off death by three months. Wait until the politicians get a hold of this one, at least the ones up for reelection. "Death panels"

One of the first and one of the most successful of the biotechnology companies, the one that put the term "genetic engineering" on Wall Street's map is Genentech, now a part of the very large pharmaceutical company Roche. Genentech recently found itself in a real conundrum.

Genentech and Roche brought to market an anti-cancer drug, Avastin, which controls the growth of new blood vessels in the body. Since tumors can only grow if they have a blood supply to bring them oxygen and nutrients, Avastin certainly seemed to hold promise for the control of new tumor growth. With such a strong theoretical background for its effectiveness, Avastin based upon preliminary studies, was put into the FDA's fast track program and received approval. Initially, at a cost of $90,000 per year it was a big winner financially for Roche.

Genentech and Roche also created a drug, Lucentis, which is used to treat a common cause of blindness in the elderly, macular degeneration. Lucentis costs about $2000 per treatment and generated about $1.6 billion in U.S. sales in 2010.

Lo and behold, some clinically oriented academic researchers, based upon Avastin's chemical characteristics and biological effects, thought it would be interesting to try Avastin in the eye as a treatment for macular degeneration which is also related to blood vessel growth. Ah ha, it worked, and according to two different major studies by well-respected scientists, one group at the governments own National Institutes of Health (NIH) and the other at Johns Hopkins, compared Avastin with Lucentis, they both worked equally well.

The conundrum for Genentech is that Avastin costs only $50 per eye for its one-time treatment versus Lucentis costing $2,000. In 2008, Medicare spent $537 million for 337,000 treatments with Lucentis. In the same year, Medicare spent $20 million for even more treatments with Avastin, 480,000. Over the last two years Medicare would have saved just over $1 billion if only Avastin had been used. Lucentis is the largest dollar amount spent for any pharmaceutical in Medicare part B. Why you may ask are doctors still being allowed to use Lucentis when Medicare (you the taxpayer) could have saved so much money for an equally effective treatment with Avastin? Genentech has launched a very intense lobbying campaign in Congress as to why Medicare should continue to reimburse docs who prescribe Lucentis for use in the eye.

To make the story even more a model for why our health care system is a mess is the eventual fate of Avastin even for breast cancer as described in the chapter about how diligently our elected representatives work on our behalf. Initially the FDA bowed to tremendous political pressure to approve Avastin for breast cancer. Eventually its lack of effect and disastrous side-effects made the FDA in a 6-0 vote to cancel Avastin's approval.

I would bet there is not a handful of readers who know the true background behind the argument the drug companies make in the media for their outrageous profits. The drug companies major arguments for their excessive profits is that they need the money to cover the enormous research and development costs they must incur to develop new drugs. Yeah, well that is a pile of crap, a massive charade hiding the truth. The largest expense line at a pharmaceutical company is marketing costs. All those kickbacks, game tickets, hot babe saleswoman who visit doc's offices, and freebie vacations, actually outweigh research and development costs (how many of you are aware of that little gem).

However there is even a larger and more dishonest charade behind their argument and it is the great dirty-little-secret of the whole medical products industry. In fact it is you the taxpayer who actually foots the bill for much of the research and development behind the drugs that the drug companies make and for which then charges you an exorbitant price. Little known is the hard fact that your taxes laundered through the federal government already foots a significant portion of the research and development behind pretty much all medical products.

The federal government through a variety of agencies such as the National Science Foundation (NSF) and the NIH hand out the grants, your tax money, that keep the scientists at Universities and Medical Schools working away on understanding the biological mechanisms of the body. Some of this work is called basic research. It is directed at understanding fundamental processes that lay the foundation for how to cure a disease.

The next stage, taking the fundamental discovery and seeing if it can play a role in a cure also happens at Universities and Medical Schools. It is done by scientists who take this basic science and come up with research programs that put pieces of the very complex puzzle of the human body together and do research specifically targeted at a disease. Their work is funded by the same taxpayer money through the NSF and NIH. All of this knowledge is open to the public through publication in scientific journals including those who work for the pharmaceutical companies. The pharmaceutical companies are the largest recipients of corporate welfare in the United States.

It is these billions of dollars a year worth of knowledge produced by researchers working away mostly on taxpayer funded grants that form the basis for the pharmaceutical companies to then add their part to the knowledge and create a pill for a specific disease. Where is the financial discount to the taxpayers who funded the research that laid the groundwork for the pharmaceutical companies to then do the final stage of the work to create a pill. Is the taxpayer funded percentage of the knowledge that created the pill 25% or is it 75%? I would expect that it is a number that is for some near 25%, others 75% and for most somewhere in the middle. Where is the discount to the taxpayer who paid this percentage of the research and development behind all these incredibly high profit-margin medications?

If one looks at the financial statements of most companies, their profits are usually in the range on the low side of just a few percent of sales. Examples of these are the large grocery store chains that sell a gazillion individual purchases in a highly competitive market for cereal, sodas, and apples. A gazzilion times a few cents profit on every apple is still a lot of money. On the other side would be companies that make profits of about ten percent or even a little higher of their sales. Examples of these would be companies that sell prestige brands where the competition may not be very strong and the purchaser is less price sensitive than for groceries.

As a retired venture capitalist I am all for profits, they are the life blood of our very innovative, productive, and job creating free-market economy. Yet drug companies with their profit margins of just short of 20% rank seventh from the top of the 215 industries ranked by Morningstar, a well-regarded financial services company. Generic drug maker profits are about 5% of sales.

Talk about free market capitalism; pharmaceutical companies violate many of its basic principles. First, there is very little competition. The doctor has most often little choice as to what pill to prescribe for your specific illness, only one has shown to be most effective. In addition, the doctor's choice in the situation where more than one drug is effective, is rarely based upon the cost of the medication. Second, you the consumer, who pays at least some part of the cost, has no say in what is prescribed. You cannot go and buy a different medication than the one the doctor has prescribed. Third, and most importantly, the person who usually pays most if not all the cost, the private or government insurer, is as the economists would say, price insensitive. The drug company sets the price and the insurer pays it no questions asked. There is nothing competitive or free-market about this.

In late June of 2011, Vertex pharmaceuticals, a high-growth biotech company that is well on its way to making the transition to a full-fledged grown-up company made two announcements that showed just how much the pharmaceutical industry is not an example of free market capitalism. Now remember, Vertex is a darling of Wall Street, its stock price is at an all-time high and it's bank account flush with money. Announcement number one is that in exchange for moving its world headquarters to a new real estate development on Boston's waterfront it was receiving $60 million dollars in state subsidies. How many laid-off teacher's salaries and school programs were cut to fund that tax-break to a company in fine financial condition.

Second, its newest drug for hepatitis C would be priced at about $50,000 for a 3 month treatment. Vertex's CEO defended the pricing on the basis that it would eliminate even more costly liver transplants for some people. I guess it knew that the argument about the recovery of research and development costs was growing thin in some circles so its only claim was to compare it to liver transplants. So what, why does that give them the right to charge such an outrageous price? Since the vast majority of the likely users would be seniors, Medicare foots this bill that has nothing to do with any of the usual bases for product costs such as manufacturing, research and development, sales, and overhead expenses, much less a competitive market. Government money in the form of tax breaks and government money for a price based upon nothing other than something vague and irrelevant as liver transplants. They could pick any price they want, they are paid, "subsidized," by government handouts in this case called Medicare, price insensitive, free market capitalism you betcha.

Drug makers have paid over the past ten years $11 billion in fines for marketing drugs for indications that were never approved by the FDA. Most of the costs for these drugs marketed illegally were paid by Medicare and most of the fines were initiated by whistleblowers embarrassing the government into pursuing the cases. Currently there is a whistle-blower-initiated case in process where the feds are going after Johnson and Johnson for $1 billion over the off-label marketing of one of their drugs, Risperdal. Surprise surprise, as of August, 2011 J&J has agreed to pleading guilty to a misdemeanor, the exact size of the settlement has not been determined but is expected to be far south of $1billion. Nice of the feds since a drug company found guilty of a felony as described in the original case could lose its ability to receive payment from a variety of federal programs such as Medicaid and Medicare

The example of another drug, NovoSeven, used extensively off-label is also mentioned in the chapter about regulatory affairs and the FDA's congressional oversight. It is a drug approved for only a specific type of hemophilia, a bleeding disorder. However it became quite popular as a general treatment whenever enhanced clotting was desired. In fact, 97% of its sales were for off-label use. A recent study was published examining its appropriateness for these uses, to quote the authors, "We found no evidence to suggest that the drug saves lives for any of the patient scenarios or conditions that we evaluated." Moreover they found the drug was associated with an increased risk of heart attacks and strokes due to its ability to promote clotting. Somewhat sarcastically, the authors also states: "There is reason to wonder how the use of an obscure recombinant coagulation factor marketed exclusively to hematologists came to be used so widely by cardiac surgeons, neurologists and trauma surgeons." Gosh, I wonder how that could have happened?

Another issue related to costs for prescription drugs and the way they are prescribed is who gets to prescribe them. This problem is especially true when it comes to medications for mental health. Psychiatry, the real psychiatry, is practiced only by M.D.s who have done an internship and residency specific to psychiatry. Psychiatry from the time of Freud has been based on the medical model, a disease of biological origins that requires medical training to diagnose and treat. From pastors to social workers and the variety of people who consider themselves "counselors," people see them for help with their emotional problems. Sometimes for the ups and downs of daily living indeed a good listener can be all that is needed; however the trouble is that those with true mental disease can not be helped by these "counselors" and things can only get worse.

Now that the field of mental health has tried and true drugs for bipolar disorder, depression and anxiety, it is more imperative than ever that patients, such as the truly clinically depressed, see a real psychiatrist. Only they are properly trained for the management of drug treatments for mental disorders. Yet right now that is not the case. Nearly 75% of prescriptions for antidepressants are given out by M.D.s with no psychiatric training, either for diagnosis or drug treatment. Antidepressants are the second most prescribed medication in the United States, second only to cholesterol lowering drugs. To make matters even more troubling, they only work for people with true clinical depression which has several diagnostic signs. The reason so many people get no relief from their "depression" is because they are simply down and go to their family practitioner or internist and he writes them a prescription without a proper evaluation for true clinical depression. The family practitioner does not have the training to manage their patient's response to the medication and adjust its dose. Why not, insurance pays for it, what the hell if it is pointless.

Just one more about drug costs. The Office of the Inspector General of the Department of Health and Human Services caught a division of Medicare paying for fake prescriptions for drugs that are high on the list of street-traded drugs of abuse. Prescriptions were written with fake physician I.D. numbers and under the names of long-ago dead physicians. Evidently Medicare does not in many cases verify the validity of the prescriptions for which it pays.

So there you have it, the nuts and bolts of the money involved in the actual practice of medicine; the behind scenes of the bills your insurer, whether it is private or government pays that are creating such a stir. In the main I expect most physicians have their patients well-being foremost in their minds. However, there are many who place that balance between their own financial ambitions and their patients care somewhere other than the patient side of the scale. For these practitioners of medicine, the folks that make the drugs, run the hospitals, and supply all the myriad of devices that are involved as implants and used in surgical procedures are all too happy to provide financial incentives to them. On top of these excess costs are the variety of unnecessary diagnostic tests from the simplest of blood tests in the tens of dollars to the more complex imaging tests in the thousands of dollars. Those who wish to enrich themselves have every opportunity. Medicare seems not to care about the fraud and abuse underlying the bills they so willingly pay.

Crying out to me in the whole issue of Medicare fraud and other abuse of the medical insurance system is why it takes reporters to find the fraud. Why have the folks at the private and government insurance programs who have this data paraded in front of them on their computer screens been so willing to ignore this fraud? For example, the doc who is at the top of the heap by a large margin for repeat spinal fusions on the same patient, I mean how hard can it be to notice that or an individual physical therapist billing for amounts that are only ever seen for entire clinics. The reason it gets ignored, it doesn't matter.

Medicare costs are a crisis that effects the whole country. Budgets, such as education, that should not be cut, are being cut because of Medicare's exploding costs. One fraud investigation could save enough money to save a city from firing teachers. It is a crisis that must be dealt with.

Politicians being the charade players that they are, especially with the next presidential election on the horizon, the news of the coming year will surely be full of fatuous pronouncement about "innovation," "free market capitalism," "competition," "death panels," and "keeping bureaucrats from making medical decisions." It will be a classic case that no matter what the Democrats propose, the Republicans will be against it, and no matter what the Republicans propose, the Democrats will be against it. They will both dip into that bag of meaningless emotional sound bites to appeal to their fans, political theater at its highest form, the best interests of the country be damned.

Enough about the way medicine is truly practiced and what goes into determining the amount charged for medical care. Time for the chapter to change its focus to a search for a way to make a meaningful change in our health care costs by taking a look at how other countries are trying to control their own health care costs. They are grappling with many of the same questions we are such as the fundamental ones: What is the role of private versus government insurers? Can competition be brought to the health care system? Should a cost-benefit analysis ever be considered in approving a medical treatment for reimbursement?

These issues are intensely political and it is hard to find studies and analyses that do not have an axe to grind. I will try my best to refer to only the most neutral analysis and descriptions as I could find in an attempt to identify the most important issues and their pros and cons. Hopefully it will allow you, the voter, to identify which talking head may be at least close to a fair-minded point of view and which others are simply trying to appeal to the Yankee or Red Sox fans out there that their team really is better than the other, the facts of the matter and what is really in the best interests of our country be damned.

As an example of what is about as unbiased an analysis as one can find, there was a recent review in the journal *Science* (the official publication of the scientists of any stripe professional association) about the costs of cancer treatment, a major part of our health care bill. The review gives a detailed history of one particular cancer patient. He did not do well on the mainstream treatments and then the issue became of whether to spend hundreds of thousands of dollars on the latest greatest treatment that even if it worked might not give him more than a few months of life.

Following much to and fro over getting reimbursement from his insurance carrier for part of the cost of the treatment, they decided to give it a try. After $350,000 for four months of treatments, there was no progress other than at least those four months, and sadly he passed away from his cancer.

The article in *Science* was also about the results that were presented in June of 2011 at a major conference for cancer specialists on other new treatments. These latest "breakthroughs" were very much a part of the national news shows in June of 2011.

A brief description of the new-wave of cancer treatments is appropriate to help you understand why they are so very expensive and also since the Sanjay Guptas of the world have to have breakthroughs to keep those ratings up regardless of their promise, the chances are very good that in the coming years, these will feature prominently on the news shows.

Although each one is different in its details, they all mostly fit in one of two categories. One is take biopsy samples of a patient's tumor along with cells from the same patient's immune system and then in the laboratory to prompt these immune cells to multiply. Ingredients are added that fire-up the immune system cells and get them ready to attack a foreign invader. Then the patient's tumor cells are added and hopefully the patient's own now abundant immune cells will learn to recognize, attack, and kill their tumor. Once enough of these cells are grown and educated in the laboratory, they are injected into the patient and if all this work in the laboratory was effective, they will then continue to attack the patient's tumor cells and also teach the rest of his immune system to attack the tumor cells.

The other, is based upon DNA characterization of the specific tumor in the patient. Similar to the procedure just described, tumor cells are recovered through biopsy and placed in test tubes. The DNA from this specific tumor is then studied, and based upon that knowledge, which cancer drugs that have a high probability of fighting the cancer can be chosen. A modification of this is to alter if possible existing drugs to be effective against this specific DNA-typed tumor. Many different drugs can be tested in the laboratory prior to deciding which one should be given to the patient.

Both of these types of treatment are known as "personalized" treatments. They are an admission that much of the previous failure in cancer treatments is because not all prostate, breast, colon, etc. cancers are the same from one patient to the next. Within breast cancers there may be 5 different types as represented by their different DNA sequences. By using a retrospective look at what tumors were killed by what specific drugs and then testing the best choices against the patient's own tumor cells one can pick the right treatment for that particular tumor. All this personalization of starting with a patient's own tumor and then using a mix of, DNA testing, growing immune system cells, and cancer cells in the laboratory is very very expensive.

These types of treatments tend to run $50,000-$100,000 dollars per course of treatment. In most cases the benefit is a few months of life. A new lung-cancer treatment is $1.2 million for an extra year of life. A part of this article in *Science* was the report that 90% of the new cancer drugs approved by the FDA over the past four years cost a minimum of $20,000 for a three month course of treatment.

The same moral quandary of balancing cost with effectiveness is present in other diseases as well. It is not just cancer, but disorders such as diabetes, heart disease, and neurological disorders where the numbers may not be as dramatic as for these new age cancer treatments, but the same issue is raised: How much to spend for how long a prolongation of mostly a bed-ridden life?

The article in *Science* appropriately not wanting to ignore the moral issues involved, quoted a well-respected cancer researcher at the National Cancer Institute, "But when you have the patient in front of you, and nothing else is working, well, I might try the crazy thing too. We used to do it with cheap drugs, but now we are doing it with really expensive drugs. The problem is they really don't work any better."

So what if it doesn't work any better, the patient's family heard about it on TV as the latest greatest life-saving breakthrough and to the drug company that sells it, it has profit margins out the roof so the marketing is relentless. Does the U.S. stand for capitalism, do we want to let "bureaucrats" make death panel decisions?" Actually the panels were a mix of patient advocates and physicians. Some years ago I came across a modest study that would not pass the true-blue standards for statistical accuracy, but the results certainly did suggest that if the patient was asked if they wanted the last few months of a treatment they said "No" more often than "Yes"; whereas the family almost always said "Yes."

The United Kingdom has made a try at grappling with this issue. They have demanded that along with the traditional clinical trials data that the company must submit to obtain approval for payment through the government funded health care insurance, the company must also submit data on the effectiveness of the drug in prolonging life. Many developed countries are working on a shared standard called Quality Adjusted Life Year (QALY) that takes into account the drugs cost and how many additional years of life the patient is given.

An important part of these programs is the comparison of one drug versus another on this measure. Comparing different drugs for their effectiveness in treating the same disease was a part of the "Obamacare" program. However, it was removed because of the sound bite you may recall hearing: "putting bureaucrats in between patients and doctors." That is how our health-care debate is being waged. That is how the future of our country's financial health as well as the health of our citizens is being decided. The bureaucrats were in reality a panel primarily of physicians with a few nonphysicians selected to specifically serve as patient advocates. How could any politician running for election not embrace such a great sounding slogan. That is how we are going about solving our budget deficit.

The simple concept of comparing how effective one drug is against another drug will play no role in determining how Medicare spends its money. In other countries that use the QALY measure to determine their payments, several of the major drug companies have begun a program of offering a drug for free for a set period to see if it works and if it is effective, then offering the drug at a reduced price for future treatments. It is hard to be optimistic that anything as productive will occur as long as politicians are involved.

Some developed countries do allow for private health care plans to compete with the government plans. Francesca Colombo of the OECD a leading think tank with representatives from 34 developed countries dedicated to promoting economic growth and democracy, in reviewing the results of a study comparing public and private plans has said: "Whatever the role played in a health system, private health insurance has added to total health expenses. It is no coincidence that the countries with the biggest private health insurance sectors, America, France, Germany and Switzerland, also have some of the highest health care costs per person." Clark Havighurst, of the conservative think tank, American Enterprise Institute, "As long as health insurers only significant function is the simple one of financing health care, government itself is probably capable of performing that role nearly as well as they do, without incurring competitions added costs."

Is competition in healthcare realistic? When your family doctor responds to your complaint of back pain, he will refer you to an orthopedic surgeon. The surgeon then sends you to an imaging center in which he has a financial interest for an MRI study of your spine. Based upon the result he decided a spinal fusion is called for and schedules it at the hospital where he does his surgeries and owns the distributorship from which the hospital buys the implements used in your fusion. Are you really going to ask if he has any financial interest in the imaging center or the distributorship from which the hospital buys the products used in your surgery?

When he sends you for a spinal fusion are you really going to say, well I would really rather try some bed rest and anti-inflammatory medications? Or if you give in and it is time for the surgery are you really going to tell the surgeon you want to call around and get quotes from various hospitals, hoping he has operating privileges at the low cost provider? How about putting yourself through a complex surgery under general anesthesia with the low-cost provider, how do you feel about that one. Hey I hear you can get a great deal in Tijuana— yeah thanks. Bringing competition to healthcare certainly in some specific ways would be great, but it just ain't realistic. The competitive pressures that keep grocery prices low do not exist and can never exist in healthcare as it is practiced in the United States. Any politician who takes about a health care system that will bring competition is full of it.

There is some attempt by private insurers to increase their profitability through something like creating a competitive environment in the health care providers. Some insurers are starting to measure outcomes of care at hospitals and relate the amount of payment to a hospitals track record. Sloppy practices mean longer stays and readmissions, so if the insurer starts to ding hospitals for below standard levels of care, it improves care and cuts costs. These measures are however few and far between. If practiced system wide it would make a small difference. However there is no across-the-board incentive on private insurers to attempt to lower their costs nor a guarantee that these lower costs will be translated into lower premiums instead of just keeping premiums the same but using the savings to increase their profit margins.

Another issue here in the U.S. related to competition is the seeming inability of the government programs to take any initiative at all in controlling medical costs. As we have seen above, Medicare has been run in much the same way as private insurers in terms of having no incentive to control their costs. It was on the one hand fascinating, but more importantly disturbing that in almost every case of Medicare abuse I came upon, it was not a Medicare employee who uncovered the abuse but an investigative reporter or a whistle blower.

Once the abuse made the paper or the evening news, then Medicare jumped on the bandwagon and of course our pals in Washington announced hearings, posters were displayed across the town, and the curtains pulled back and the Congressional Theatre opened with that age old ritual of playing to the audience of either Yankee or Red Sox fans. I was stunned to come across the law banning outsiders access to Medicare data. Those reporters who have gained access have typically done so through legal action and or negotiations with Medicare defining the precise data they will be allowed to see.

There is an example of the perfect storm of greed having Medicare as its playground. Recall the comment about the first hurdle you must jump over to get a job as an investment banker: "Sell your mother." Well one of them came to run a health care company called Tenet that was mainly in the business of owning and operating hospitals. This fellow had a fine career as an investment banker, buying, selling, investing, you name it. Imagine someone bright as hell with the only goal in life to make his pile of money as big as possible who is running a company that has as one of its major sources of revenue, Medicare. Does "kid in a candy store" come to mind?

One year after rising to Forbes magazine's top position on their Executive Pay scale he was at the top of Forbes CEO Pay Dishonor Roll. The stock in Tenet had dropped 70% in that year and was to drop even further amidst of a flurry of irregularities found in Tenet's billings to Medicare. Yet, and this is the wonderful part, in that last year, prior to his resignation, this CEO took home about 190 million dollars in pay, 110 million or so in exercised stock options and 80 million in a combination of salary, bonus, and perqs. Yes he took it home and put it in the bank after running a company engaged in Medicare billing fraud. The Tenet shareholder committee ran an ad in the CEO's local newspaper demanding he return the money. Old saying, "the best predictor of future behavior is past behavior." Now that is an investment banker that makes his profession proud.

If we can go back to our friend the stent that is put into clogged blood vessels to create a pathway for the blood flow, one example based upon their use sort of summarizes why this whole darn issue of healthcare is so recalcitrant to being fixed, the behavior of those on the front line, the docs. It involves a high quality study, the results of which were published in 2007 in the New England Journal of Medicine.

The study compared equivalent patients, one group received a stent plus the traditional medications for chest pain and the other group received just the drugs. It spanned 2,287 patients over five years. The results showed no difference between groups. The patients that received the surgery and the implanted stent did no better than the comparatively cheap drugs by themselves in controlling the chest pain.

The day the results of the study were announced, the stock of the companies that make stents fell. Over the next month the use of stents also fell, but surprisingly over the next few months, their use came back to the level before the study was published. Stents were a major source of revenue for the hospitals as well as the surgeons who put them in.

It is estimated that if the study guidelines were followed, it would save $5 billion of the $15 billion spent each year on stent surgeries. A cardiologist in referring to insurance companies ignoring the results of studies by well-respected physicians that are published in first class journals that point to specific ways to make a big hit against health care costs said: "There's no incentive on the part of the insurance company to do that, They would cause an uproar on the part of the physicians saying insurance companies were attempting to interpose themselves on the medical process."

A hot off the press story that will probably follow the same sequence as the stent story involves another medical device involving the heart, pacemakers. A recent study found that about 40% of the patients who under current guidelines would receive a pacemaker receive no benefit from them. They would have the same health outcome as patients who did not receive the device. These are patients that can easily be identified by a specific measurement on the EKG study that is a part of the standard work-up for a person having heart problems. At a minimum of $25,000 per implant, stopping the use of the device for these specific patients would save Medicare about $500 million per year. Or looked at another way that is half a billion dollars out of the pockets of the hospital, the surgeon, and the device maker. Do not hold your breath that anything will change.

In some cases Medicare is just doing what the laws put in place by our politicians tell them to do. They are not allowed to consider a treatment's actual benefits, especially in comparison with other treatments, when deciding how much to pay doctors for doing a certain procedure. In this case of stents, cost savings through a competitive comparison of treatment effectiveness was thrown in Medicare's face, yet ignored. They were just following the laws made by the politicians who are on the take, bribed by companies that make these products. Oops we are in the United States not some third-world country after all, I mean they get "campaign contributions."

Since private insurance carriers generally base their reimbursement on Medicare rates, Medicare's imperviousness to abuse sets the standard for the industry. The new health care law had changes to these policies and encouraged the use of effectiveness studies to be a part of payment decision—again, that is what provoked the "putting businessman in between the patient and the doctor" and it was removed to get enough votes for passage. Remember the quote from the *Economist*, "Americas propensity to pay has one important benefit: it encourages investment in research. Drugmakers recoup their investments in America; other countries take a free ride." Go Yankees! It is truly all one great big charade.

If it were not so sad, a recent article in the Los Angeles times (6/13/11) was really kind of funny. In England there is currently a lot of teeth gnashing over the state of its own health care system, mostly a government run system. The general political tide in England has some currents of "privatization" as the latest buzz word with politicians calling the current system "Orwellian" and "evil." The more interesting phrase for us in the U.S. is their term, "American style" for the shift to a privatized system.

However, in spite of the sound bites, polls clearly show that "American style" fills its people with tales of third rate care or no care at all for the bottom tier, second rate care for the middle tier, and care equal to the English system as available only to the very rich. As described in the article, "For a people accustomed to free healthcare for all, regardless of income, the fact that millions of their cousins across the Atlantic have no insurance and can't afford decent treatment is a farce as well as a tragedy."

As one would come to believe hearing many American politicians describing the "socialist" system of countries such as England, it is a system of unimaginable horrors. Yet in that very same county as described in the article, "So frightening is the Yankee example that any British politician who values his job has to explicitly disavow it as a possible outcome. Twice." To quote the conservative Prime Minister David Cameron, "we will not introduce an

American style private system." "In this country we have the most wonderful, precious institution and also precious idea that whenever your ill…you can walk into a hospital or a surgery and get treated for free…It is the idea at the heart of the NHS (National Health System) and it will stay. I will never put it at risk."

So what is going on, our politicians who oppose Obamacare point to the nationalized systems and call them garbage, unimaginable horrors of "death panels" and even worse? Yet, their politicians point to our system and say in effect, "over my dead body will such a system occur here in England." Gee, do you think it is just in the nature of any issue that politicians grab onto as a way to win votes that the only right answer is the one that they can use to invoke emotional feelings about my team versus your team? Could it be that what is in the best interests of the country plays no role and is subjugated to their own personal needs to make themselves big shots by being elected to office? Naaaahhhhh, not politicians.

Now if one wanted to start with a fresh sheet of paper and redo the entire health care system, the one known as the "public utility" model would be a fine one to consider. At some point, the folks who run the country decided that everyone has a right to certain basic services, such as electricity, natural gas, water, and sewers. These services in most cases are provided by private companies. However, to insure that everyone receives these services, the government regulates them very closely to insure an adequate level of service at a reasonable price consistent with an appropriate profit.

In exchange for giving up the chance for rapid growth in the stock price as would be the case for a company making computer chips, the investors in a public utility receive a reliable dividend, much like interest on a CD. If in fact the city served by the utility does grow, the stock price will tend to grow along with the growth in the number of subscribers to the utilities service. If the company needs money to expand its services, it can make an issuance of new dividend paying bonds or preferred shares in order to expand and meet the demands of new subscribers.

The public utility model is an interesting one, a blend of public and private. The company can utilize the private capital markets to raise funds. It has investors who receive proceeds from its efficient running and it can expand and the stock price will rise as its subscriber base expands. Yet it is regulated by the government under the theory that all citizens have a right to reliable and reasonably priced electricity and natural gas. What if we applied the same thinking to a citizen's right to having their broken leg fixed or receiving treatment for a heart condition, a citizen's right and not just a privilege for those who can afford it.

What if such a plan or others that would in fact fix our health care system once and for all were put in place? It could easily be structured to bring real competition between what drug is prescribed, what surgical procedure is done, which imaging procedure is used and at just which facility all this occurs and health care costs would drop dramatically. However, all this would have a profound effect on stock prices, initially fall and then stabilize. For the individual who has as significant portion of his savings for his retirement and his children's college education invested in a fund that includes stock in companies, they would take an initial hit.

There is a joke that is applicable to so many issues: A woman is walking down the street at night and sees a well-dressed man crawling around on his knees under a street light obviously looking for something. She asks: "Excuse me, what did you drop, can I help you look for it?" The man replies, "I was waiting for the bus and I dropped my change." She then says: "Why are you looking here, the bus stop is up the street." The man looks up at her and says, "I know that is where I dropped it, but the light is better here."

So we must remember that this whole vitriolic dialogue with seeming no sure solution to the health care cost problem can only occur within the framework of not impacting the stock price of health care stocks or the revenue of physicians. Now how the hell do you do that? Find a politician with the willingness to take a bite on the bullet of setting profit margin limits to companies involved with providing health care products and services. You can't because if they had that type of moral courage they never would have become a politician and won an election in the first place. I hope you will now be able to sit back in your seat in the theatre and watch the drama called "Healthcare Costs and the Budget Deficit," starring your elected representatives unfold before you. The players for the Yankees and the players for the Red Sox, each one will speak their lines, like finely targeted guided missiles to strike deep within the emotional heart of each team's fans.

Here are some of the fundamental issues to keep in mind when you try to decide which approach is the lesser of the evils. On the rare chance that at least one politician will actually address the types of issues raised in this Chapter, the issues that will lower the actual costs of health care instead of just shifting it from one pocket to another, then stand up and cheer and pull the lever next to their name.

1, If health care is a right and not a privilege then some form of insurance must exist and all citizens must subscribe. It is through spreading of costs across as many people as possible, some of whom will be heavy users and others light users that rates can be kept low; therefore it will be necessary for all people to have insurance. Also, it is known that if there are those without insurance, when they need care, it is just an additional burden on the government.

2, If an insurance programs only purpose is to simply take in premiums and send out payments to providers then there is no reason for it to be a for-profit enterprise. A nongovernmental not-for-profit or a governmental agency ought to be able to handle the paperwork just fine.

3, Since currently prescription drugs, physicians billing rates, medical tests, product costs, hospital fees, and any other bill generated by the health care system are at rates that appear excessive against any standard measures of profitability for the companies that provide them, something must be done to put pressure on these excessive profit margins.

4, History has shown that government agencies do not manage costs effectively and have a tremendous inertia to not disturb the status quo. Whether it is the Defense Department keeping an eye on its costs or Medicare sitting on a bundle of fraud and never recognizing it, governmental organizations have a lousy record of controlling costs.

5, The key, whether it is a private insurer or a government program is to in some way provide an incentive for the insurer to lower the costs they must actually pay to the care providers. Increasing premiums on the private side or printing more money on the public side can not be the solution when the costs rise. Whatever entity is the insurance provider, it must have the authority to reach into the health care system and make whatever cost as well as utilization changes as are needed to bring revenue and expenses into line with general standards across industries. If that is done the savings must be passed on through lower premiums for insurance.

6, Healthcare cannot be completely free. The user must have some skin in the game. An income based co-pay must accompany all health care utilization.

VII. DEADLY GAME OF CHARADES

Today, July 19, 2011, the text on the bottom of the TV screen was that three Americans had been killed in Afghanistan and it was featured by the talking heads of most of the news shows. I had just worked on the Media chapter, a part of which raised the issue of the media's, on a comparative basis, obsession with death in Afghanistan and Iraq while all but ignoring the many fold deaths over the same time periods on our nation's roads. I have spent some time trying to understand why this very disproportionate time and effort announcing and commenting upon deaths in our wars compared with deaths on our roads. Is this strange disparity in reporting deaths a charade of some sort?

One the one hand, soldiers who sign-up for the military are knowingly putting their lives in harms way and essentially rolling the dice. On the other hand, someone who hops in the car to go to the grocery store, or even on a highway vacation trip, does so with pretty good statistical assurance and expectation that they will not die. Yet 30,000 of such innocents are killed every year. Any death is of course a tragedy but when someone makes the conscious choice to put themselves in harms way, that certainly cannot be a reason why when it happens the media dwells on it more than when a life is taken by someone engaging in activity where that harm is well down the probability list. If five American soldiers were killed tomorrow, or even one or two in Iraq or Afghanistan it would lead every major news network broadcast and be prominent on the text at the bottom of the screen. Yet when five high school girls were killed in a crash because the driver of their car was texting, barely a mention if any.

Have we just become immune to deaths on the highway so that the folks who sit around meetings where they decide what goes in the newspaper or on the TV news each day just feel that no one will care. Oh yeah, someone died in town today in a car crash, happened a whole bunch all over the country, about a hundred each day, not a big deal. Versus, "oh no, three people died in Afghanistan today, that's a headline worth a certain bump-up in market share, let's make it the lead story."

What makes the media's silence on the traffic deaths seem even more bizarre is that it would not be very hard to prevent at least 50% of those deaths. At a minor increase in costs and inconvenience to the consumer, a variety of modifications to our cars would make a significant dent (gadzooks, what a word choice) in the road kills of people. In fact, when we stop our involvement in Iraq and Afghanistan, the government should take just a small percentage, certainly less than 10, of the money we will no longer be spending on the wars, and subsidize the safety improvements to cars bought in the United States. Just that would save more American lives (I think politicians use the term, "precious American resources") each year than were lost in all the years of these two wars. If the news coverage of our wars in Afghanistan and Iraq reflects our concern over the deaths of Americans, how can we not afford the trivial amount to save that same number of lives each and every year.

To make matters worse, over the past few years, the automobile manufacturers are starting to develop complex new internet access systems for cars that no one is denying will make them much more dangerous and cause the death toll to rise. Yet, so far, there has been little outcry by the folks who have the power to legislate against adding things to cars that will without a doubt make them more dangerous. Nor has the media, through their power to control what concerns occupy the American mind, made any mention of the deaths sure to come.

Right now, communication systems such as cell phones for talk and texting along with video displays that function to provide real-time location and control of a variety of functions such as audio systems and climate control through driver interaction while the car is moving are killing people on the roads. Imagine if thirty years ago, someone said that in thirty years you will be able to dial a telephone, hold it to your ear and talk while driving, type messages and interact with a touch sensitive television screen while you were driving at any speed on any road no matter how congested under even the worst of weather conditions. They would think you are out of your mind.

The statistics on deaths and injuries related to cell phones are hard to gather with pin-point accuracy. After sorting through various estimates, it would appear that of the 30,000 road deaths in 2008, 6000 were directly attributable to a distracted driver; about 20 percent of those are related to cell phone use. Of the half-million injuries in 2008 resulting from distracted driving, about 5% are attributable to cell phone use. I have avoided guesstimates based upon "derived" statistics, in particular from groups with an axe to grind on the issue.

The accidents and deaths from distracted driving, can only be about to significantly increase since many manufacturers have already begun to announce the upcoming wondrous new ways that their car's dashboards will become portals for cyberspace. Ford which has been a leader in this area with a system branded as "Sync" has just released their next version, "My Ford Touch." Its aim is to take every user function of the car now controlled through knobs and switches on the dashboard, even the seat controls, and place them on a screen with a touchpad on the steering wheel. One of the testing gurus of such technologies is Walt Mossberg, who in commenting on his use of Ford's new system wrote, "but (after speaking highly of it) Ford's new user interface has so many options and functions that I believe it presents a challenging learning curve. Learning the new system can be distracting while driving... My advice is to learn these in the driveway gradually."

Research in Motion, the maker of BlackBerrys hopes to use a new set of products and software brought to market specifically for the automobile as a way to gain some of the ground they have lost in the cell phone and tablet markets. It recently purchased QNX Software Systems, one of the leading companies in providing the electronic systems behind many electronic functions that the driver controls in the car. RIM's push is to provide the ability to read emails, launch apps, and access a variety of stored entertainment from the cars dashboard. One article that I read even suggested that the RIM platform would be excellent for video games, OMG!

Thilo Koslowski, an analyst with the well-respected cyberspace research group, Gartner, said, "internet-connected autos will be among the fastest-growing segments in four years." Many functions will become available, such as making dinner reservations while driving, hotel reservations while on a road trip, using a variety of apps, select which entertainment will come over your audio system and even appear on your monitor, take part in Twitter and blogs, and last but certainly not least, update your Facebook listing. Automobiles are a competitive marketplace and it will only take one brand to push the limit and eventually all will have to give you the ability to play games while driving.

Ray LaHood, the Secretary of Transportation in the United States has already launched the first salvo, "There's absolutely no reason for any person to download Facebook into the car." It will be up to the National Highway Traffic Safety Administration, a part of his organization that will be responsible for setting the rules about what can and cannot be accessed while driving. So far Mr. LaHood has been unable to get federal rules written about even using a cell phone and texting while driving. People will most certainly die every year from trying to drive while typing away for a text or twitter message, trying to solve the glitch on the touch screen in their GPS system or opening an app to make a hotel reservation.

If it bleeds it leads. Seen the bleeding from distracted driving leading on the TV news or front page of the newspaper? How many of you know of the woman in 2009 who while speeding came upon a line of cars stopped at a construction project. Since she was paying her bills on her "smart phone" at the time she never looked up and plowed into the line of cars. She killed one of the people doing nothing wrong but being the victim of corporate greed and legislative moral irresponsibility thanks to lobbyists.

Maybe the next one will be your husband or wife, son or daughter, mother or father, or fiancé. What death could be more senseless than one that occurred because someone could just not resist reading their latest text message or paying a bill? How about it, if it really was someone that was a part of your life, you may be the very next person that devotes the rest of their life to starting or just joining a national organization trying to fight the lobbyists from the automotive industry and electronics industry for legislation outlawing these deadly activities. We are alone amongst most other developed countries in our dealing with these issues. Bribery, graft, and corruption, not here, oh no, we called it lobbying.

There is a drug that has the following characteristics:
1, It has effects primarily on the liver, the stomach, and the brain. Chronic use destroys liver function and leads to death. In the stomach it erodes the lining and can cause an ulcer by itself, but is primarily known for making much worse the ulcers of people who have them from other causes. However, it is on the brain where it has its major impact. Compared to other drugs that effect the brain's chemistry such as Prozac for depression, Xanax for anxiety or every other psychoactive medication whether for panic attacks, bipolar disorder or the other host of behavioral problems treated with medication, this other drug is a sledgehammer. It destroys your ability to control your movements and shuts down the inhibitory part of the brain, releasing a variety of normally regulated behaviors, primarily interpersonal aggression.
2, More deaths are caused by overdosing with this drug than any prescription medication.
3, This drug is implicated in more rape (41%), felonies (73%) child beating (67%) wife beating (80%) and murder (83%) than any other drug.
4, It is implicated as the cause of 15,000 traffic deaths, 37% of all traffic deaths each year, and over half-a-million traffic injuries each year.
5, When its direct medical effects, behavioral effects and its level of usage are taken into account, it is the most dangerous drug in regular use in the United States.
6, The drug is legal, one does not need a prescription, it can be brought anywhere from every neighborhood's grocery and "convenience" store to the similarly ubiquitous special establishments whose primary purpose is to sell only this drug and to sell you as much as you like, typically until you go unconscious.

7, The drug is advertised everywhere. The advertisements show it as a wonderful drug to take and that taking it will bring joy and sexual adventure. Much of this advertising is targeted at the young.

Of course the drug being described is alcohol.

Can it be true that a drug with this potential for carnage is readily available to anyone above a certain age (18-21 from state to state)? How can this be? Once the effects of smoking on our health were well documented, it took several decades but at least a partial ban on where people can smoke cigarettes finally was enacted and a major campaign started to alert people to its health risks. Cigarettes only major risk to our health is primarily lung cancer with also some limited effects upon our cardiovascular system. Has anyone smoked a cigarette and then gotten in their car and because they were impaired from smoking killed an innocent family in another car. The same is true for rape, robbery, murder and the whole other list of mayhems caused by people who are drunk. None of these effects occur from smoking, yet smoking is illegal and alcohol is perfectly legal, even celebrated in advertising. A very potent charade. Drink alcohol, get drunk, have a good time.

A statistic that is regularly used by the FDA as a critical issue in determining whether or not to approve a drug is called its "safety ratio." This ratio compares the amount of the drug that is needed to exert its desired effect to the amount of the drug that must be taken to cause death. The safety ratio for heroin is six, alcohol 10, LSD about a thousand, and marijuana estimated to over a thousand. Marijuana's ratio is estimated since so few people have ever and I mean ever died from an overdose of marijuana.

In fact, marijuana's detrimental effects upon our bodies in adults are hard to find. Those that have been reported are usually its impact upon adolescents who have smoked chronically. In reviewing studies, long-term memory impairment and diseases associated with the airways, lungs and trachea are the two most typically described. The impact upon our airway would result from anything that is burned and sucked into the lungs.

One effect that is heavily debated is whether marijuana is a "gateway" drug that once used prompts the user to search for more effects from drugs such as cocaine and heroin. The other side of the argument is that these folks would have probably found their way to cocaine and heroin even if they had never used marijuana. Perhaps what is so important about this lack of bad news about marijuana is that any scientist worth his ambition could become a hero to a large segment of the population and get kudos, research grants, and have almost rock star status to the media if he could find a truly compelling negative effect of marijuana. They have been trying for decades, so far a dry hole.

In contrast to illegal marijuana, it is abundantly clear however that legal alcohol is an incredibly potent and easily abused drug that has consequences not just medically to the user but also to the rest of society from the infliction of harm to others. An additional cost to alcohol use is its effect upon society which in the end shares some of the financial costs brought on by the abuser for the damage to themselves as well for the suffering inflicted by them upon others.

Alcohol is far more dangerous than a whole list of drugs that are carefully regulated by the FDA and available only by prescription from a pharmacy. As previously noted it is heavily advertised as a positive drug to take and as easily available as buying a carton of milk. How can marijuana be against the law and the subject of such social outrage at the very thought of legalization by the same society that daily drinks the incredibly more dangerous drug alcohol.

The way the media reports on death is one of the grandest charades. It is a grand charade involving Americans being killed on our roads by the tens of thousands each and every year but not a peep. One death in Iraq and Afghanistan or by a terrorist and it leads. Who dies is far more important to the media than how many die. The "who" is directly related to its impact upon readership and ratings and thus the media's profit. Is it fair to blame the media, they, as they should, care about what would enhance their profits?

If the public really cared about Americans dying no matter how it happened, then the media would care as well. If the point is to stop Americans from dying by the media's bringing awareness of their deaths to the general public, then road accidents should be at the top of our list. However, stopping Americans from needless death is of no concern to the media. The facts speak for themselves. A tiny fraction of the money saved when the wars in Afghanistan and Iraq wind down would save more Americans from dying in their cars in just one year than died during the almost decade-long duration of these wars. But since no one cares, the media has not chosen to make this a subject.

If the American public did care about how many Americans were killed on our roads and how relatively little effort it would take by the car companies as well as how relatively little money it would take to dramatically reduce these deaths, then the media would put it front and center. Or perhaps what we have is a chicken and egg phenomenon. What has to come first, the public being concerned and the media then recognizing the opportunity and putting relevant stories on their broadcasts and in their papers, or does the media first have to decide to create awareness of the problem by placing the issue in front of the American people.

The statistics are pretty impressive about what happens when the car companies and law enforcement community takes safety seriously. Whether it was initially seat belts and then followed up with airbags, these innovations have had a significant effect upon injuries and deaths in automobile accidents. Even more impressive is the sequential drop in carnage due to drunk-driving as enforcement and publicity campaigns have become sequentially more aggressive.

There is far more to be done on both fronts, keeping drunks from driving, serious fines for using distracting devices as well as protecting innocent victims from damage when they are in an accident. All that is needed is the interest to do so and we all know how that interest is created. If a single child's disappearance can rivet the nation, how about 30,000 of us being killed every year when it would not take all that much to cut it down by 50%. Give a damn, take a stand and save your own life from this ludicrous charade.

Allstate Insurance as one might imagine has its finger on the pulse of automobile deaths regardless of the cause. Allstate has a great concern because being able to reduce these deaths would do wonderful things for their profit and thereby their stock price. In early 2011, Allstate ran a full page ad in newspapers all over the country. The ad was mostly a simple drawing of 747s stretching out to the horizon with lines of people boarding. The large type text read: "If 12 fully loaded jumbo jets crashed every year, *something would be done about it.* EVERY YEAR, MORE THAN 4000 TEENS DIE IN CAR CRASHES." In smaller print, "When even one plane crashes, the story is in the headlines for weeks. But the equivalent of 12 planes full of teens dying every year is barely a blip on the national radar." Alcohol and distracted driving are the major contributors to these deaths. You go, Allstate

That the incredibly dangerous drug alcohol is perfectly legal and its use celebrated in advertisement yet the dramatically more benign drug marijuana is illegal is the very definition of the charades that run our country.

VIII. CHARADELETTES

Art

Today's art market is little different from today's stock market, more charade than substance. Once upon a time stocks were valued based upon a company making profits and art was valued based upon the visual experience it provided the viewer. Stocks have now become more about the "story" behind them and less about the substance of the business they represent. Art today has made a similar switch from substance to story. Also shared is the number of people with a mutual self-interest in playing this game of charade. In the art world, dealers, auction houses, galleries, and museums are all in on the creation of new product for consumers to purchase and from which they prosper. Here is a brief history and how it came that what is called art today is a charade of what art was universally thought to be.

A painting is done on a two-dimensional space, usually a canvas with a certain width and height. A sculpture has three dimensions, width, height, and thanks to being able to chisel away at the wood or stone, a third dimension, depth. For the first several thousand years of what is called art, that was it, either a painting or a sculpture. The degrees of freedom for the artist were what could be created on a two dimensional canvas or in the three dimensions of stone.

In the beginnings of art as an object for aesthetic appreciation, a work of art was usually a very close representation of real things, such as a person or a landscape. A painter or a sculptor strived to accurately depict its subject matter. It was judged as a work of quality by how close it came to the real object and how pleasant a visual experience the viewer felt when looking at the work. Over time, painting and sculpture began to evolve away from being judged primarily on how well it depicted its subject and relying more on the visual impact it made.

Around the turn of the 1800s into the 1900s, even though the image still held some resemblance to the object being portrayed, some artists began to focus more and more on just creating aesthetically pleasing works of shapes and colors. Mondrian's paintings of different colored squares and rectangles would be the logical endpoint of this type of art; just color and form. The goal was to create an aesthetic experience even if the work was completely independent of any even part-way representation of an actual object.

At the same time, some artists in their attempt to express their unique vision of the experience of "seeing" created variations on the painting of form and color that were abstractions of the real object. Braque and Picasso pioneered one of the most well-known styles of this "abstract" art, known as cubism. Cubism, was so named since the artists treated any object as if it were a six-sided cube and the artist attempted to show objects from several sides at once integrated into a continuous image.

After cubism had been wrung out, painters entered an innovative period called abstract expressionism. Abstract expressionism made the expression of emotion the primary goal of painting. It abandoned any attempt to portray an object or even traditional shapes but simply spread different colors around the canvas in drips, drabs, and splatters in an attempt to evoke in the viewer an emotional experience.

Sculpture followed along in a similar vein, from its beginnings as a near duplication of an actual object, to just a three dimensional form that was designed to create an enjoyable visual experience in the viewer. Both sculpture and paintings had a variety of variations on these themes. For example, Andy Warhol showed us that even objects from daily life had an artistic value when put onto a two dimensional canvas. Jason Seley took automobile bumpers and welded them together into pleasing sculptures. However, all was constrained within the confines of two dimensions for painting and three dimensions for sculpture.

Now, as everyone knows, the artist's job is to earn a living through creating their work. The eccentric surrealist artist Salvador Dali has been quoted as saying that one can judge a painter's greatness by how much money they made. Those artists who were able to convince a gallery to show their work for sale, if their work created the right experience in the viewer's mind, were able earn a heck of a good living. In the old days this might sadly occur only after they were dead, but once art collecting became a cool thing to do, showing off ones art collection became a way to achieve status and meant that artists were discovered and feted while still alive. Making and selling art became a very big business, making mega-fortunes for the artists who made the work and dealers who sold the work.

Since this evolution of art occurred over the last several hundred years, museums popped up to showcase art from bygone eras. People paid money to go see paintings by the superstars of bygone eras. Collectors could get big tax deductions by donating art to these museums. The art would be displayed with a label carrying the donor's name. In addition, very rich people could donate the money for a museum and their name would go on the museum. Less well-heeled donors could put up the money for rooms within the museum and their name would be displayed along with paintings on the wall of the room. Among the high-end folks this became a competitive enterprise to see who could donate a whole museum better than the other guy's museum. One level down was to donate a bigger room than the other guy's room.

By the second half of the twentieth century, art had become a global and very complex industry. Fortunes could be made and lost by betting on which artist would become a biggy and be shown in the right museums. The dealer's with a track record of finding and displaying the next Picasso's work are fought over by beginning artists to showcase their work. Simply having one's work displayed at the right gallery is most of the way toward success as an artist. Collectors work special deals with galleries to get first-crack at the art world's next superstar. In some cases collectors and galleries work together with artists to orchestrate their launch onto the art scene.

A relationship parallel to the one described in the chapter about Wall Street between a company (artist), the investment banker that handles its IPO (gallery-opening night show), the analysts (critics) who write the reports and the private equity investors (galleries known for discovering next big thing) who funded the early stages of the company (artist) is little different from the introduction of a new artist to the marketplace. The auction houses that specialize in art are somewhat like the New York Stock Exchange or the NASDAQ exchange. The "John Q. Public" investor in art buys from a gallery. The "institutional" investor in art or other well-connected high-end investors do not buy from galleries but from auction houses that specialize in art.

So as we neared the end of the twentieth century, an entire industry with many parts had developed around the creating, buying, and selling of art. Art that in the basic form had not changed for hundreds of years, two-dimensional paintings and three dimensional sculptures. New and fresh product was created every few decades or so as artists found innovative ways to express their unique artistic visions of reality within these two forms.

However, eventually there is just so much blood one can wring from a stone. The industry was turning in on itself, there was very little truly new and different coming along. The big money was being spent and made just trading the same masterworks again and again. As people had larger piles of excess cash on their hands thanks to this or that investment bubble, prices soared to levels thought unimaginable just years before they really did happen. What can be created on the surface of a two-dimensional canvas or can be created even in three dimensions however, had pretty much run its course. There were very few new IPOs in the art market.

A situation occurred in the art world, not unlike that of the investment banking world in the l980s. The investment community was running out of new companies that could be marketed to investors on their profit and loss statements and underlying asset values, the traditional way investment decisions were made. Instead, new companies were created that maybe someday would cure cancer or make a fortune selling groceries over the web. Hey, no risk no reward, get in on the ground floor, when this baby takes off …

The investment banking system went to work. IPOs were sold based upon glowing analysts reports about phantom companies and everyone was fat and happy. So taking a page from the investment banking playbook, in their need for new product the art industry decided to redefine art. A charade of value was about to be launched upon the culture vultures who identify their status in the universe as collectors of cutting-edge art. The galleries, critics, auction houses, and museums who themselves feed off these vultures led the cheers on the sidelines.

A new form of art was brought to the public, one that added a fourth dimension. One of the first such objects of the new definition of art was a dining room table set for dinner created by Judy Chicago in the late l970s. Neither a painting nor a sculpture of a dining room table, but just a dining room table set for a dinner. Now we all have seen dining room tables set for a lavish dinner, whether in our own homes or in restaurants, nothing new there.

In the case of the new art, it is no longer the visual experience of viewing the artist's work, which in many cases has nothing visually special about it, can seem very mundane, and even in some cases, unpleasing to the eye. For the new art, a fourth dimension was added, an explanation from the artists about the very special social insight provided by the dining room table. If you went into a museum and all you saw was the dining room table, you might think you pulled into the wrong parking lot and went into a restaurant. However, once you read the script, you would appreciate how this dining room table symbolized some very meaningful insight into social relationships.—or not.

All it took was a prestigious dealer to show it in their gallery and the collectors, museums, and auction houses all stood up and gave it a salute, with a sigh of relief, as the great blues singer Lightnin' Hopkins said, "good times here, better down the road." The collectors wrote checks and the auction houses created the exchanges for secondary buying and selling after the gallery launched the IPO of the art. Museum goers have not embraced such "installation" art quite as warmly as the art connoisseurs. The still want to have the simple and pleasant visual experiences of gazing upon the Da Vincis, Goyas, Rembrandts, Mattisses, Picassos, De Koonings, or Rothkos. If a description of the importance of this work in the history and evolution of art was on the wall next to the work, well that was nice too.

Perhaps sometime in the future maybe the rooms of a museum will have an installation in each room (installations tend to take-up a lot of space). Instead of a guidebook telling you what paintings are in each room, when you walk into the museum you will be handed a little WiFi device that will deliver either through an ear bud or on a screen the story telling you why the pile of sunflower seeds on the floor is an important insight into some aspect of society. Just that pile of sunflower seeds is touted by the stock analysts, oops I mean critics and galleries, as the most important work of today's hottest Chinese artist, WeiWei.

In fact, why have a dining room table or a pile of sunflower seeds on the floor at all. The visual experience is ordinary and trivial to what the new wave of "installation" art is all about. The importance is the text written by the artist explaining the social insight that can be gained by looking at the installation. Since the installation is usually an object or collection of objects arranged in a way that the viewer comes across in their daily lives, why not just sell the copyrighted text over the web, the "collector" reads it and every time they see a dining room table, they can have the intellectual experience intended by the artist.

Has art finally made itself into such an arcane viewer experience that it can only be appreciated by having the viewer being told what it is they should be experiencing? Is this new art simply a product created by an industry that had run out of new offerings for investors and collectors to buy, auction houses to display, and museums to showcase? Is todays art a charade of anything that art previously aspired to, the evoking of a natural visual experience on the part of the viewer? Another charade created and promoted by a mutuality of self-interest.

<u>Charities</u>

Charities do wonderful things. They feed, provide medical care, and house those who cannot provide themselves with such basic needs. When a disaster strikes they are often soon on the scene helping those who have suffered a loss. In addition to providing desperately needed services to humans, some charities help animals suffering from neglect and even work to save a species headed for extinction. In a similar vein some charities purchase especially beautiful and ecologically important land so it will be preserved in its pristine state for future generations. Yes, charities in the most part are incredibly wonderful and valuable organizations. In the United States, the government has recognized the importance of charities by providing donors to the charities a tax deduction for the amount they donate.

Yet, there is a charade aspect to some charities. An aspect that occurs in many organizations, not just charities that begin with the best of intentions. In spite of such noble ambitions, some of these organizations move into losing sight of their purpose and simply go along preserving little but themselves in the form of the salaries for the people that are employed by the organization. I almost feel badly in describing examples of charities that are mutating into such self-serving organizations since in the main charities are wonderful and our world would be much diminished if they did not exist.

For example, in the Haitian earthquake a professional dancer, Fabienne Jean, had her leg badly damaged. After a battle to save it, eventually it became gangrenous, and her doctors recommended it be amputated. Although it meant giving up her career, she eventually agreed and that was that. The doctor who did the surgery was in Haiti on loan from Mt. Sinai in New York. After the surgery, Ms. Jean remained in Haiti, just another displaced person living in squalor. Her original doctor found out about her condition and strongly recommended that she come to New York for an additional surgery as preparation for the fitting of a prosthetic leg, and treatment in the first-class rehabilitation center affiliated with Mt. Sinai. Work began on getting all the paper-work completed for her admission into the U.S.

However, a New England company that made prosthetic legs also heard about Ms. Jean's plight and offered to get involved. They had a foundation that received donations and provided prosthetics for indigent people such as her. All expenses would be covered and it would all be done in Haiti. They began to pressure her to turn down the Mt. Sinai offer and let them take over her care. In fact, they even threw some monkey wrenches into the process of getting her cleared for entry into the U.S.

Talks went back and forth but eventually little cooperation emerged between the two groups competing for the dancer. An article in the New York Times, 4/13/2010, "For a brief period, Mr. Acton (of the New England company's foundation) and Mount Sinai appeared to be working in tandem…But later he conditioned that offer on his group's remaining her prosthetic provider, and he said his board of directors was concerned that Mount Sinai was trying to steal a high-profile patient…The cooperation broke down." The lead doctor on the Mt. Sinai team in sending an update to his team, wrote, "Her ability to dance will help them cash in." She ended up staying in Haiti and receiving the prosthetic leg from the New England Company. She is receiving rehabilitation therapy from a high school senior turned therapist and hopes to open her own boutique someday. Man, how can stuff like this happen?

A paper published on May 24th of 2010 in the prestigious British medical journal *The Lancet* reported on a recent study that showed progress on two fronts in the battle against early childhood deaths in impoverished countries. One was a review of past statistical sampling techniques and if errors in the process were corrected it showed that there had actually been one million fewer children dying each year than had been previously thought. In addition, great progress had been made in the past two decades in lowering the number of children that had been dying. Prior to the reports publication a variety of charities that make their living off fund raising over children dying in third world countries appealed to the authors not to publish their findings since it would hurt their fund raising efforts. Leading the charge was UNICEF, a charitable organization with the United Nations.

A pretty darn sad story is how charities fight with each other over naming rights for their charity and their marketing slogans. The Susan G. Komen For the Cure Foundation used the "for the cure" slogan to label their fundraising events. A variety of others have come up with variations on the Komen's "race for the cure" with their own "juggling for the cure," "Kayak for a cure," "bark for the cure," and "blondes for the cure."

The Komen foundation has sent them all threatening letters and takes them to court if they persist. The Komen Foundation has been similarly aggressive with other organizations using its branding color, pink. Their attorney defends all this litigation with, "We see it as responsible stewardship of our donor's funds." Komen is really serious about this, taking to court a group raising money for lung cancer with a kite-flying contest of hand-decorated kites. It called the event "Kites for a cure." The court battle also wanted to deny the kite flyers any use of the color pink.

Lance Armstrong's Foundation, uses "Livestrong" as the slogan for its charity and associates it with the color yellow in all its materials. A woman whose son, nickname of "head" had died of lymphoma and she wanted to start a group with HEADstrong as its slogan. Mr. Armstrong's charity got wind of this and sent her a letter, a part of which advised her that "strong" could never be used in a way that made it stand out and that the color yellow could never be associated with her charity. In addition, it wrote to her attorney, "Your client's use of the color gold is of great concern to LAF because it appears to be very close to the color yellow."

I mean "come on children, grow up." In fact I think it time to make this section of the chapter short and sweet, or maybe short and bitter, the more I started to lift the rug, the uglier it became. Wall Street, and politicians I mean what did you expect, scumbags under every desk, rich and powerful yes, but scumbags never-the-less. So here are just a few more examples, you will get the point.

Contributing to veterans, especially in our troubled economic times, what could truly be more noble. We have to admit that many who sign up voluntarily for the military are not on the fast track to fame and fortune. When they return home from putting their lives at risk for their country, and living under life-stress for two years in some pretty primal conditions, it should be no surprise they need help of pretty much every sort. How can you not respond to a charity called Wounded Warriors. It turns out two different charities share the same name and have dueling websites. One does have Inc. added to its name and the other ends with Project; however some donors gave money to one thinking they were giving to the other. It went to federal court and a judge ruled in favor of one over the other to the tune of one having to change its name and pay the other $1.7million. The decision is under appeal. Do you think the lawyers donate their time, well do ya?

How about Sunshine Kids Club of California raising money for kids with cerebral palsy versus the Sunshine Kids Foundation raising money for kids with cancer. The one for cerebral palsy in response to a threatening letter from the one for cancer offered to reference the cancer group on their own website just in case someone went there by accident. According to court documents, the cancer group's response was that they "would be clearly remiss in its stewardship if it permitted dilution, tarnishment, blurring, destruction, or weakening of this mark [trademark]."

The ultimate charade is not just one charity spending its money on litigation against another charity but a charity that simply uses an unusual percentage of its money for its own expenses and gives away very little. The classic example is the professional athlete making millions of dollars a year and looking to avoid taxes but putting a big junk of that money into a charity he starts.

A wealthy athlete claims to "want to return something back to the poor neighborhood and help the kids." Some really do, and the financial reports of the charity are pretty much in line with the acceptable percentages for how much gets spent on what. However, some also have these percentages way out of whack and are found to simply be tax avoidance vehicles when most of the money funds a variety of living expenses and pays salaries to family members for bogus jobs.

Recently, a lot of publicity was generated when "60 minutes" did a segment exposing a charity run by a fellow named Greg Mortenson who claimed to be setting up schools for girls in Afghanistan and Pakistan and wrote a book detailing his own harrowing Afghan experiences that led him to his charitable epiphany to pursue these efforts. None other than Jon Krakauer who knows a thing or two about the mountains in Pakistan and Afghanistan from his own well documented mountain climbing feats had some initial involvement with Mortenson but then got very nervous about what he was finding.

Lo and behold, much of Mortenson's personal saga that sets up the whole charitable effort was full of holes. An examination of the charities finances showed it to be primarily a vehicle for funding Mortenson's own private-jet lifestyle. Some schools may have been built, but even trying to track those down has been a sketchy enterprise. This was a high class charade. In the beginning the President of the United States, Barak Obama, donated $100,000 of his Nobel Prize winnings to the cause.

So beware folks, it would appear that some charities require just as much homework before making a donation as you would before investing in a stockbrokers recommendation. They're everywhere, they're everywhere, those charades.

Victimless Crimes-Gambling & Prostitution

It is not just in the United States, but in many places around the globe there are towns that either because they are in the mountains at high-quality ski resorts or along the coast's prettier beaches they attract people of wealth. In some cases these towns are more than just resorts but are near areas with significant commercial activities to attract year round residents as well. Although this may irritate the feminists, it is simply a fact that these towns, and any that have a relatively high percentage of wealthy men, also attract an unusually high-percentage of attractive women, whether naturally or thanks to the skilled hands of a plastic surgeon.

In all of these towns there are certain high-end restaurants with sizeable piano-bar like areas that attract men and women looking to get to know each other. A hypothetical conversation between a man and a woman he finds attractive might be about how he has never been to Tahiti and would really like to go but would hate to go alone. Thirty minutes or so later, telephone numbers are swapped. Next week the couple meets for dinner and after dinner they take each other for a test drive. If both are happy with the experience, flights will be booked and a hotel room (that is singular not plural) is reserved. If the man does not offer, the woman will bring up the fact that she would need some new clothes for the trip and he hands over some cash. A few weeks later they are lounging on the beach in Tahiti. Will they ever meet again other than for the next trip, probably not.

In other sorts of places, the town will a have street where scantily clad women parade up and down the sidewalks looking for men to pay them for sex. In the same neighborhood typically near a motel there are bars where these ladies may go for a bit of refreshment. The women are committing an illegal act and often times are arrested for prostitution. In between the subtle exchange of money for sex in the first example and the more blatant exchange in the second example are a vast variety of such activities that have sprung up thanks to the internet. Some are simply not too disguised offering sex in exchange for money. The type of activities offered and the price for each is described. Others have a thin veil of disguise such as massage or companionship services. However, it is not secret what they are about.

As mentioned before, one of the fascinating things that occurred as I went from a general idea for the book to refining it into specific types of charades and then doing the research to find out if the details really supported my ideas was just how right I was, even more so than I ever imagined. Writing this book has truly been the "gift that keeps on giving." And so it was in late summer of 2011 that I came across the following in the list of news stories on my AOL home page: "Seeking Arrangement: College Students Using 'Sugar Daddies' To Pay Off Loan Debt."

Evidently, with the dramatic way tuition costs have soared at multiples of inflation over the past decade, college debt is overwhelming many students ability to pay. Some women are turning to men to exchange their companionship for money. I guess the sites are pretty good at matching people because most of the men end up getting laid on the first date even though they are much much older than the women.

There are now websites specifically dedicated to such arrangements. The article comes right out and says, "women passing through a system of higher education that fosters indebtedness are using the anonymity of the web to sell their wares and pay down their college loans." Quoting the founder of one such website for these hookups, "Over the past few years the number of college students using our site has exploded…College students are one of the biggest segments of our sugar babies (on the sites men are 'sugar daddies' and the women 'sugar babies') and the numbers are growing all the time."

A sugar baby who attended school in Manhattan, after her first hook-up with an older man in a Greenwich, CT mansion is quoted, "I never thought it would come to this…I mean, I had just gotten money for having sex…I needed the money." A sugar daddy said, "But I can't walk into a bar and go up to a 25-year-old. They'd think I'm a pervert. So this is how I go about meeting them."

A founder of the one of the larger of these websites was attending MIT business school when he saw attractive girls at school with men who were clearly many years older and much richer than he and that led him to start his website, initially not focusing on just college girls with older and richer men. However, when he examined the demographics of the women who listed themselves on his site, he then modified the site specifically for college girls looking for help paying off their student loans. A variety of websites for women looking for Sugar Daddies, quote numbers of around 30%-40% for the percentage attending college.

Oh, and just to show that I embrace diversity, it would be unfair not to mention that the same dramatic growth is occurring in hook-up websites for gay men as well. In frustration, one such participant when being told by a school official that he had better step-up paying his debt or he would not be allowed to register for the nest semester said, "I just wanted her to understand what the expense of NYU was really costing us…You have no idea what some of us do in order to stay here." He also described these sites as "virtual street corners."

It seems that recently the media has chosen the headline "the illegal slave trade, trafficking in women for prostitution" as the "if it bleeds it leads" *du jour*. Certainly they are not referring to college girls, the hot babes of resort towns, or the women on the web sites who are often well over 30 just looking for a little extra spending cash. So what is this thing called prostitution. In part it certainly is too young girls duped into prostitution through promises of jobs and a better life in a far off and distant land who end up being treated worse than a dog on the street. One can only applaud the most aggressive police action targeting this debasement of a human being.

However, that is not really what most prostitution is about. Instead it is an active choice by women to offer themselves as sexual partners in exchange for money. Just as is true for cosmetic surgery, it is a woman making a free choice about what to do with her body. A variety of groups, from feminists to Bible toters are vehemently against this activity and aggressively support legal action to arrest both men and women who take part in prostitution. Is it a criminal act when two willing participants engage in a behavior that harms no one? Is it a part of our examining how governments spend their money that we want our law enforcement and border patrol agents to spend their time arresting and prosecuting people who are doing things by their own free choice and that bring harm to no one else?

Prostitution is somewhat like marijuana. Its availability and its use is everywhere. It is so since law enforcement spends little time prosecuting it unless it is flaunted in their face or they receive complaints from "outraged" citizens about a certain street corner. In the case of marijuana, its legalization is now openly discussed, for prostitution it will have to percolate for a while longer, only in the public eye when a politician ,TV talk-show host or evangelist gets caught doing what a whole bunch of other people do, from college girls to wealthy businessman.

A really crazy patchwork of legal and illegal is another of the victimless crimes, gambling. This one is on the front burner of politics and in some cases has even been taken off the stove and is now out in the public for everyone to taste. In Nevada, gambling is the state's biggest industry.

There can be no question that a lot of people like to gamble. In the United States, Native American peoples that have a formally recognized history as a tribe and now have a reservation are exempt from almost all state and federal laws while on the reservation. Several decades ago, tribes realized that they could build Las Vegas style resorts and casinos on their tribal land. In the main these have all been a tremendous success, the profits bringing tremendous gains in the quality of life on the reservation. Further proof of people's desire to gamble, wherever and whenever it is available.

Other states such as Mississippi, Alabama, New Jersey, California, and Missouri have made attempts at state legislation for legalizing gambling. In some states it is legal sort of, only certain types of gambling in certain locations. In other states such as New Jersey, extending gambling outside of Atlantic City has run into a lot of hurdles. New gambling casinos are seen as a threat to the existing ones as well as protests from the horse racing establishment who do not want competition to their own legalized gambling.

In addition to Nevada, one state, Kansas, has taken the brave step and made casino gambling legal. They have stuck their toe in the water by making the casinos a state owned enterprises with a professional management company hired to run the place. Of the profits 27% goes to the state and the rest goes to the management company. So far it is all working out just fine.

In spite of the objections to gambling on moral grounds, the evidence is clear that Americans will vote with their pocketbooks when given the opportunity to gamble and what better way than in the privacy of your own home, just you and your computer. In 2006 the U.S. Congress passed a law prohibiting online gambling that involves interstate commerce, focusing on the financial transactions crossing state lines while moving around in cyberspace. It is a cat and mouse game over internet gambling. One site popping up only to be issued a cease and desist order and then another one pops up.

Sports betting is legendary. A major source of revenue for Nevada casinos is the "sports book" to which a large space on the casino floor is dedicated. Although only briefly mentioned in the Chapter about "student athletes," betting on college football and basketball is every bit the equal and from important game to important game, even exceeds the amount bet on professional sports. Much of which is done out of the sight of the law. In fact, some of the mega-scandals in college sports involve payoffs in an attempt to fix college games. Informally, there are few businesses in the country where betting on sports through "office pools" does not take place.

So how come it is mostly illegal? We let people do other things they enjoy such as playing golf, going to the movies, or surfing. How come other things they enjoy such as gambling are illegal? In prostitution maybe it matters that two people are involved, but gambling can be done all by ones self. In fact, prior to the era of big-time professional golf with lucrative endorsement deals and TV revenue, most of golfs better players earned their living by betting. It was well known which country clubs would arrange matches between wealthy amateurs and games top pros. Country club pro shops knew the names on both sides of the transaction and were the pimps and their courses the brothels of golf.

Gambling does no harm to anyone other than the person making the free choice to gamble and put his money at risk. In fact, sometimes they may actually win which brings not just money but the thrill of victory. Why is this against the law and as with prostitution why is precious government money spent keeping people from doing something that they enjoy?

Prostitution and gambling, victimless crimes, a potential source of revenue through government taxation, and a potential source of great pleasure to those who want to participate. No one is involved other than those who make the free chose to participate. Auto racing and a variety of other very dangerous sports are legal even though occasionally people are seriously injured, maimed for life, and even die. Why do we ban only some things that involve risk? What would happen if all of a sudden the government outlawed investing in the stock market? I would bet more money has been lost and lives ruined through foolish investing than gambling? The more damaging one is legal and the benign one illegal. Imagine a politician in the South proposing to ban NASCAR because of its dangers.

On the periphery of the argument against these activities is the claim that it is not just the participants who get hurt, but others as well. For example, gambling hurts the family of the gambler, gambling can be addictive, and as with prostitution, gambling attracts an undesirable element. Prostitution can lead to sexually transmitted diseases and women being enslaved. These are all valid arguments, sort of. Playing tennis can lead to broken bones. Surfing can lead to drowning. Reading too much can damage eyesight. Mountain climbing and auto racing can lead to deaths. Typing can lead to carpal tunnel syndrome. All of this is true, but, in our society, individuals are free to act in ways that put themselves at risk. Especially to act in ways that the risk, whether to themselves or to society in general are very small. Especially in ways where the risk to themselves and to society can be minimized.

Legalizing gambling and prostitution would bring tremendous revenue to cities, states, and the federal government. Legalizing gambling and prostitution would mostly rid it of the undesirable element that in some types of these activities it does indeed attract. Legalizing gambling with creation of rules and regulations would certainly make a dent in the aspect of gambling and addiction problem for those gamblers for whom it is an addictive activity. The same could be said for the dangers of STDs in prostitution.

What cannot be changed, and may very well prohibit the legalization of these activities and the bringing about of the benefits are politicians. Give them an issue that they can moralize about and appeal to peoples emotional feelings and they will clutch it to their breast and milk it for all it is worth. Remember prohibition and the morality crusades of the Temperance Union. If that is not an issue that was created purely by politicians as a rallying point for voters, I am not sure what is. Everyone was still drinking even when it was illegal, just like gambling and prostitution, and legalizing it has proven to be a tremendous source of economic growth and tax revenue. Laws against victimless crimes in which people nationwide participate whether it is legal or illegal, what a charade.

Neocolonialism and Modern African Charity

Sub-Saharan Africa has struggled to leave the third world and enter the second, much less the first. Some countries may briefly raise their status and seem on the road to some semblance of stability, economic development, and decent life for their people only to have a rebellion replace the ruling party and a new "strongman" to emerge with the inevitable sliding back down into rampant disease, poverty, and lawlessness. I wonder how many Swiss banks owe a large-part of their "private banking" business to this seemingly never ending revolving door.

When initially explored by European and Arabic adventurers primarily looking for slaves, ivory, previous stones and metals, and other natural resources to be exploited, Africa was a loose confederation of tribes. Few countries existed; it was a single tribe at its simplest and tribal confederations at its most complex. As a result of the European and Arab outsiders superiority in means of war, the Africans had little choice but to accept the will imposed upon them by these exploiters.

This colonialization changed much of Africa. The colonizers tried to group a variety of tribes together into countries, just as had happened in Europe many hundreds of years previously. In some cases, if one believed that the European way of life was superior to the African ways, then it was felt that this imposition of lifestyle brought a quality of life such as health-care, schooling, and policing that was from the outsiders perspective at least, an improvement to African ways. However, in the 1950s and 1960s questions began to be raised, especially through the United Nations, whether or not it was appropriate for these foreign powers to colonize and control the lives of Africans who had led their traditional ways of life for centuries before their "discovery." As a result, the Europeans left and returned control of the land back to the Africans. Agreements were reached for joint control of the mines, oil fields, and other commercial activities that would require some time to hand them over to the indigenous peoples.

In many countries this handing their lands back led to a gradual slide back into the tribalism, warlords, and general loss of the rule of law, health care, and education. In response, to the poverty, famine and disease that emerged, a variety of charitable organizations set up programs to try to improve the daily lives of Africans. Trillions of dollars were spent over decades.

Sadly, the longer it went on the realization hit that the victories over poverty, filth, and squalor were few and far between. The charitable organizations and donor countries began to take a second look at how their money was being spent. One glaring result of all the aid, was the siphoning of money by the rulers to friends and family to buy political loyalty, with perhaps more money ending up in secret Swiss bank accounts than being spent on a country's people. Family and friends of these strongmen lived a glamorous life on the French Riviera and other glamor spots around the globe while their citizens for whom the money was intended sat in the dirt dying from dysentery and starvation.

Sooooo, there began a new wave of charitable help. Former President Bill Clinton, rock star Bono, and business star Bill Gates went about giving talks about a new approach of philanthropy in Africa. Their approach was to put boots on the ground along with their money. These boots would insure that the money got spent the way it was intended. These boots would keep a very close eye on every dollar and where need be even white man's boots would be in charge. Instead of writing a check to the King, the money would remain under the control of the charity until it was time to put the money in the hands of the people building the schools, distributing the food, and providing the medical care.

The question is this. The fall of colonialism was in part based on the philosophy that people from other countries had no right taking control of an African country just because they could. Colonialism was philosophically immoral. It was the indigenous people's country, others had no right to impose their will, standards, and life-style expectations. Is what Clinton, Gates, and Bono are up to, just another form of colonialism? Are we now once again, only because we can, imposing our will upon Africa to conform to our expectations of a way of life? We will only give them money if they spend it on what we want them to in the way we want them to and if it means we "invade" and run the show—so be it.

There is nothing new about this situation. It began in the 1800s with missionaries coming to Africa to in part convert them to the white man's way of life, but primarily to infect them with white man's religions. It was not that Africans did not have religion, they certainly did, some beautiful and complex religions. However, they were not the right religion. In some cases it was indeed, convert or we will kill you. Does anyone know how to say, "what would Jesus think?" Then followed the era of people coming to Africa with the best of intentions to help them solve their food, educational, and medical failings, at least failings compared with European standards. Then came the era of economic exploitation, diamonds, ivory, etc.

Is the current new wave of philanthropy where the outsiders impose their will on Africa to do it our way or no money a reversion to the "white man knows best?" Is it just a game of charades masking a return to the old colonialism? I am fully well aware that when people are starving, dying of treatable diseases brought on by infrastructure issues that can be solved, we ought to have a moral obligation to do our best to alleviate human suffering. However, is it finally the right time to ask, just how much money has to spent over how many decades of mostly fruitless efforts before we begin to take the attitude as is developing over our weariness in Iraq and Afghanistan that maybe it is just time to leave people to sort out their own lives? A very very difficult issue. As I write this, the pictures are on every night of the famine in Somalia and reports of warlords preventing food to be delivered to refugee camps, it is to painful to watch.

Perhaps the answer is an international force of dramatically overwhelming superiority that under UN mandate comes in and takes over a country that has been deemed unable to provide its people with the basics of food, shelter, medical care, rule of law, and education. A team then comes in and runs the country. The bill is paid through the "exploitation" of the country's resources. No more bank accounts in Switzerland and houses on the Rivera. The folks on the donor dole will scream bloody murder.

Gradually over decades the country is turned over more and more to local control. Let us just stop this century-long game of charades and fix the problem on behalf of the suffering people who in the main lead lives of poverty not even imagined in the developed countries and no different than they did decades ago in spite of a many decades long game of charades and trillions of dollars spent.

Self Help

Well after that cheery discussion let us turn to something that is just as much a charade, but the stakes are lot less, a cupla bucks out of people's pockets and maybe a few weeks or even months of false hope. The titles of the books with their associated CDs and other stuff to buy will usually have words such as "lessons," "secrets," and "how to" in the title. The rest of the title will involve concepts such as "get rich," "make millions," "find happiness," and "fulfill your dreams of…" They are the materials loosely grouped under "self-help."

They are purchased every year in many billions of dollar, the U.S. alone accounts for $10 billion a year. The people who buy them usually feel their lives are wanting in one way or another and if they buy one of the books or CDs they will find out how to go about satisfying that want. What is most bizarre about all of this, and perhaps the central core of the charade of self-help books, is that if any of these books in its own subject, such as *The Secrets to Becoming a Millionaire in Real Estate* or *Ten Secret Lessons to Finding True Love* were really worth anything other than as source of income to the person who wrote it, there would never be another book because that book really does work. In most professions, there are usually a few standard text books for every field and its subspecialty, whether the medicine, law, or engineering. They have it all worked out and explain the details of how to treat this disease, the precedents involved in a certain point of law or how to design a bridge that won't fall down. No additional books are needed.

Some people take this information and become good doctors, lawyers, investors, or engineers. The point being that if any of these "self-help" books were worthwhile everyone who reads them would be rich, have a life-long marriage, or whatever the heck they promise you. It is the nature of things that everyone cannot win, they are zero sum games. It is in the nature of the investing business that some people will lose. It is the money they lose that makes others winners just as the money made by those that win has to come from somewhere, and typically it is from those that lose. There are only so many A+ members of the opposite sex available.

The only place a person can find the important reasons why their life is not working out the way they want is in the bathroom every morning when they look in the mirror. It most certainly will not come from the 83rd self-help book published that year on the "true secrets for finding wealth and happiness." To once again fall back on Shakespeare, this time in *Julius Cesar*, "the fault dear Brutus lies not in our stars, but in ourselves, that we are underlings."

Nice Guys Finish Last

"Nice guys finish last," a saying made popular by Leo Durocher the former player and manager of the New York Giants, a baseball team for those nonhistorians of the game. The charade is not that this saying is wrong but that it is right, very right. The charade is those who create a public persona that they are "nice" guys. For example, gosh don't those anchors of the morning news on TV and the daytime and late-night talk show hosts seem like just such warm and swell people.

Have you ever thought about how many people would give anything to have their job with its million- dollar plus annual incomes and countrywide if not also world-wide adulation. Have you ever thought about how many people who actually have a job just like theirs on small local stations lie in bed at night wondering how they can make it to the big leagues.

The above is just one example of a highly competitive profession. One where a very select few make it to the top rung. A very very select few compared with the number who aspire to reach that rung. Have you ever thought about what separates the winners from the also-rans. Sure, there can be no question that the winners are extraordinarily talented, amongst the elite. It is not only talented, but as is especially true in a visual medium such as television, won the genetic lottery for genes that make a person physically appealing. However, I would bet that there are many people out there in local TV talk-show studios around the country that are also good looking and have the core talents necessary to perform the job.

It is not just the core talents specific to that job that make people outstanding in their field, but a couple of other personality traits as well. One is of course ambition, a burning desire to be number one. Second, and the central issue to this discussion, is a certain type of personality that allows them to strategically plot their way through the crowd and have the tenacity and fierce competitiveness to what some would call "worm" their way to the top by relating to the decision makers in just the right way, and when necessary to use sharp elbows on their competitors. There is a woman, now near the end of her career, who worked her way up through network news to talk-show and interview stardom that was once described by one of her colleagues as something along the lines of, "she is the last person I would want to run into in a dark alley when only one of us could make it out the other side."

This being said, there is the occasional Michael Jordan, Albert Einstein, or Oprah Winfrey who although also having the ancillary talents that are required to win, are just so extraordinarily talented in the core abilities of their profession that they stand alone as number one.

If someone were a nice guy or gal, a sweetheart who would rather settle for what is fair than having themselves standing alone at the top of the pyramid of success, then they already have 2.9 strikes against them. In any human endeavor there are simply too many people who want the top spot than there are top spots. From businessperson, scientist, cellist, poet, or Senator, they are all intensely competitive careers and once the truly inadequate have been cast off the ladder to success, there are more with equal core talents for the task than there are positions for them to fill.

The ones that make it do so, because they are not "nice" in the sense that most people use the term. They make it out an intense desire "to make it" that overwhelms any notions of doing the "right" or "nice" thing and it is replaced by doing only that which allows them to win. So all that warmth, cheer, good natured charm and banter that is a part of their performance on television, or the kindly, grandfatherly mega-billion investor, just get into a room with a closed door when the time comes to do business, they did not get where they are by being nice people.

In fact, academics have studied whether nice guys actually do finish last. The researchers focused on a quality called "agreeableness" which seems probably a major component of being considered "nice." Those who were rated below average earned 18% more than their peers. To quote one of the co-authors, "nice guys are getting the shaft." Several other studies, measuring salaries and promotions have reported similar results, those found less agreeable receive higher pay and are preferred for promotions.

One issue that must be pointed out is that in large organizations, disturbing the status quo can be dangerous, at least depending upon the personalities of those in the higher ranks. Some higher-ups actually look for the personality that finds ways to do things better and shake-up the system. Just the act of raising such issues that are viewed positively by the higher-ups, to one's peers could cause the perceived troublemaker to be rated as disagreeable. However, in some organizations, shaking up the status quo is perceived as a threat by those at the top, so someone below them who is perceived as disagreeable by their peers would also be viewed as a "trouble maker" by those above.

Nothing could be a more clear-cut example of the corporate culture's role in defining what is thought of as "disagreeable" and whether or not it is rewarded than the recent problems in the auto industry. Ford threw out its senior management and brought in a new boss from Boeing with a reputation for shaking things up and thinking outside of the box. Just the act of bringing in someone from aerospace was viewed with great skepticism to the sclerotic halls of Detroit. However, as we all know, Ford was the only Detroit auto company not to need a bailout. General Motors on the other hand was and forever will be known as the perfect example of a "do not rock the boat" and "no thinking outside the box allowed" management team. It took the government pushing them into bankruptcy and dramatically shaking up the management team to get them on the road to profitability.

In business, being disagreeable and rocking the boat could be the accusation by the team players against the guy who is finding fault with a flawed system. If he is proven right, his critical nature will help him find success. It is therefore no accident that in a competitive environment nice guys do and should finish last. A cautionary note for all you nice guys out there.

IX. IF IT BLEEDS IT LEADS:

TALKING HEAD CHARADES

I have been a car-guy ever since I was maybe ten years old. It was this interest that probably almost thirty years ago made me start to think about just how much of what goes on in our culture is really just a charade. A charade created to serve the self-interest of one or the other of the major institutions that create the things that occupy our minds. In this book I have focused on the three dominant institutions, Wall Street, Washington, and the media that are playing a game of charades that through mutual self-interest serve to reinforce each other.

At the center of it all of course is the media. Who determines what we think about, what we know that is going on in the world, what dramas of daily life are of concern to us, what is coming over the horizon that will affect us? All these questions have one answer, the media. I mean other than the issues right in front of us, that our refrigerator has only a half-carton of milk left and we better stop at the grocery store, that which occupies our active minds is mostly created by the information placed before us by the media. They are the great filter of all that goes on, from across town to across the globe, and determines what we know is going on and therefore what gets our attention to care and think about.

Back to cars. My first real charade moment was when one car magazine broke the rules of professional courtesy with other car magazines. A magazine had become known for its "Car of the Year" selection. An honor that would get mention in this well-read magazine and be touted in all the winning car company's ads. Well, another magazine exposed that a certain brand, I seem to recall it was Saab, was approached by the award-giving magazine that it would be selected as car of the year, but that a condition of the award was that Saab had to agree to mention of the magazine's name in such and such a prominent way in its ads along with certain other terms related to co-promotion of the awarding magazine. Saab turned it down over these conditions. So the magazine found another car manufacturer willing to go along. They did not change the award to the "Car of the Year—Sort of." In the Summer of 2011 as I write this, Saab is teetering on bankruptcy, hah hah, just like Bear Stears turning down Paulson's offer, so much for standing on principle. Anyway chalk up my first real understanding of a national, in this case even global charade of a mutual self-interest, the media with a car manufacturer.

Next up was a media charade that really got to me since it was about a matter that to me was of cosmic importance, a person's character. A car magazine, well what could you expect, but a person's moral character was at least to me different. At the height of the Monica Lewinsky scandal, the President had still not come clean (strange word to use given the subject, a stained dress). He gave his first speech to the nation on the matter and it was pretty darn weasely. The talking heads were less than thrilled and it began the descent that eventually led to the "that depends on what your definition of 'is,' is."

I am not sure if it was minutes later or hours later after his initial weasley speech, but the president's public relations team issued a clarifying statement. A young CNN reporter, Wolf Blitzer, stood somewhere outside of the White House I think it was, and said he had just received a press release clarifying the President's remarks. He mumbled some words, adopted a body language posture, and read the release that out-weaseled the initial weasely remarks. Wolf Blitzer's tone of voice and body posture clearly showed his distaste for the whole thing and without a doubt it was clear what he wanted to say was, "do I really have to read this crap and talk about it seriously." However, as a trained professional with ambition he did.

From the time of the origin of the legend of people selling ownership of their soul to the devil to fulfill their ambitions, it has been a theme from novels, drama, poetry, film and every other description of the human condition. It was clear that from that moment on, the media owned Wolf Blitzer. He had made a decision, to actively and purposefully take part in a charade, a third-rate charade of "cover you're a_s" piled upon "cover you're a_s." It was blatant to one and all.

The devil has rewarded Mr. Blitzer with selling his soul to the media's game of charades with his serious reading of the White House statement and he is now a hard-core and full-fledged member of the media's game of charades; today he is the mainstay of CNN news cadre of talking heads. A deal with the devil that Saab was not willing to make and look where they ended up.

Mr. Blitzer's deal with the devil piled on top of the car award was building the pile of straw on the camel's back that would just take one more straw to break it and cause me to devote the better part of a year to doing the relevant research and writing this book. The last straw was the one already mentioned in the chapter about Wall Street's game of charades and how CNBC enables the game to be played.

Two aspects of this enabling were in particular a motivator for this book. One has been long ongoing, the bit about when a senior executive quits, the official press release always gives a bogus reason that has nothing to do with the real reason. So what one might say, but the real reason is usually related to the company from which they are resigning and it is usually very relevant to people's decisions about whether to buy or sell the stock in the company. The CNBC folks know that, yet they read these press releases without even a wink, giving it their *imprimateur* of validity.

However, it was the tech-bubble scandal and the feigned shock, "shock I tell you, shock," of the CNBC talking heads that the research analysts working for the investment banks were really just shills promoting the stock of the banks clients that bordered on downright fraud. I mean come on, everyone anywhere near the business knows that is the role of the research analyst. Yet, CNBC's talking heads played along. In this case their high profile played a significant role in the destruction of wealth held by the average person who can only follow their brokers recommendation and listen to CNBC for their information, lambs to slaughter.

Look, the world is a competitive place. Each car magazine wants to be first with a road test of the latest model. By being negative in a car review that means some other magazine will get first crack at that company's next new model. If Mr. Blitzer did not go along with the farce, no more interviews or scoops with highly-placed administration officials, much less keeping his job at CNN. If the talking heads at CNBC do not take part in the charades, what power player would come on for an exclusive interview? It is an interlocked world, you go along with my game of charades and I will go along with yours and we will both prosper.

This is the way it goes, no one can argue with that. However, I also think, would like to think, that most people assume that the mainstream media is to a greater rather than lesser degree giving us an accurate description of what is going on out there. What we know about the world that leads us to vote for this or that person, what causes us to invest our retirement or our child's college money in this or that stock, and what leads us to purchase this or that car is all determined by our assumption that the media is not going along with a game of charades. This is not a joke, the integrity of the media has very serious real-world implications.

This next conversation about the charade of the media is about as ugly a subject as there can be. I thought it was so important that I intended to devote one whole chapter to it. However, once I made the commitment to writing this book, created a general listing of chapters, and then began to do the detailed research, I found on some of the "minor" charades so much more than I ever imagined that the scope of the book expanded dramatically. So it became a part of the chapter about the way the country responds to its citizens deaths and how these deaths are portrayed in a way to be of most benefit to the media. Since it directly involves the media, a brief mention here.

Our country is deeply involved in two wars and at least one other skirmish. One of the wars, Iraq became the absolutely dominant media topic of the day. Over the past eight years, about a trillion dollars has been spent on this war and 4500 Americans have given their lives. In addition there have been hundreds of thousands of Iraqis that have died as well as more than 1500 troops from other countries. In Afghanistan the cost and casualties so far are about1600 killed and the cost is running about $100billion per year.

The plain fact is that in these same years, over 30,000 Americans died in automobile accidents every year. Sixty times more than were killed on average each year in the war in IRAQ. Did you ever hear any discussion of this carnage, Sixty times as many people dying on the roads as were dying in Iraq? What gives?

"If it bleeds it leads," is the time honored saying by even members of the media about how they choose what to talk about as we tune in to find out what of importance is happening out there beyond our personal reach that we ought to know about. In 1986, the automobile manufacture Audi was suddenly the bleeding lead because its cars were accelerating out of control of anything the driver could do, causing injury and loss of life. People bled and the story led. Audi had been around as a European car company for long before WWII. It was only in the 1960s that it began to make itself known in the American market. It did so with great success. A well-deserved reputation for fine German engineering etc. etc. That medias claim that you could die in one of its cars through no fault of your own nearly destroyed the company.

Surprise surprise, it turns out not to be true. There was no unintended acceleration; drivers had just made errors. It took Audi twenty years to build its sales back to where they were just before the media fell in love with the "unintended acceleration" story. You would have thought the media would have learned its lesson. But no. Fast forward to early 2010 and it was Toyota cars that were now accelerating out of control, more bleeding, and more leading. This time even Congress and Ray LaHood, the Secretary of Transportation, jumped on the bash Toyota bandwagon.

The magnitude of Washington and the media's response to the Toyota story must in part be related to the fact that for the past twenty years and more, Toyota has been kicking sand in the face of the American auto industry that was recently on the brink of mass bankruptcy. What an opportunity for the politicians. Yeah, those no good damn Japs, they may sell a lot of cars, but they are death traps, "Buy 'Merican" was the in-between-the-lines message. The senior management of Toyota was called before congressional hearings. Tough questions were asked. Toyotas management philosophy was pilloried for having produced such reckless behavior. The baby of journalistic integrity was thrown out with the bathwater of Jap bashing. Multi-million dollar fines were levied. Shifty people with those shifty eyes were hiding the truth that they knew their cars were death-traps all along and never did anything about it. Congressional hearings as theater truly turned into a theater of the absurd.

One of the leaders in pushing the Congressional hearings was Darrell Issa of California. One of his colleagues commented, "Darrell recognizes a good issue when he sees one, and getting Toyoda (President of Toyota) to come was a good issue." Grandstanding and showboating, dumping all over them no good "furriners" makes for great political theater. A charade of perfect mutual self-interest.

The lawyers also jumped on the bandwagon. Special sessions were held in courtrooms as attorneys would plead their case to be chosen to represent the litigants in Toyota trials. The Wall Street Journal, March 26, 2010, headlined an article, "Lawyers Play Speed-Date in Toyota Law Suit Tussle."

The ultimate opportunity for piling on came when the allegations by drivers against Toyota spread to their hybrid the Prius. So now we have the ability of politicians to not only beat up on those damn Japs, but the no good hippie environmentalists as well. The drums in Congress beat ever louder. The hearing became showplace trials for all the faults of the evil Japanese empire. The dramatic story of a California highway patrol officer helping a driver slow his Prius from 90 mph to a stop was the top of the news. This was one of details, a slam dunk, the driver even recounted how he reached down to make sure the floor mat was not in the way and even tried to grab the gas pedal to make sure it was up. He made a 911 call and supposedly followed the instructions of the 911 operator about shifting into neutral. Toyota had to issue a recall of all Prius cars.

All someone had to do was a little background check on the driver to find out the truth. He was in deep financial trouble, having just previously filed for bankruptcy and the car was about to be repossessed. Even worse he had been previously convicted of filing false insurance claims for stolen possessions. Tests showed that a driver of his size could never have reached down to the bottom of the foot well to touch the gas pedal. The car's electronic brain records every move, he never shifted into neutral. The wear pattern on the brakes was inconsistent with hard braking. Another Prius episode that occurred in Harrison, New York, followed a somewhat similar pattern. All forensic tests showed the driver's foot never left the gas pedal, to quote the National Highway Traffic Safety Administration, "There was no application of the brakes and the throttle was fully open."

What was even more shameful if that can be imagined was an ABC investigation, one could just hear the talking head as the break for commercial, "wait till you see what we uncovered in our tests of Toyotas electronic problems, stay tuned, it will scare you to death." Well it turns out that the segment of scientific tests that showed exactly how unintended acceleration could happen in a Toyota were faked. It was so bad that when the cars tachometer that shows engine speed was right up near its maximum of 6000 rpm that would have been well-over 100 mph in top gear, in the same shot the gear lever could be seen to be in the "Park" position. ABC later apologized.

It is not as if we did not have a template for all this. The Audi case for example, and there are others of false claims of unintended acceleration just being driver error. The parallel is even to the point of the media staging a phony test. In the case of Audi it was a 60 Minutes segment that they later apologized when it was leaked that the transmission had been altered to make the case. For Toyota it was just short of $50 million in fines, numerous lawsuits that have to be defended and eight million cars being recalled at a cost of $100 million to Toyota. Its senior managers being grilled in front of Congress for knowing about this "defect" killing Americans and trying to hide it. Toyota's debt was downgraded by the ratings agencies causing their borrowing costs to rise.

So far, the first trial to reach a conclusion, Toyota won it. Eventually the same guy who pilloried them in the beginning, Ray La Hood admitted that it had all been a matter of driver error. At one point early in the fiasco he went so far as to recommend that people not drive their Toyotas, later changing his tune, "We feel Toyotas are safe to drive." No defects were found in the mechanical side of Toyotas nor in the electronic system. It had all been one great big hoax played upon the American people by its media and their representatives to Congress. Why? Because the only thing that matters to the media is ratings and to the Congress issues that they can use to make emotional appeals, true or not, to win votes.

Although only a part of the broader meaning of "bleeds" in the media national anthem, "If It Bleeds It Leads," the media's coverage of issues related to medicine is shocking and shameful. Perhaps it is my own many decades in both the academic and business sides of medicine that makes me react doubly strongly to this particular aspect of the media charade. I really really do know the details on this one—been there done that. It is reflected not just in the seriousness and accuracy of the coverage but the topics. For a medical topic to find its way to the media, it is not about how many people are effected by the news, but how "hot" a subject is it, and how does it fit into the social *zeitgeist* of the day. Autism, breast cancer, and AIDs, now there you have three subjects that are at the top of the media hit list, driven in most part by the entertainment industry in general and celebrity in particular involvement with the subject.

A rogue scientist published an article in 1998 about the relationship between childhood vaccines and autism. A celebrity, with an autistic child then picked up the cause and the media was off and running with little bother to look into the actual evidence behind the claim. For a few years this was one of the subjects "*du jour*" for the media: childhood vaccinations cause autism. Both the researcher who made the initial claim and the initial claim were discredited. The journal that published the paper withdrew it in early 2009. An editorial in the prestigious journal, the British Medical Journal, described the original paper and the research behind it as "an elaborate fraud." Yet a study published in early 2010 showed that 25% of parents still believed in the link between the vaccinations and autism. The author is quoted, "Now that it's been shown to be an outright fraud, maybe it will convince more parents that this should not be a concern."

Childhood diseases such as measles that have been consistently near zero in developed countries thanks to vaccinations showed a jump in response to the initial publicity. We have the sickness of many children and even some deaths to thank for the toxic mix of junk science and the media's drive for ratings.

Women's breasts, from the frivolous such as "wardrobe malfunctions," and Pamela Anderson's to the serious as in the possible toxicity of silicone breast implants and the proper timing of mammography, are another subject that is sure to gather instant media attention. In the case of silicone breast implants, for some reason, a large segment of the pro-abortion group that has as its rallying cry a saying about a woman's body being her own and with it goes her right to choose how she treats it, somehow when it comes to making a choice about breast implants is very much against them and was all too happy to jump on the bandwagon that those made of silicone were toxic.

Since I want to keep to the rule of being as apolitical as I can I will not mention that those women who work in the media for certain major stations tend to be on the pro side of the abortion issue. Nope, you will not see a statement such as that made here. Be that as it may, the media sure made a fuss of the implant toxicity issue. Made a fuss even though at the time there was no evidence of a relationship between silicone implants and toxicity. Made a big enough fuss that in 1990 the FDA had to temporarily suspend the use of these products, until additional studies were performed. Additional studies were indeed performed and sure enough, just what most people knowledgeable in the facts of the matter thought turned out to be true. Breast men the world over breathed a sigh of relief. No harm done by having breast implants made of silicone. Whoda thunk it given the initial drum beat?

The medias hunt for charismatic news stories, regardless of their relevance to its viewers was never more on display than their coverage of a debate in the medical profession over the proper age to begin screening for breast cancer with mammograms. A preliminary study done by the U.S. Preventive Services Task Force (USPSTF) under the auspices of the Department of Health and Human Services about when a woman should have mammography for screening for breast cancer suggested a review of the current guideline to begin at age forty and consider a delay until age 50.

Obamacare was hot and heavy in the media as the push was on to get Congressional approval for his health care reform package. It was the time of talk of "death panels," and "medical rationing" by putting bureaucrats in charge of making health-care decisions. Some politicians and media outlets found out about this first-step in an evaluation report and used it as a case in point of bureaucrats making health care decisions. Politicians made speeches and media talking heads egged them on. The medical community recoiled in horror as the government backed away from the whole program to study what is the appropriate time to begin screening. One well respected radiologist simply said, "Politics got in the way of the science and best public health practice" and another who had been on the initial study group, "I am a big believer in science and evidence…I thought people would really embrace the new science and say 'Wow, this is really good.'"

The whole issue about mammograms just drifted off into the vapors where it really belonged. A panel had issued a report calling for a reconsideration of the guidelines for mammography. A preliminary study written for and of use to doctors. No decision had been made, it was a subject fit for debate amongst the medical profession and then a final decision and report would have been made.

Other than its pseudo-relevance to Obamacare it never would have been mentioned. The coverage was destructive since the physicians who had volunteered their time to participate in the study I am sure came away more convinced than ever "that no good deed goes unpunished" and swore never to go near any hot media subject ever again—who needs this in their lives. Never reported on a national news broadcast was the fact that in July of 2011 the American College of Obstetricians and Gynecologists issued their final guidelines, which are the ones that most physicians follow, start screening at age 40.

AIDS however, is not an issue of this or that diagnostic timetable nor an elective cosmetic surgery procedure, but is a deadly disease, and an infectious deadly disease. The things that plagues are made of. It has been probably the most discussed disease in the media ever. This happened even though in the developed countries at least, the number of deaths is relatively small and it is primarily a disease of a small subset of the population. In addition it is not a mystery how one gets the disease. Do not engage in that very voluntary behavior and you will not get the disease. It is not exactly a plague transmitted in mysterious ways or transmitted in ways that people must act. Do not engage in unsafe sex and you will not get the disease, it is your choice. Yet the media covered it as if the fate of the world's population was in the balance.

Those facts having been said, a discussion of how the media has used AIDS for its own purposes and how the gay community has used the media for its own purposes shows us the best and the worst of the effect of the media upon the national dialogue and the dangers of when two powerful institutions focus on something of mutual self-interest.

The gay community is much more highly educated and much more affluent than the population in general. Well organized, able to put money behind their efforts, and with influence within the media profession, the gay community brought AIDs awareness to the top of our national consciousness. A fascinating part of this is that as diagnostic tests became reliable and cheap, and effective drugs were developed that would dramatically slow the disease and in many cases even suppress it for a lifetime, the public began to lose interest in the disease. In response, the gay community very effectively used the media to perpetrate a revival in the public discourse with two issues. One was that AIDs was beginning to spread amongst the heterosexual community and then after that one lost its media legs they brought out its growing prevalence amongst seniors. Both of these eventually faded from the media's focus since although certainly areas of concern, the statistics show the prevalence in the elderly and heterosexual communities to be low and stable. However, because AIDS is a hot topic, the media certainly was not shy in initially blaring the headlines.

Now, in comparison with other diseases has AIDS received more than its proportionate share of media attention? Certainly it has. However, this public relations effort by the gay community worked. Not two decades after the discovery of the disease, there are now both diagnostic tests and medications for the disease. It is not over, the medications just suppress the disease and it is only the rare case that it is suppressed to the point that the patient can stop taking the medication. In addition, there is no vaccine. Although much of the publicity about AIDS certainly never would have happened if did not afflict an affluent, educated, and vocal subset of the population, the publicity certainly did bring about a far greater research effort to find medications than if it had not been so well publicized by the media.

Unfortunately the above discussion is relevant only to the developed countries. In the third world, the disease is in many cases of plague proportions. However, that subject is beyond the scope of this book. Fortunately several nations of the first world and private foundations have taken up the challenge and are providing the infrastructure and funds to try to solve the problem. Relatively speaking there has been very little bang for the buck as discussed in the section about colonialism in the chapter about "Chardelettes."

There are many diseases out there. Many diseases that are at worst deadly and at best bring about a lifetime of care by others. A lifetime of a pretty miserable quality of life. They are not a disease of an affluent, educated, and vocal subset of the population so they receive very little attention. They have at best a foundation that funds some research on a cure begun by a family with a member afflicted with one of these "orphan" diseases. The pharmaceutical companies ignore these diseases since the market size is small and the media drumbeat that could prompt government funding for research has no prominent person involved to drive such an effort. It is a really sad part of the whole story of funding for medical research. On the one hand this relationship between the media and research into cures for disease worked great for AIDS but there are many equally deadly diseases about which not a murmur is heard and little progress is made in finding a cure since the markets are too small for the pharmaceutical company's attention.

CNN bills itself as the "worldwide leader in news" and maybe that is so. If it is so, then it has a tremendous responsibility. Worldwide it does more than any other institution to determine what it is that occupies people's mind on a "worldwide" basis. On January 24th, 2011, it ended a segment with a big truck going along a snowy highway, the last words from the talking head before the commercial were, "wait till you see what happens next." On its sister station Headline News, on May 11, 2010, the lead story was about a young girl who slipped and fell during a Nashville flood and was partially sucked into a small culvert, she screamed and her father immediately pulled her out. The talking head actually apologized for making that the lead story. In spite of that, the tease for the first commercial break was about an airline losing a dog and whether or not it is ok to read *Playboy* at work. That is how the electorate in this country learns about the issues affecting their lives.

Take any major networks prime-time news broadcast, ABC, CBS, or NBC for example and well over 50% of the stories are really features about attention grabbing subjects. I am coming across more and more the use of the term "nonfiction entertainment" when I read articles about the changes that have occurred in the past decade to what now passes for a news show on television. The loss of "gravitas" in the subject matter was forewarned in the loss of gravitas in the people delivering the news. It is now a hair, cleavage, white teeth and giggler talking about the "if it bleeds it leads" topics of the day when we tune in to see what is going in the world out there that we ought to know about. Even the Simpsons did a great parody on the state of the news in their "Girlie Edition" episode.

I am all too happy to accept that television is a for-profit making enterprise. Most of the television stations parent companies are publicly traded. Their stock is in the retirement plans and college-education funds of their stockholders. They have a responsibility to their shareholders to maximize profits. If no one watched there would be no advertising revenues. They have evolved in the direction they have over the past decade because that is what the public want to see. It is the free market at work.

However, we live in a globalized world. In part our lives are affected by what goes on across the globe. Our livelihood is dependent upon the goings on in the world-wide economy. When we have a decision to make related to our being able to support ourselves and our families, it would be nice to be able to make that decision with some awareness of the economy and the forces at work to send it in this or that direction over the next few years. Similarly, if we are of the age where military service is an option, or the parent of a child of that age as well, understanding the events around the globe are very important to our decision making in that regard. The list is a long one where our knowledge and understanding of global events can lead us to make better decisions about our own lives. We need to find out somewhere what the heck is going on out there.

A quick answer is of course the world-wide web. It is not fair to be focusing on television as the only portal for our knowledge. Unfortunately the world-wide web has a major flaw, how do you tell the credible source from the nonsense. This is not just about whether the facts are right, but also germane to the people expressing opinions. However, today, the same criticism can justifiably be applied especially to cable news shows. Point of view is a thread that runs through their reports.

We will soon be electing a new president and a substantial number of Congressmen and women. They will be making very important decisions on a variety of issues that will directly effect the quality of our lives such as education, health care, and what to do about our wars. These elections will also determine the effectiveness of our response to the emerging competition from China, Russia, India and Brazil as well as our ability to influence world events in a manner that will make them turn out in our favor.

Our fall from grace as a global competitor is the subject of the chapter about our status as the #1 country in the world. One of its themes is that looking at the cold hard facts of our health care system, our educational system, and other sources of pride show us to be fading to the bottom of the top ten and in more cases than we would like to admit even out of the top ten. Is the lack of a credible source of news and conversation about issues important to our future a part of what has sent us in a downward direction?

Perhaps the world of the U.S. as the dominant country will indeed not end in a bang but a whimper, a whimper by a six o'clock newscaster saying, "don't change that channel, you won't want to miss what happened to that doggie and its bone, coming right after the commercial break."

X. POLITICIANS: CHARADES

AS A WAY OF LIFE

In the chapter about Wall Street we learned that when it comes to a choice between the good of the country or their own self-interest, no question Wall Street finds the answer by looking in the mirror. But really, no hard feelings, investment bankers just trying to earn a living, eking out a few bucks here and there. I hope that even before reading the chapter about Wall Street, most readers understood that Wall Streets main job was to make money for Wall Street and if along the way they made money for Main Street, well that would be nice too. Anyone who has used a stockbroker knows they make money when you buy and then again when you sell, no matter if their recommendation made you money or not.

So good deal or bad, the investment bankers make tens and maybe even hundreds of millions as commission on the sale. That is an investments banker's agenda, self-interest, so what if their constituents get screwed. So really that is their job, push to the limit of the law, play both sides of the street against one another and with the help of cadres of lawyers, stay out of jail.

What is so troubling about the goings on in Washington is that most people believe that Washington is supposed to be acting in the best interest of their constituents, all their constituents—different from investment bankers. Yet as will be described in chapter and verse to follow, politicians are no more serving Main Street as are the investment bankers. Indeed, their primary interest is simply to be who they are, politicians, election after election seeing to it that they get elected, again and again.

Of course getting elected is about how much money a politician can raise to pay for those TV and radio spots. If you think your $25 even $100 contribution plays a role, sorry, just a drop in the bucket compared with the corporate donor. It is a hackneyed saying, as old as the industrial revolution, but politicians are owned by corporate America. Sadly, the more expensive election campaigns become the more influence is had by those who contribute the most, it is just in the nature of things. Who would know better than Alan Simpson, the legendary now retired Senator from Wyoming who said: "The God here in Washington is the God of reelection."

Nowhere is the conflict between Main Street and corporate America' ownership of Washington played out more dramatically than in the way

Washington uses regulation to find a balance between the profit needs of America and the protection of America's citizens from getting screwed. From pharmaceutical companies to oil drillers to the investment banks, the rules by which they should all play, ostensibly rules written to resolve the inherent conflicts in a company whose main job is to maximum profit made off the people who buy their products. That the pharmaceutical company's drugs will do what they are supposed to and not cause more harm than good, that the oil companies will produce their oil without harming our health and destroying our drinking water or the oceans that the fish we eat live, that planes will stay up in the air, and that the stockbrokers will be reined in from conning us into making foolish investments is all up to the regulations put in place by our government.

Let us get one thing clear: If pharmaceutical companies in the old days did not sell a lot of "snake-oil" and sell drugs such as thalidomide that produced horrific birth defects, the oil companies did not cause the litany of environmental disasters since the first well was sunk and the first barrel of crude refined, people did not die by the hundreds a year in coal mines, and that investment bankers did not sell bogus stocks and charge usuress interest rates, there would not be regulations. In the good old days of the Pittsburgh steel industry, men had to bring a white-shirt to work so they could change in the middle of the day and the streetlights were kept on 24 hours because of the soot in the air. **THAT REGULATION EXISTS AT ALL IS SIMPLY A RESULT OF CORPORATIONS OWN ACTIVITIES THAT PROVED THAT THE "FREE MARKET" DOES NOT WORK IN THIS REGARD. THEY HAVE NO ONE BUT THEMSELVES TO BLAME FOR EACH AND EVERY REGULATION.**

If people want to buy a garden rake or trash can they can hold it in their hands to see how sturdy and effective it will be. Even if they thought wrong, not much lost. However, how about the consumers ability to know what brand of hip implant they want to spend tens of thousands of dollars and the rest of their lives walking around on. Nope, simply impossible for the person to know if it is to be trusted, and as we have seen, in some cases even the doctor doing the surgery is not exactly to be trusted since he too has financial skin in the game. So, the government created the Food and Drug Administration (FDA) to pass judgment on products we eat and medical products we put in and on our bodies. If it were not for the FDA, every pill we take or hamburger we eat could be a game of Russian roulette, losing not money but our life if we made a wrong judgment. A variety of other regulatory agencies were put in place to protect people from industries that had previously put their customers well-being in jeopardy. Regulation put in place by our representatives in Washington acting out of concern for the welfare of their constituents. Hey, reading that over, it sounded pretty good. Nice story, sounds good, but is it mostly a charade?

The next many pages will be a recounting of some really wonderful examples of how well our regulatory system works, not! After reading it, you may wonder, "What the hell are these politicians talking about that we need less regulation, the ones we have are a joke, useless, people are dying on the oil rigs and in the coal mines and from eating tainted food." I have to say, the more research I did the more appalled I became at just how dismally Washington's regulatory apparatus works. It was not what I expected to find. Regulations and charade should be in a Thesaurus for having the same the meaning. The politicians really have only one interest in mind, campaign contributions, little happens that is not covered by that umbrella. In comparison with corporate America's contributions, Main Streets are barely noticed. So here goes, take a tranquilizer before reading this.

The FDA is the regulatory agency that is supposed to protect our interests and make sure the drugs we take do what they are supposed to do and do more good than harm. To make sure this is accomplished, the FDA is mostly staffed by physicians and Ph.D.s in fields relevant to medicine. Under their guidance companies do studies of drugs and submit their findings for study by FDA panels composed of specialists in the drug's area. These panelists then make a recommendation to the FDA higher-ups which almost always follows the panel's recommendation. Or so thought I and most Americans.

A company in Hackensack, New Jersey called ReGen developed a mesh that could be implanted in the knee to help people grow new cartilage that had been lost or degraded. They made their submission of studies on the safety and effectiveness of the product, the FDA examined the material and in December of 2008 gave the product its approval for sale.

In March of 2009, the Wall Street Journal published an article raising questions about just what went on in the approval process. In fact, four Democratic Congressman from New Jersey had brought considerable pressure to bear on senior officials at the FDA and this lobbying played a significant role in getting the device approved over the FDA's own staff's recommendation of rejection of the application.

Based on the WSJ article a new deputy commissioner of the FDA began an investigation of the approval process. The investigation concluded that the FDA had been influenced by the politician's pressure and that the approval should not be given. However, under the Congressional rules for how the FDA operates, there is a list of specific reasons why the FDA can reverse a decision. Political pressure shaping the decision is not one of them. The Congress put these rules in place.

Avandia is a drug to treat people with diabetes. It is sold by the international pharmaceutical company, Glaxo, one of the biggest in the world. Avandia's sales in 2009 were $1.2 billion. Sales of at least a billion is the general benchmark for "blockbuster" status, Wall Streets term. A 2007 study in the British Medical Journal reported a significant increase in heart attacks amongst those who took Avandia, a statistically significant risk well above what would have been expected even in a population with diabetes. The Senate launched an investigation in the FDAs process of approving Avandia and its response to reports of this side-effect. So good work for the Senate.

The Senate's report showed many troubling things. Glaxo's folks had known about this side-effect all along. Glaxo's own employees as well as people at the FDA had complained to their superiors about it being ignored. The heads of the FDA did nothing about reversing their initial decision. The Senate report found that at least in this case there was an inherent conflict of interest, those who had seen evidence of the cardiac risk in the initial studies for approval, yet approved it anyway, would be reluctant to admit their error. Most importantly, there was no system in place at the FDA for information required after the approval, when the drug had been in use for a period of time, to be used to bring about a reversal of the initial decision.

The Avandia case also brought to the Senate's attention another fundamental problem with the FDA process. The studies at medical schools and hospitals upon which the FDA approval is based are paid for by the company that makes the drug. Of the authors who participated in the Avandia studies that were favorable, 87% of the authors had financial ties to Glaxo whereas of the authors without financial ties only 20% were favorable. Sounds like a fine way for a regulatory agency to reach a conclusion

A situation involving a drug initially developed by Genentech and then brought to market by the company that acquired them, Roche, also shows just how "squirrely" this drug approval process can be. Avastin, was approved for specific cancers in which it is administered alone and is effective. Roche did a clinical trial where it wanted to see if Avastin was also effective in breast cancer when combined with an already approved drug, Taxol. The hope was that Avastin would improve Taxols effectiveness

The application was made to the FDA for approval at a time when there was much political pressure on the FDA, in particular about cancer drugs, that the FDA was being too hard-nosed and not letting terminal cancer patients take their own risks that their lives might be saved. In the clinical trials Avastin showed at best a minimal improvement when given in combination with an already approved drug for breast cancer, Taxol, compared with Taxol alone. In addition, there was evidence suggestive of troubling side-effects from the Avastin. Bowing to pressure, the FDA approved the drug but called for further testing and data collection focusing on the side effects once the drug was in use,

The follow-up found the side effects of internal bleeding to be life threatening and reduced life expectancy even in patients with breast cancer. Moreover, the data upon which the original approval was based, much of which consisted of X-rays, was sent out this time for review by doctors not paid by Roche and their review found no benefit of the drug upon breast cancer. The FDA this time revoked its approval. Needless to say, the lobbyists are now back at work, an appeal process is underway.

All of this was going on when the Obama health-care overhaul was front and center. In the fine spirit of bipartisanship, and keeping nothing but their constituents in mind, a group of Republicans raised hell that the only reason the FDA rescinded the approval was the cost of treatment with Avastin, $88,000 a year (see the Chapter about medical costs for further discussion). Forget about the fact that the drug was of no help and would cause some people to die from internal bleeding and that a drug, Taxol, was available that was helpful with comparatively minimal side-effects. Yea for my team on this side of the political aisle and boo for your team on the other side, enjoy a slow death through internal bleeding. The FDA approval process certainly is a neutral body just looking at the facts. No wonder the politicians are using the sound bite about allowing bureaucrats to make health care decisions so front and center, they do it themselves. As the famous cartoonist Walt Kelly's character Pogo was so fond of saying, "We have met the enemy and it is us."

When a drug or a medical device/implant receives FDA approval, it does so for a specific use. No big surprise there, less well known however is that any physician is free to use any approved drug or device for any other condition that they wish. Even if the drug, device, etc. has never been tested for this use or not. I am not joking. The one caveat to all this is the rule that manufacturers can play no role in encouraging the docs to go down this "off label" track. Gosh, I wonder how a doc would even get the idea to try a drug for a different disease than one for which it received FDA approval, gosh I wonder?

Pharmaceutical companies employ vast armies of salesman who haunt doctor's offices, hospitals, and medical schools giving out free samples to encourage docs to use their company's products. These companies also hold off-site continuing education seminars usually in places such as ski resorts or the Caribbean, which of course makes the expense of attendance a tax deduction if you are not a big enough prescriber of the company's drugs so they pay for it. The docs who give the presentations are the same ones who receive a nice grant to run the clinical trials. In all this salesperson-physician interaction is the wink-wink conversation about hypothetical uses for this or that product—hypothetically speaking of course.

Occasionally one of these salespeople has a moment of conscience and blows the whistle. This happened in the case of a treatment for a heart problem called atrial fibrillation. Someone had the bright idea, that using a catheter inserted into specific areas of the heart and with just the right amount of energy released at the tip, a productive short circuiting of the electrical currents causing the problem would occur. Lo and behold it turns out a device to do this already existed and was FDA approved for fixing a different problem. However, it had never been the subject of clinical trials for atrial fibrillation fixed by "ablation" so was not approved for that use.

In 2009, 25,000 cardiac catheter ablations were performed in the United States, all with an unapproved device right under the FDA's nose. Why bother having an FDA if this is allowed to go on? Well, a brave young lady, Elaine George had worked in sales for companies that made one of these products and blew the whistle on them. You see she had attended training sessions where for all practical purposes she and her colleagues were trained in the "wink-wink, nod-nod" school of salesmanship to the physicians.

One such company, AtriCure, settled with the federal government and ended up paying a $3.8 million fine. Elaine gets $688,000 for blowing the whistle. Estech, another company selling these catheters settled for $1.5 million, of which Ms. George will receive $226,000. Ms. George has lawsuits currently pending against three other companies alleging they also marketed these devices for the off-label use of atrial fibrillation. As Oprah would say or words to that effect, "You go girl."

There seems little question that in some cases, this procedure with this device does work. However, does it work better or worse than other treatments that are available? Are there more dangers to using this treatment compared with other treatments that work just as well? Are there certain age patients who are more appropriate than others? Is there a level of disease that responds to this treatment, perhaps advanced disease versus just the beginnings, for which it is more appropriate? You see, these are all the questions that controlled clinical trials will answer. With no trials, no one is keeping score of who gets better and who doesn't, much less just how much energy needs to be released just where in the heart to produce the desired effect. Needless to say, all these off-label uses have a tremendous impact on inflating health care costs.

Now to those outside of medicine, they may not realize that medicine is no different than investment bankers, car mechanics, plumbers, or anyone else who provides you a product or service in exchange for your money. Just where they fit on the line between balancing your interests and their own financial interests is a function of their own personalities, their character. Some involved in the business are appalled at the state of affairs on the off-label use. Ms. George claims to have attended a training session where the trainer showed them how to use a model of the heart to demonstrate the use of the company's device for treating atrial fibrillation. When she questioned the legality, she was told: "Don't worry about that. This is how you sell it." Another company's materials given to salespeople, in referring to its device: "represents the opportunity to own the category for surgical atrial fibrillation."

But is this about business and Wall Street or about medicine? One of the leading manufacturers of the heart devices said at an investor conference referring to the treatment of atrial fibrillation, "a fast growing underpenetrated market." Another company at the same conference, "may be the best growth market in the medical device space for the next 5-7 years." A medical device analyst with an investment bank said that of the $100 million spent on cardiac ablation devices, nearly all are for treating atrial fibrillation." Oh, by the way, about 80% of patients with atrial fibrillation are effectively treated with much much much cheaper drugs. All of this off-label use occurs right under the FDAs nose. They attend the conferences and are intimate with the practice of medicine. Short of a whistle-blower or investigative journalist rubbing their nose in it, they do nothing. A good friend went blind for a week, nearly permanently from a "cowboy" doc treating his diabetic retinopathy with an off-label use of a drug. This is not just a matter of statistics, but our health at stake.

Time to leave the FDA behind in its own dust of incompetence. Of course the government regulates far more than just medical stuff, it regulates in the exact same efficient and neat and clean manner a whole variety of things that has brought us the already discussed BP disaster, Lehman disappearance, and Wall Street shenanigans. Now time for a quick tour of a few more examples of life-

and-death regulatory home runs as well as just some examples that really have to make you wonder who does the job interviews in the government.

A gas pipeline exploded in San Bruno, CA in September of 2010 leveling 38 homes, more than 50 were injured and eight were killed. A representative of the trade group for utilities, the American Gas Association said at hearing into the blast that it was probably due to an anomalous defective pipe and no need for general safety concerns. The hearings were held by the National Transportation Safety Group safety group which has a division that is responsible for pipeline safety. They concluded that in fact it was defectively welded pipe that caused the explosion, deaths, and carnage.

Pacific Gas and Electric (PG&E) which owns the pipeline was supposed to have given the pipeline a periodic inspection but did not since its robotic system could not fit into this type of pipe as was case for at least 60% of its pipes. In fact, nationwide there are 187,837 miles of older pipe that were installed before any standards were even put in place as to the quality of the pipe used to carry natural gas. Well fine, let's accept that some pipe is too old to inspect and being old will eventually leak, but in most cases, these leaks are smelled before they explode and of course one would expect a system to be in place for early warnings to be taken seriously and immediate inspections and appropriate warnings given to those who might be affected.

The system is an abject failure, numerous cases are on record of calls being made by residents about the smell of gas that went unheeded and lives were lost in the subsequent explosions. In San Bruno, it turns out that PG&Es record keeping system showed the pipe that blew up to be seamless and therefore not needing the type of check-up schedule that the welded seam pipe that it was would require. But the back-stop did work, residents had called in complaints about a gas-leak smell in the neighborhood but no went to check. Eight people killed and 38 houses destroyed and the California Public Utilities Commission fined PG&E six million dollars for lousy record keeping and deliberate noncompliance with safety inspection, but said it would lower it to 3million if the company met its deadline for completing inspections and updating its records on their pipeline system. PG&E has revenue of 1.8 billion dollars a year and will end up getting fined 3million dollars when eight people died. So what comes first, regulations, or people dying?

The most recent coal mine disaster in the United States was April 2010 at the Massey Energy Company's mine in West Virginia where 29 miners were killed. Investigations following the disaster found several disturbing facts about the regulatory efforts for coal mines. As in the BP oil disaster, much of the policing of coal mines is left up to the coal companies themselves to report their own violations. Equally troubling is the finding that even when the coal companies reported their violations, the federal safety officials from the Mine Safety and Health Administration (MSHA) went out of their way to look the other way, sort of the like the MMS regulation of the oil drillers. The MSHA set limits as to how many mines a year could be ranked in the worst offender category, one mine per field office, and three mines per district. No matter how bad mines were, only so many could be listed in the top category worthy of being put under a strict enforcement of safety rules watch.

Of course after the Massey fiasco, as is always the case, hearings were held and pronouncements made. Labor Secretary Solis said: "reaffirms what we already knew: The pattern of violation process is badly broken" and that MSHA had better work on "regulatory and administrative fixes." The head of MSHA said that it was necessary for the agency to "change the way we deal with persistently problematic mines this year." Wait a minute, so the regulatory folks in Washington knew the monitoring and enforcement process for coal mines was "badly broken," but nothing was done.

A slick ploy used by operators in a variety of industries is simply once they get in trouble with regulators, to close shop and open up under a different name. A few years ago this came to light when a nurse's incompetence led to numerous deaths in the hospital where she worked. It seems this was nothing new, two other states had revoked her license. However there was no central data base to allow here future employer in a third state to find this out. So it has been going in the coal industry. Pile up a stack of safety violations, shut down, and reopen under a different name. As a result of the Massey deaths it is proposed to create a data base whereby operators who had been shut down would not be allowed to work in the industry again.

Prior to the catastrophe in Massey's West Virginia mine, they were under the scrutiny gun for a mine in Kentucky. They had six roof falls in 5 months and 2000 safety violations in 2 years, but still the regulators could not shut them down other than on a temporary basis and Massey was fighting and winning the fight against even that move. Under the regulatory system, a mine has a laundry basket of challenges it can reach into and use in court against any safety violation. Nothing can be done until all appeals have been heard which can take years—after the report of a dangerous safety violation that puts miners at risk. In addition, at Massey at least, inspection and safety reports were routinely found to be filled out to cover up any violations, only as a result of actual miners testimony at hearings was this uncovered. The federal inspectors never checked to match the reports with the underground facts. After the West Virginia problem, Massey gave up its legal fight and voluntarily shut down the mine.

In the Spring of 2011, federal inspectors conducted an UNANNOUNCED believe it or not inspection of another West Virginia mine owned by Massey. One of the inspectors commented, "nothing short of outrageous" to describe the conditions he found. From a safety standpoint it was a catastrophe with miners at risk from numerous chronic and acute dangers. "Unannounced," well at least not formally. In May of 2011 the head of security for the mine received his third felony charge. He had trained the guards at the mine to use their walkie talkies to contact the workers in the mine as soon as the inspectors arrived at the gate.

My intention in writing this book was to simply use the BP oil spill, the Lehman Bros bankruptcy, and an example or two from the FDA to show how much of a charade exists in the regulatory function of the folks in Washington. However, while doing the research on that charade and the other chapters in the book, it was a gift that keeps on giving. The deaths in the San Bruno case and Massey mine explosion showed a regulatory system that was pitiful. Regulatory agencies completely asleep at the wheel, knowing problems existed both in the regulatory rules and out in the field, but nothing happens until someone dies. Below are some others that found their way to my attention and will just be briefly described.

A new way for getting oil and natural gas out of shale has been developed, called "fracking." Through injecting liquid under pressure into the shale it fractures and gas and oil are forced into the cracks and find their way to the surface. It has shown itself to be very productive. Unfortunately as you may know, most of people's drinking water comes from underground aquifers. It only stands to reason that the chemicals injected to fracture the shale will mix with the water.

Amazingly, no agency was interested in this issue. Citizens whose drinking water suddenly turned icky, at times even containing enough natural gas that one could light the faucet, started asking questions. It turns out that one of the main ingredients injected is diesel oil. Diesel oil cannot be put in the ground anywhere, not leaking from gas station tanks, not in landfills, it is illegal. Separately, of course there are rules on the books about safe drinking water etc. etc. Citizens raising hell with their congressmen has finally brought this to the governments attention and they are at least beginning to look into just what it is that is being added to our drinking water. The Department of Energy has created a panel to look into the issue. It is headed by John Deutch, former CIA boss and even with current and former business relationships with companies involved in fracking he has said. "that the regulatory system wasn't moving rapidly enough and decisively enough to resolve some of these questions" and it appears as if the panel will recommend stringent monitoring of drinking water and full disclosure of all chemicals injected into the ground. What comes first, people being able to light the water coming out of their faucets or regulations?

The FDA database is full of information on drugs currently in formal clinical trials. Wouldn't people who play the stock market like to know what was going on before it is formally released. An FDA chemist decided to let his fingers do the tapping on a keyboard to the database and in four years made himself just short of $4 million dollars. Come on FDA did it not occur to someone that such information which should be confidential anyway in terms of patients medical information have some security to this information.

In late 2010, the Inspector General of the Justice Department issued a report on the new FBI computer system, Sentinel, that was going to make it easier for the various policing organization to share information so that the right hand not knowing what the left hand was doing which led to the failure to stop the 9/11 attack would not happen again. The total budget was to be $455 million. As of the report, $405 million had been spent and the project is at least two years behind schedule and at least $100 million over budget. That is the good news. After 9/11 a project called Trilogy was put in place and three years and 170 million dollars later it was so bad that it was canceled and Sentinel was started.

On the same homeland security front is the much publicized high-tech border security fence to make us safe along the border with Mexico. Using the highest technology of cameras, motion sensors, and a laundry list of other gizmos, the U.S. has spent $600 million with little to show for it that actually works. In fact the Department of Homeland Security froze spending in early 2010.

In 2009, a small fire was noticed in the rugged country to the East of Los Angeles. It was nearly contained in one day. On the morning of day 2, a veteran fire-fighter from the Department of Forestry flew over the fire and called in a request for specific water dropping aircraft and the locations where water needed to be dropped that should end the fire threat. There was no one to answer the phone. After many calls, later in the morning he got someone to answer the phone but it did not matter. The answer was that it would be several hours before the planes would be available. He upped the ante by describing the critical nature of the moment—if the fire was not stopped where it was, moving into the next canyon system could open up a major disaster. He was right, the fire made its jump and became the largest fire in LA county history with the loss of two firefighters lives. Recordings and collaborative witnesses fully backed the firefighters inability to get the Forest Service to respond to his requests as well as his opinion that it was now or never in terms of containment.

Same stuff, different place and time. As with many government agencies, they rely on private contracts for supply of the aircraft used in wilderness firefighting. In 2008 a private contractor's helicopter crashed during a fire-fighting effort in northern California. Nine people died. An investigation showed that the company supplying the helicopter lied about its weight empty (allowing it to charge more for a higher weight loaded—meaning more people could be carried). The investigation also brought to light conflicting rules about who inspects such contract aircraft, certifies their airworthiness, and keeps track of the safety records of the companies that the U.S. government does business with for the supply of aircraft.

At a Connecticut power plant in early 2010, during scheduled maintenance to make sure pipelines that carry liquid fuel are clean of debris, natural gas was blown through pipelines. It is a warranty requirement of the company that makes the power plants turbines. If debris were in the fuel lines it could damage the blades of the turbines. Natural gas has traditionally been used for this purpose. However this time an explosion occurred, killing six and injuring 50.

The federal agency, Occupational Health and Safety Administration (OSHA), did its investigation and issued a strong letter suggesting that an inert gas, such as Nitrogen, be used for this purpose in the future. It did not ban the use of flammable gases even though the investigation clearly showed that residual natural gas was responsible for the explosion and found it to be an "inherently unsafe" method. An officer of the agency said they would love to issue a ban but that regulations require specific studies be performed before such an order can be issued. The manufacturers of these turbines stepped up and ordered all customers to substitute oxygen or nitrogen for natural gas. The Chairman of the chemical industry's own group, the Chemical Safety Board responding to the failure of OSHA to ban the use of natural gas for procedural reasons said, "I believe there should be an emergency response to an emergency situation."

Following up on the San Bruno gas pipeline explosion, other gas companies in California were asked to show their records of pipeline safety inspections. One of the biggest, Sempra Energy could not find records of inspection for 450 miles, 28% of their pipelines that run through populated areas. These are inspections required by the federal and state government rules. How come no one over the many years has ever checked to see if they were following the rules? Why bother writing regulations if no ever checks that they are being followed?

How about the way these regulatory agencies and other major governmental institutions deal with investigating people, sometimes their own employees who either through ineptness or calculated evil cause harm to occur. Although not about regulations, remember the Army psychiatrist, Major Hasan who went on a shooting rampage at Fort Hood, killing 13 and wounding 30 in November of 2009? It is just a perfect example of the way government agencies deal with internal personnel issues. It makes you think it is nearly impossible to be fired from a government job. At one point in his training to be a psychiatrist he was supposed to give a presentation. He did, and it was all about quotes from the Quran advocating torment and death to non-Muslims. This was not for the University of this or that, but at Walter Reed, the military's main hospital. Later, while on a fellowship he delivered a lecture to one of his classes based upon a sympathetic view of Ben Laden and the 9/11 bombings. The class booed him and the talk was stopped.

At last the FBI began to look into the guy and found his relationship with a former American turned Al Queda recruiter with whom Hasan exchanged numerous "fellow traveler" emails. His supervisors at Walter Reed were scared by Hassan and the FBI was investigating him. Yet his file is full of supportive documents full of politically correct gibberish such as, "illuminating the role of culture and Islamic faith within the Global War on Terrorism," and "His unique interests have captured the interest and attention of peers and mentors alike."

There right under their nose was a dedicated jihadist and everyone threw up their hands in surprise when he got a gun and shouting in Arabic "God is Great" within a military installation moved down 13 people. How could this have happened?

I can't resist, here is another example. Recall that pathetic guy who tried to blow up his SUV in Times Square and only managed to create a smoke bomb. To the FBI's credit they tracked him down within 24 hours and found him at 3pm on a Monday returning to his home. His home and his block were surrounded waiting for him to emerge and be arrested. Thanks to the secrecy within the FBI and news organizations putting the country's safety above their own self-interest, several news trucks, the ones with the satellite dishes, were soon parked on his street. The suspect managed to leave his home in the suburbs undetected and board a plane ready to escape. The feds had lost him. Fortunately alert security at the airport identified him and he was captured prior to takeoff. The investigation that occurred into how the FBI lost the guy resulted in nothing.

It is indeed a sad story, the lives lost, and vast amounts of money wasted in what ought to be pretty simple regulatory and government affairs. In reality the regulations seem to be written for evasion. Government money spent in multiple iterations of the same incompetence. Now let us throw into this mix the kinds of people and amounts of money that are involved with the investment banking industry. Government employees going toe-to-toe against the geniuses of Wall Street who out of their own greed, drove Lehman Bros into ruin, created the CDOs, CDSs, and the other seemingly magical financial instruments that brought the worldwide financial system to its knees. It is a grotesquely one-sided game as we all found out in the meltdown of 2008 and such relatively minor failures as the Madoff scheme. The government regulators had whistle blowers pounding on their doors, and yet they did nothing.

Let's start with perhaps the most slam-dunk of all financial regulations. If anything is supposed to level the playing field it is the rules against insider trading. Everyone is supposed to have the same information and then let the ones who can make the best sense out of that information win the game. However, if some folks know something "material" to a company's future prospects and everyone else does not then the game is truly fixed.

Unbeknownst to me until I started researching the area for this book and I would bet that at least 90% of the U.S. population is unaware of is the very special relationship between insider trading in the stock market and members of Congress and their employees. The laws DO NOT APPLY TO THEM. Yessiree, those folks who deal daily with the regulation of private industry, from the drug companies to the oil companies, much less the investment banks themselves, can use that information known only to them about regulations and the companies they regulate to buy and sell stock in these very same companies.

The chief of staff for the top Republican Congressman on off all things, the House Appropriation Committee on Standards of Official Conduct was one of the top traders in Congress, making 2,291 trades in 2009 and 1,888 in 2008. The Chief of Staff for a Democrat made a total of 300 trades over 2008 and 2009. The details are as bad as you can imagine. How can it be that the people who set the rules of the road and are privy to the most relevant of nonpublic information are immune from insider trading?

This information about the Congressman and their employees stock trading is available to anyone who wants to go through the hassle of filing a request for disclosure of information with the government. It makes finding the right form on the IRS website look easy and the information is usually a year out of date. However, that does not mean that our loyal representatives who we elect to look after our welfare and whose salaries and perks we pay are not hard at work on this issue.

A bill sponsored by two representatives has languished in Congress for four years. It would place the representatives and their aids under the same insider trading laws as the rest of us plain folks and require that disclosure of any equity trades be made within 90 days. When proposed 4 years ago only 14 other representatives would endorse it. The current version of this legislation has attracted only six supporters. In spite of the efforts of these two members of Congress for the past four years, currently it is dead in the water and they are even unable to get hearings scheduled to discuss the matter. What more do you need to know to convince yourself that the entire Congressional system is one big charade of pretense. A similar bill was introduced in the spring of 2011. Who knows?

Another major game of Washington charades is how they handled the bursting of the bubble in technology stocks. As discussed in some detail in the chapter on Wall Street, this is the bubble fueled by the "independent" research analysts who wrote the reports touting this or that stock. It turned out they were really working for the investment bank that took that stock public and were simply trying to pump up the price of the stock.

As part of their investigation into the phony reports of stock analysts that created the great technology bubble, the Securities and Exchange Commission (SEC) decided upon some regulatory actions to lessen the self-dealing in the process. Under great pressure from lobbyists representing the investment banks, the original SEC plan was watered down.

In fact, the SEC did give some fines, a joke compared with the amount of money involved, to some of the most egregious analyst charades. Fortunately district federal judges keep a watch on these goings on and must approve the SEC settlements with these firms. Two such district court judges, Jed Rakoff and William H. Pauley, stepped in and refused to give approval to the watered down agreements unless the investor protections as in the original agreement were put back in place, yay! for them.

Strangely enough, we have judges to thank in more than one example for stepping in to try to get the people's representatives to work on behalf of the people. Barclays, a British Bank, has a large presence here in the United States. It is notable for having picked up the largest pieces left over from the Lehman bankruptcy and integrated them into its own activities. It is also well known for having played a significant role of knowingly laundering money for a variety of countries under sanctions, such as Iran and Cuba by creating fake transaction records. Initially the government had settled with Barclays for a "deferred prosecution agreement." They would have to pay a fine of $298 million only if over the next few years they did not stop laundering money.

A federal judge called the deal "a free ride" and a "sweetheart deal," and stopped it, telling the government to go back to the negotiating table. Another judge put a stop to a deal with Bank of America and got the fine bumped from $33 million to $150 million and another put a $75 million deal with Citigroup on hold and told the government to get a better deal. Well, at least now when the folks doing the deal for the government someday send their Resumés to these investment banks they can say, "the judge made me do it."

The SEC's work on behalf of safeguarding the American public from dishonest investment scams really seems to know no limits. Of course what could be more important than the SEC making sure that when a company does an IPO, its representations are accurate. In early 2009, a Ukrainian company applied to the SEC for approval to sell stock to the public and it was approved. An investigation showed that the company had one employee, a 79 year old massage therapist, and only $100, yup no thousands, millions, or billions, just plain old $100.00, enough for a nice dinner for two these days. In this case it was the capital to build a chain of health spas.

Another such Ukraine related company, Ukragro, took the same path, using the same law firm as the previous deal. Soon after "going public" the company declared a 60:1 stock split and acquired a gold-mining claim in Nevada. A newsletter, Intelligent Investor Report, then issued a buy recommendation describing "proven gold deposits" and exclaimed the stock "could soon be flying past $15/share!" I can just hear the telemarketing boiler-room pitch: "A chance to get in on the ground floor…." In fact it turns out that the same small law firm in Seattle was behind eight other launchings of SEC approved publically traded companies in the prior two years. The sole employee of the gold mining company was the same woman's name as in the chain of health spas filing.

Boy I sure do feel safe knowing the SEC has my back.

As well you should, especially after the little publicized Stanford affair. In comparison to the Madoff boondoggle, Allen Stanford's Ponzi scheme was small potatoes, only $7 billion dollars. Yet what makes the Stanford case even more frightening than Madoff, if you thought Madoff showed grotesque incompetence on behalf of the SEC, Stanford doubles it. Between 1997 and 2004 the SEC investigated Stanford's investment business four times, and each time concluded it was a fraud. As early as 1997, a Fort Worth SEC examiner told her branch chief, "keep your eye on these people because it looks like a Ponzi scheme to me and someday it's going to blow up." In 2003, the National Association of Securities Dealers sent a letter to the SEC and in all capital letters it alerted them to the fact that Stanford's investment company "WILL DESTROY THE LIFE SAVINGS OF MANY." Yet they did nothing. A recent investigation pointed the finger at the former head of the SECs office in Fort Worth for quashing the investigations each time. It was the Madoff scandal that brought focus on the SEC's grotesque handling of Madoff's Ponzi scheme and the subsequent investigation brought the Stanford case to light. Once again, when it comes to the government, reality is even more bizarre than fiction.

Let's try taking a look at the actions Congress took or is contemplating taking as a direct result of the most serious financial crisis since the great depression. As you may recall from an earlier chapter, much of the crisis was precipitated by the way banks created a variety of instruments tied in a variety of degrees of separation from, or "derived" from, very shaky mortgages. The banks put their own money and the money of large investment funds such as pension plans and mutual funds into these instruments. Once these shaky mortgages started to default, the chain of events looked like one of these incredibly complex domino structures that only needs the lead domino to fall and the impact of the first on the second spreads out into numerous side arms of dominoes.

Key to this cascade of failure, directly and both indirectly, was the ability of banks to invest their own money in these very speculative financial instruments. A banks solvency is based upon it having enough money to pay off its depositors if they come in to withdraw the money in their accounts. That is the origin of the term a "run" on the banks. If word got out that a bank had made very poor investments with its depositor's money, no one wants to be the last one in the banks door to get their money before their bank has no more money. So since the banks had made bets with their depositors money on risky mortgages which were now failing and had invested money in some of these exotic financial instruments that were in some way derived from risky mortgages, and when word started to reach Main Street that some banks were in trouble, massive failure was looming. To avoid a panic, that is why the federal government stepped in to prop-up most of the troubled banks to prevent the kind of "run on the banks" that caused the great depression.

Paul Volker has held many offices related to finance in the government as well as having been a very well respected head of the Federal Reserve. Soon after the banking crisis he proposed a rule that came to be known as the Volker Rule. It would prohibit banks from investing their own money in risky financial instruments as well regulating a banks relationship to hedge funds that also were investing in these risky instruments (in fact after the depression such a rule the Glass-Steagall act had been put in place but it was rescinded in 1999 in order to allow banks to make risky investments with their depositors money). Volker took a hard line and had support from many in government, at least when it came time to making speeches at congressional hearings. Five former secretaries of the treasury, from both Democratic and Republican administration, penned an article in the Wall Street Journal giving strong support to the Volker rule: "Banks benefiting from public support by means of access to the Federal Reserve and FDIC (Federal Deposit Insurance Corp.) insurance should not engage in essentially speculative activity unrelated to essential bank services."

However, by now you must have expected this was coming. When it came time to actually put the rules on paper, congress started to whittle away and do the usual creating back doors, self-policing, leaving the details to the agencies, and all the typical shenanigans that would allow them to say they fought for this and that and worked on behalf of Main Street against the evil investment bankers. With visions of sugar plum fairies in the form of banks making their usual large campaign contributions dancing in their heads, those bright guys with those bright million dollar a year lawyers behind them saw to it that the regulations were surprise surprise, a charade. When news of how watered-down the bill became was announced in July of 2010, the shares of the major banks shot up.

In fact, one of those financial analysts, a banking analyst at Morgan Stanley said in terms of the investment banks that the rules were "better than expected." The CEO of the Securities Industry and Financial Markets Association commented when he learned that 200 items in the Congressional bill overhauling the securities industries would be left for the regulators to do the details, he said, "The bottom line here is that this saga will continue." One of the million-dollar lawyers for the securities industry, "I view the legislation as a whole as starting out as being horrendous, now its merely very horrible." A consultant to the financial industry, "it could be much worse."

But of course, writing new legislation is a major process, still ongoing in summer of 2011. Perhaps it is being unfair, but after reviewing so many examples of the sequence that begins with a major screw-up whether oil drilling or investment banking that then proceeds through a multiple stage process from hearings through final bill writing and ends up years later with final language, the whole process really is laughable. As an example of just how peculiar this process is, there are in the spring of 2011, four different regulators writing their own version of the Volker rule. The final rule will be created out of negotiations amongst these four different government groups. Lobbyists for the banks pen the actual words used in the final legislation.

I expect it is no accident that the process of regulation writing is this contorted. Perhaps it is that way for really two major reasons. One is it gives individual politicians multiple opportunities to take part in the drama, to say their lines for the sake of sound bites for media ads come the next election. Second, it gives the power players involved in the industry, directly themselves or through their campaign contributions and lobbyists, multiple bites at the apple just in case along the way, new stuff gets put in that they want changed.

Goldman Sachs as one might imagine has former legislators and regulators as part of their lobbyist teams. They know the people writing the rules and know the system as well as anyone. In the case of the Volker rule it is a take no prisoners event. The man doing God's work, Lloyd Blankfein himself is working the halls of congress and most importantly has the privilege of private meetings with Mary Schapiro, the head of the SEC. At stake is several billion dollars in revenue if the Volker rule as presently written is passed. You know whats are puckered in the investment banking world. A Goldman lobbyist has been anonymously quoted for obvious reasons, "They're totally freaked out about Volcker," "People are working on that a lot, with agency staff, with lawmakers, you name it." We all know who the "you name its" are.

If regulation was adequate and the regulators did their jobs, the meltdown of 2008 could have never happened. It had not happened since 1933 because of the Glass-Steagall act that was then repealed in 1999 thanks to the great pressure by Wall Street's lobbyists. So hearings were held and fatuous sounds came out of Washington. New regulations and pronouncements, yes we have your best interests at heart, our only concern is with you, Main Street U.S.A.

The hearings were called "Americas Financial Crisis Inquiry Committee" and they released their report at the end of January 2011. Since the six Democrats and four Republicans had only our best interests in mind, that is why they came out with really two different reports. The one supported by the six democrats put the blame on the financial industry, from the investment bankers to the bond rating agencies and Washington regulators who allowed deregulation to rule the day. A dissenting report was supported by the four republicans focusing blame on everyone. However it took special aim at a previous Democratic administration that had increased homeownership with easy mortgages in the 1990s as a part of the agenda. You see, this report also blamed Main Street for failing to meet their mortgage responsibilities. Go Yankees, go Red Sox, what the hell.

A very close friend, a tough-guy Wall Street lawyer went to get a mortgage on his vacation home. He wanted just a straight 20% down mortgage. When the sales guy in the bank could not persuade him to sign up for an adjustable this or that mortgage with less money down but a larger mortgage, they called in a "Vice President" to make the pitch. My friend held them off. I can only imagine what chance Joe Average would have when they go in for a mortgage. "Adjustable rate, oh yeah, but don't sweat the small stuff, never happen." Sure its all the homeowners fault for signing up for the tricky adjustable rate mortgage. You betcha.

Some wonderful quotes from the report that show their remarkable insight and why Congress gets paid such big bucks: "dramatic failures of corporate governance and risk management at many systemically important financial institutions were a key cause of the crisis." I guess that means as in the management of Lehman Brothers running it into the ground. Another quote: "stunning instances of governance breakdown and irresponsibility." I guess that means as in the SEC failing to catch Madoff and Stanford. Boy are we glad so much time, effort, and money was put into the report that showed such brilliant insights that banks failed because of bad management and people lost lots of money because the SEC was asleep at their jobs.

So, in terms of the way Washington is looking out for Main Street when it tries to invest its money, the outlook is not great. Wall Street is run by a group of very bright, aggressive, ambitious folk who have no one's interest in mind other than their own. Most of the time their interests and the interests of the investor are not the same. They just want to get the investor to invest their money in Wall Street's products. If these products go up or down is not the concern of Wall Street, they make their money either way.

As previously described, looking into the regulatory function of the government, from the perspective of incompetence and charade is a gift that just keeps on giving. Here is a brief look at some other stranger-than-fiction things that popped up while investigating Wall Street regulations.

Mortgages given to folks with no money down and little checking into their financial status were at the heart of the whole financial crisis that once started took down the country's economy. So in late Spring of 2011 what does the credit union for a government agency, NASA, do, it offers mortgages with no money down. The exact thing that Congressional hearings railed against as the evil empire behind the financial meltdown is now being done by a government agency. In response to criticism, a government official said the mortgages would be given only to "highly qualified" buyers. Yeah right, that is why the only way they can get a mortgage is with no money down—because they are so highly qualified financially. It is hard to believe some of this stuff.

Most folks from Main Street that buy stocks buy them in a way that allows them to profit only when placing a bet on their going up. However, there is a way, called going "short," that allows an investor to place a bet that the stock will go down. If it does goes down, the investor makes the difference between the stock price when the short is placed and the difference when the short is taken away. Conversely, if the stock goes up and the investor then cancels the short, the investor owes the amount between the price of placing the short and higher price when the short is removed. Some very large investment funds do only "short" sales. They step in when they think a particular stock is way overvalued and the price will soon drop.

Now since most money going into the market is a bet on stocks going up, many on Wall Street would like the naysayers to disappear, it is not good for a business based on the concept of an ever-rising stock market that some experts are betting on stocks falling. As the financial crisis set in, the shorts placed big bets on the continuing failure of the sub-prime mortgage market and its cascading negative effect on the stock of companies in the mortgage business and those banks that played around with all these exotic instruments derived from the mortgages. The shorts made fortunes.

The very same folks who pound the table about "free markets" being the basis for all good put much of the blame for the failure of the banks on the shorts. Better them than blaming a grotesque failure of financial regulation. The SEC in a 3-2 vote, as a part of the financial overhaul did not ban but did put severe restrictions on the shorts. So much for free market capitalism. No sir, don't you believe it, stocks will never go down, invest every spare penny in the market, after all, the SEC has your back. What tech bubble, what Ponzi schemes, what derivative instruments, betting on stocks going down, outlaw it.

OMG! The SEC in early 2011 adopted a rule that demands that every three years corporations take a vote of their shareholders on the executive pay packages. The SEC finally listens to the rage on Main Street, that the same folk who drove their companies into bankruptcy or needed billion dollar bail-outs to stay afloat, maybe should let their shareholders have a say in what they get paid. Not so fast buckaroo, yes they did put in place that regulation but as with most other regulations it is just a charade. The companies indeed must take this vote but the rule says the result is nonbinding. I am truly truly not making this up. I am sure many politicians will in speeches and campaign ads use the fact that they put in place a law giving shareholders a say in executive pay—you betcha.

How can these things happen you may ask? Well this is how, just ask a Mr. Aguirre who once worked as an enforcement lawyer at the SEC. He thought he had discovered a case of insider trading involving a major hedge fund, Pequot Capital Management. As part of his investigation, in 2005 he sought permission from the higher-ups at the SEC to interview one of the gods of Wall Street who later became CEO of Morgan Stanley. Permission denied. Soon after his attempts to go after what he thought was a slam-dunk insider trading case, he was fired. In June of 2010 the SEC paid Mr. Aguirre $750,000 for wrongful termination. In fact, the founder of Pequod eventually paid $28 million for insider trading.

Gosh, recall the Stanford Case in Texas, when the SEC was hit between the eyes with allegations of a Ponzi scheme and their own investigations concluded it was true. Well that was 1997-2003 when it was quashed by SEC higher-ups. Hmm, were there any Texans involved in the government during that time? Stanford made millions in campaign contributions both locally and federally. Let's hear a big round of applause for the SEC.

As for other disputes where Main Street gets taken advantage of by those of far greater power, financial resources, and legal expertise, Washington has given the Main Street investor the opportunity to strike back through arbitration. A well-respected Wall Street Journal columnist, in a December 12, 2010 column described a woman's experience in arbitration. Now after having read this far along in this book, do you really believe this is a straight deal?

In his column, Mr. Zweig states: "For many investors, Finra (Financial Industry Regulatory Authority) arbitration seems to resemble a medical-malpractice case heard in a court run by the American Medical Association, with a jury made up partly of doctors. In describing the woman's trial and tribulations, Zweig writes, "Ms. Matser says she worked on her case for much of the past four years. 'I lived on less than $16 a day, for my food, my cat's food, all my expenses.' Ms. Matser says. 'If it weren't for the 99 cent store. I don't know what I could have done.' Bravo for Ms. Matser, an American hero, she won $20,383.60. She also developed shingles due to the stress." Isn't anything that Washington does real, or is everything truly just a charade?

So the next time a politician announces to the world that they have put this or that wonderful thing in this or that bill just approved by Congress, just remember what arbitration is really like, the ability of shareholders to vote on executive pay that is not binding, and what happened to the Volker rule in between the time it was proposed and actual put in the fine print of legislations. Ugh!

Just this sequence of politicians touting their horn and then when it came time for writing the bill very little has changed is also true of the highly touted new "consumer-friendly" rules governing credit cards. In 2009 Congress passed the Credit Card Accountability Responsibility and Disclosure Act of 2009. The main focus of the act is to protect the consumer from egregious fees for minor offenses, to make sure the consumer is fully aware of what the offenses are that trigger fees, and to insure timely notification when new offenses and fees are put in place.

Sure you may rest easy, this time maybe the mouse has a defense in place for the cat, thanks to the mouse's supposed protector, Washington. Yeah right, as described by an economist at the Federal Reserve Bank of Chicago, "Card companies are figuring out how to replace old fees with new ones. It's a race between regulators writing ever-more-complex laws and credit-card companies setting up ever-more complex fees." How right he is. Guess who will win? Ghee, you think maybe it's the folks who pay the reelection bills.

According to a Pew study, between July 2009 and March 2010, the median annual credit card fee increased 18% and the median cash-advance and balance-transfer fees jumped 33%. Just how bizarre can all this get? A bank called First Premier has a program where it issues cards to people with poor credit, in this case cards with a limit of $250. However, they tack on a processing fee of $95.00. The cat and mouse of it is that the fee is tacked on before the card is even used. So if the card holder goes out and makes a first ever charge of $200, it triggers overdraft related fees based on a $45.00 overdraft. As reported in the media, when interviewed about this case, the president of the bank said the new

Federal rules only apply to fees charged after the account is opened. The cat wins again.

The cat just keeps on winning. The rules that kept the "boiler room" stockbrokers, the telemarketers of Wall Street, from hyping junk to the average investors are being washed away by Congress. It is setting up a platform for con artists to start a company, own the majority of the stock, then fire up a public relations blitz for the newest thing from a cure for Alzheimers to social networking and have legions of phone bank workers selling stock to the public. Of course the stock the average Main Streeter will be buying at $10.00 per share, "a chance to get in on the ground floor before this thing takes off," is the stock bought for pennies by the folks who started the company.

Why, why is it this way that Main Street always gets screwed? Surely there must be some folks in Washington up to do battle with the giant cat on Wall Street or in the corporations offices. The answer may really not be all that complicated. In fact it is the ultimate example of a mutuality of self-interest between Wall Street, the media, and Washington that the answer is not that well displayed in public. Just ask Ross Perot.

It is so well disguised that it is talked about freely in the media in the context of third world countries that are kept mired in their misery because of graft, bribery, and corruption in the economies and government but never spoken of in the same sentence as is Washington. In fact, Washington is no different than any of the others. In fact, graft, bribery, and corruption are so rampant, so potent a force, so sophisticated, and so ingrained in how Washington works that it has been institutionalized with its own sanitized name, LOBBYING.

Yes, that is why Main Street does not stand a chance and will never stand a chance unless the system is changed. The politicians of Washington hold hearings that are really no more than theater. In the case of a catastrophe, the Senate puts on its play, the House of Representatives puts on its own play and the relevant Congressional committee that is supposed to be overseeing the industry that caused the catastrophe puts on its own play. Each play is about the same subject, the same characters are interviewed, the same events rehashed, all simply to put on a play for the audience on Main Street. Regulations are proposed and a second round of soliloquies is given over the media for the benefit of the voters on Main Street.

The regulations are a sham, a charade to keep Main Street quiet. The final language in the regulations is not finished until months and even years after all the dramas unfold. It is this final language put in place unknown to Main Street that creates the back doors and qualifies the what, when, and were of how these regulations can be applied. Why is it done this way, because the corporations subject to these regulations have these politicians in their pockets. Hundreds of millions of dollars are needed to put on an effective campaign for office. The money is spent on creating TV ads, buying network time, and holding the focus groups to test this or that position on this or that issue with the voter and then to test the effectiveness of the ads.

From where does this money come? Not from the individuals on Main Street. No, the vast bulk of this money comes from corporations, millions of dollars at a time. The main corporate sponsors are the investment banks on Wall Street. Without their money, what we know of as todays political campaign would simply not exist. It is the lobbyists who act as the transfer agent between the money in the corporate pocket and Washington. You give a large enough sum of money and you own the politician. There is a direct correlation between the amount of money given by a corporation and the specific committee a politician is on. If they are on a committee that regulates a company's industry, then that is where the money goes.

At the top of the investment banker's concern list is the derivative markets. Who cares that it destroyed the U.S. banking systems and its economy. Derivatives were the major contributor to their profits. This is an amazingly peculiar world. Many of you will recognize the name of Barney Frank a democrat from Massachusetts who is first-up when it comes to investment banking bashing and to get the label of "socialist" from the talking heads of extremist talk-shows. The head lobbyist of Goldman Sachs in Washington is one of Frank's former assistants. A prominent member of the lobbying team is Richard Gephardt, formerly one of the leading Democrats in the House.

Damn, this whole thing really sucks. A revolving door from Congress to lobbying for Goldman Sachs and from Goldman Sachs to Treasury Secretary: Hank Paulson with Busch and before him Richard Rubin with Clinton. How could anyone ever expect the right thing for the country to get done?

As initially written, the new bill to overhaul the regulation of the investment banking industry had put many new disclosures on derivative trading, effectively moving them out of the shadows and into the public arena for all to see who is doing what to whom. Most importantly, as mentioned previously, the new regulations prohibit the investment banks from investing their own money (actually their depositors) in a risky class of derivatives. Once the lobbyists got their teeth into it, Congress watered it down substantially. Melissa Bean, a Democratic representative from Illinois, after hearing the changes that had been made to the bill due to lobbyist pressure prior to a final vote, was furious and is quoted as saying, "Are you flippin' kidding me."

Even the kind old grandfatherly sage from the corn fields of Nebraska, Warren Buffett put his money on the table when it came down to derivatives. This legislation writing is sometimes pretty darn focused, especially when an influential Senator such as Ben Nelson from Nebraska has a say in things. It seems that Mr. Buffet's investment group, Berkshire Hathaway needed some help on the particular type of derivatives in Berkshire's portfolio. Since Berkshire is Mr. Nelson's largest campaign contributor, surprise surprise who threw his considerable influence to getting the bill changed so Berkshire's derivatives would be unaffected.

During the height of the financial meltdown something that those of you who listen to the financial news channels seemingly heard discussed hourly, the term "mark to market." Here is what that is all about. At the time the meltdown occurred, the accounting standards required that companies valued the assets and loans on their financial statements at their fair market value as of the date of the financial statements. This is no different than when you go to the bank for a loan. They want to know how much your assets are currently worth, your house for example, or the investments that you hold. At the time the housing market started to soften, if banks had to list their mortgages at their value right then and there, their balance sheets began to take on a terrible smell.

Some folks, Larry Kudlow of CNBC in particular, began to pound the table that this was unfair. Instead of marking assets to their current market value they were contending that since the downturn in housing was only a temporary glitch, it would be more fair to value these and other assets at what was paid for them or what they would be worth some time in the future when the current troubles had disappeared. Temporary glitch in the housing market, have they no shame?

Imagine if you went to a bank for a loan and owned shares of a Company X for which you paid $100 per share but was currently valued at $30 per share and tried to make the case to the loan officer that he should still count them as worth $100 per share. That is what the major financial institutions were asking from the legislature. Current fair market value should no longer matter, but some other measure of value such as what they had been worth or might be worth in the future is the right value to use. In fact that is what the accounting rules makers did. Bowing to a lobbying campaign from the banks, they changed the rules. So when you see assets valued on a bank's financial statements, that value has nothing to do with what the asset is currently actually worth, but will represent only what the bank paid for it, even if it were during the biggest bubble in that asset classes history. Confidence inspiring isn't it.

And now for another quicky list, this one of recent lobbying efforts and what they produced, even in regards to tanning salons.

As a part of the Congressional theater of hearings following the financial crisis, one of the plays was about consumer protections. The previously discussed changes to credit card fees was one of the acts in that drama. Another act had to do with consumer loans. Although some car dealers are still family enterprises, most dealers across the country are franchise-like operations of major companies, owning tens, even hundreds of dealerships. They have a big lobbying presence. Guess who was in the original bill about what had to be disclosed in the loan application and after intense lobbying their loans are no longer a part of the bill. Yes sir, loans made by car dealers, exempt from the new regulations, you know, the trivial stuff such as full disclosure of penalties, interest rate adjustments, etc.

In the old days, rural areas were just that, rural with their population scattered across long distances and not exactly known for their affluence. To help provide phone service to these folks, the federal government had subsidies available to phone companies to motivate them to put in the poles and string the lines so all could have phone service. These days, many of these areas are now the centers for ski resorts, hobbyist ranchers, and are known as some of the most affluent areas in the country, or even just solidly well–off and populated by those with second homes. The Federal Communication Commission proposed to phase out this subsidy of $2.9 billion over the next few years. The phone companies put their lobbyists on the case and it is now dead. Yours truly has a cabin in a reasonably prosperous area in the Rocky Mountains on the border of a National Park—you get the picture, and a smile came to my face when I had my phone put in and as part of the paper work received a notice of the federal phone subsidy on my line.

A UPS jumbo jet crashed and both pilots were killed because of a fire in the cargo hold. It turns out that many crates of lithium ion batteries were the cause of the fire. Everyone knows of the danger of their spontaneously overheating and catching fire. Yet they are not categorized as hazardous materials for special treatment during aircraft cargo transportation. There has been an effort to get legislation through Congress requiring these batteries be treated in this manner yet an intense lobbying effort by the battery manufacturers, cell phone makers, and their trade association has stalled the legislation.

As we all know, cars are now controlled by computers. The local mechanic must now educate himself into the lingo of computers much less invest in electronic diagnostic equipment. Similarly, the generic individual part that could be replaced is rarely the source of trouble, instead all is electronically integrated and a small part can rarely be replaced, instead the central "brain" is tossed out and another put in. These types of diagnostic procedures and programming of new complex electronics cannot be done by a private shop without a great deal of manufacturer information. The car dealers are happy as many local mechanics find themselves having to refer their customers to the dealer for repairs. Recent studies have shown that many local mechanics actually take the car themselves to the appropriate dealer rather than lose the customer for those maintenance issues that they can handle.

Some local mechanics have tried to outfit themselves both intellectually and equipment wise to be able to handle these computerized vehicles. To do that however requires the manufacturers to release the various computer codes. Citing this or that reason the manufacturers are loathe to do it. Recent attempts at legislation by lobbyists representing independent repair shops has been beaten back by the larger club of the lobbyists for the automobile manufacturers and car dealers.

Sometimes it is a heavyweight match, big clubs bashing away at each other. Such is the case in the multi-year struggle over an airborne laser weapon. The pentagon has tried and tried to get the program itself shot down, saying, "There's nobody in uniform that I know who believes that this is a workable concept." So far, $5.2 billion has been spent on the project, echoes of government computer programs should be ringing in your head. The history of this thing reduces one to tears. Intense lobbying by defense contractors to their congressional representatives have kept this thing alive. It continues to this day.

It is a complex issue how far should the government go in regulating an individual's private behavior. For example, Congress wanted to put a tax on the most sugared-up of the soft-drinks. The statistics on consumption of these beverages and health problems such as diabetes are pretty convincing and they do represent the single largest intake of sugar in people's diets. Of course the correlation between representatives who went the extra mile to see to it that this legislation never saw the light of day and contributions through lobbyists from the soft-drink industry was 100%.

Only two more of these to go. First a silly one, tanning salons, unless of course you are a lone entrepreneur who has put their whole life savings into a single store. Almost as important as the diabetes epidemic and trying to reduce the intake of sugary drinks, but maybe not quite as far reaching, was a similar effort to tax tanning salons because of their risk to our health from skin cancer. It turns out that some of the megafitness center chains also have tanning salons. Their lobbyists managed to get this defeated, at least as far as the chains go. However, the local onesy or twosy tanning salon owners will have to add a 10% fee to their prices and then send the government that tax involving the usual unintelligible language and myriad forms.

Of a larger concern are the lawyers, especially those who spend their days in court suing people in business such as doctors and corporations. As a professional association, lawyers have given more donations to federal candidates than any other profession. One would think for example that a necessary aspect of any health care bill is to try to attack the costs associated with "defensive" medicine, whether it is the cost of malpractice insurance, the added tests just to build a legal defense just in case of a malpractice suit, or the size of awards. No surprise that health care overhaul included none of this. A legendary plaintiff's lawyer once responded to a newspaper quote that claimed plaintiffs lobbyists were "all but running the senate," when he said: "I really strongly disagree with that. Particularly the 'all but'."

What really seals the lid on the nastiness of how lobbyists really determine the regulations under which the rest of us lead our lives is the documented fact that many times, the lobbyists actually write the language of the regulations. As described by the CEO of Google, Eric Schmidt, "The average American doesn't realize how much of the laws are written by lobbyists…It's shocking how the system works."

An egregious specific example is described by Thom Hartmann in his fascinating book, *How Corporations Became "People" and How You Can Fight Back*, on p. 195: "And in one of the most notorious cases, a fellow who worked for the legal group of a multinational chemical and agricultural-products company quit his job and went to work with the FDA, where he wrote a regulation that allowed that company's product into the food supply; quit the FDA and went to work for the USDA, where he participated in writing regulations eliminating labeling of the product for consumers, and then quit the USDA and went back to work for the law firm representing the multinational." Another example, Senator Lisa Murkowski of Alaska first put effort into getting a specific piece of EPA regulation taken out of the executive branch and put into the legislative branch. She then allowed two lobbyists for large energy companies who had once actually previously worked for the EPA to write the specific rules that regulated regulations of emissions of greenhouse gases.

It should come as no surprise that an organization such as the American Legislative Exchange Council (ALEC) exists. It is funded by major corporations and holds an annual meeting at a resort location where state legislators, lobbyists, and corporate execs can all come together and get to know each other. Much of what goes on is centered around putting the right lobbyist together with the right corporation and then the lobbyists buttonhole the right state representatives. During the course of these meetings they draft outlines of legislation that will then be put into final form by the lobbyists prior to their being submitted for approval. So it is not just a few times that lobbyists actually write regulatory legislation, there is even a formal mechanism for getting all this done.

California is at the top of the list for institutionalizing the process. The term "sponsored" bill means written by a lobbyist and accounts for 42% of those introduced in the Assembly and 33% of those in the Senate. In the 2007-2008 session, only one representative Tom McClintock, a republican from Thousand Oaks (suburb of LA) refused to introduce a sponsored bill. From the plumbing manufacturers association writing legislation that allows them to do the tests to show faucets are lead free to a local billionaire doing away with a challenge to his plans for a new football stadium, that is how it works in California.

About 50 years ago, a professor at a college course in American History that focused on "social institutions" once told his students, me being one of them, that corruption got worse the smaller the body being governed. He claimed that in the worst case, small towns, everyone knew and might even be related to everyone so all questionable if not actually illegal deals could be kept quiet. The larger the governmental organization the greater the chance that someone was keeping an eye on what was going on. I think he was right. I have had only one experience to be involved in a legal challenge to a government, my small city of about 18,000 people. Amazingly we won, we fought city hall and won. I was stunned by what I learned. They had been breaking the law for years, just no one noticed.

It is hard to find humor in such a sad situation, really tragic, I mean how our country is run. However, I did laugh when several times in reading articles about lobbyists writing bills, one thing I started to wonder about, so did some of the writers of these articles: If the legislator knows so little about the subject, how do they respond to questions when on the floor of the legislature. In some cases, even during the open legislative session, the representatives would actually turn to the lobbyist and have them answer the question. If the representative I guess had some sense of shame, they would set up hand signals for the lobbyist to let them know which questions were okay to answer and which ones to dodge.

So if the kinds of things described above that involved citizens handing money over to politicians in exchange for favors were reported from Iraq, Afghanistan, or Nigeria, surely the words bribe, graft, and corruption would be included. Not us however, we are squeaky neat and clean. Let the people's voices be heard through the ballot box. No sir, not us. In fact, bribery, graft and corruption are indeed just business as usual in this country. It is so much a part of our governmental system that we have even adopted a much nicer sounding term, "lobbyist." In describing the situation in California, a former Assemblyman, Joe Canciamilla said, "It's like being in a Middle Eastern bazaar." It reminded him of walking through the marketplace with hawkers shouting out at him trying to get him to sign up for their bill and the bill from the guy two stalls down.

Please, one last comment, do not think this is anything new to the United States. The term "lobbyist" came to be used because President Grant (served 1869-1877) would end his day having a drink in the lobby of the Willard hotel. Those who wanted special favors from the government would join him for a drink and plead their case. Really no different where today in this or that third world country, the warlord holds court and villagers comes to plead their case and ask for his help.

That is how our country gets run, at least in those ways that Congress can control. In terms of our daily lives, from automotive repairs to the banks and even tanning salons, the rules and regulations that they write set the ground rules for most of our activities. From what I have found in my investigations and have put in this book, it appears that without a doubt, our best interests are absolutely not being represented by the people we elect to do just that, represent us. Instead they are truly owned by the corporations that donate to them millions of dollars for their reelection campaigns, to once again quote Alan Simpson, who if anyone has been there and done that qualifies to be the judge, "The God here in Washington is the God of reelection." That our politicians represent the people is the grand charade of this country.

As a Summary of all that is in this chapter, and as a "don't take my word for it," is an interview between Anderson Cooper, and Eliot Spitzer, former Governor of New York and Attorney General of the State of New York along with Matt Taibbi, financial writer for Rolling Stone Magazine that happened on April 14, 2011 on Mr. Coopers "360" show. Here is an excerpt of that interview (underlines inserted by J.G.):

Cooper: So two-and-a-half years since Wall Street brought the economy to death's door and guess how many senior Wall Street executives have gone to jail? Well, the answer is none. None has even been charged with a crime. ...Well, Michigan Democrat Carl Levin says Blankfein and other Goldman executives who testified before the Senate subcommittee lied and should be referred to the Justice Department for possible criminal prosecution. (what is then described is testimony from Goldman execs demonstrating the previously described selling to clients mortgage back derivatives that Goldman new were garbage and bet on their loss of value, J.G.).

Cooper: Joining me now, CNN colleague Eliot Spitzer ...and Matt Taibbi. Eliot, do you believe Goldman broke the law and lied?

Spitzer: Yes, I do. And I know people are going to say how can you say that as a lawyer? I have read this report. It confirms our worst fears about double dealing, lying. Goldman Sachs has zero, none, nada credibility in my book. They have scammed the American public, lied to Senator Levin's committee.

Cooper: But is there a smoking gun in this? Is there really clear evidence of a crime?

Taibbi: I think so. I think the only reason that this is even controversial, that we're even asking the question should they be in jail is because this is the financial services industry and this stuff is complicated. If this was any other industry. If this was a car dealership for instance, basically what happened was imagine you're a Ford dealership and you get a whole inventory full of Broncos that have defective brakes in them and you decide not only to sell them, but to give bonuses to your salespeople to sell these defective products. And then you go out and sell life insurance policies on the drivers of the cars that you sold. That's exactly what happened here in a nutshell. They had defective merchandise. They had these terrible mortgaged-backed deals that they knew were going to blow up and they unloaded it as fast as they could on their clients while they bet against them.

Spitzer: When I was AG (Attorney General) back in 2002 and 2003, and went after these companies for the same thing, lying to the public about the quality of the stocks, they said, we get it, we have learned. Bunk. They did the same thing year after year after year because they saw a penny they could pick up. Outrageous.

Cooper: Matt, two-and-a-half years after this. No one has gone to jail; no one has even been prosecuted on charges.

Taibbi: Well, but they have sure gone after Barry Bonds and Roger Clemens.

Cooper: Those are easy pickings and—

Taibbi: I mean the entire history of this whole era clearly demonstrates that the Justice Department has no appetite whatsoever for taking any cases against any of these Wall Street executives, even when they have very good evidence and very strong cases. The failure of regulators is just extraordinary. You have documented this incredibly well in "Rolling Stone."

Taibbi: Sure. Absolutely. The regulators were completely asleep at the wheel and in some cases they were tremendously understaffed and didn't have the resources or the wherewithal to take on these jobs. A great example being AIG, whose regulator was the Office of Thrift Supervision; a saving and loan regulator was regulating the world's largest insurance company and they had one insurance expert on their entire staff.

Spitzer: Although I will tell you an interesting story. We went after AIG, got them to get—the biggest settlement in history. Their accounting was a fraudulent scam, top to bottom. I was called and told back off by the US attorney in the Southern District, we will take care of it. They never did, never did it. Tim Geithner, treasury secretary, apparently reported in today's "New York Times" was calling people saying don't bring cases, it will unsettle the markets, so they let these guys go free. Meanwhile, he signed off on $12.9 billion to Goldman to cover a bad bet they made.

Cooper: Do you think politicians are scared of going against Goldman Sachs?

Taibbi: Absolutely. Goldman Sachs was the number one private campaign contributor to Barack Obama's presidential election campaign. It's one of the single biggest campaign contributions to both parties in Congress. So it's a rare event when, you know, an establishment politician like Carl Levin decides to basically open up a shooting war against a company like this. It just doesn't happen very much because the consequences for these politicians are so severe, and that's one of the reasons why they have lasted so long.

Spitzer: Anderson, before I sued, went after Merrill Lynch, which was the first case we filed many years back, I was told by their lawyers—this is a direct quote—"Be careful, we have powerful friends."

Cooper: Do you think the Justice Department will prosecute?

Spitzer: If they don't, shame on them. If they don't, the Attorney General should resign if he can't bring this case.

Cooper: You think it's an easy case?

Spitzer: Anderson, it is so outrageous to me, the deeper we dig and the more fundamental the violations we see that these investment banks hiding behind the patina that they would take care of the public interest in regulating the stock market, time and time again scammed and deceived on our tax dollars are paying those grotesque bonuses that we still read about.

Cooper: I remember there was a quote in one of the articles you wrote, Matt, and I don't want to quote it word for word, because it was quite, well, descriptive, but it was somebody saying that basically if one of these guys was sent to prison, that would stop these shenanigans from happening again, that that's really all it would take. If somebody was held accountable, it would have a cooling effect.

Taibbi: <u>Yes absolutely, I talked to one guy who was a former SEC investigator and he said basically if you start sending Lloyd Blankfein or one of those guys, put one of those guys in a real maximum security prison for six months, this whole thing would be over very quickly. The whole situation would be cleared up. But the problem is, there's no incentive for these guys to change their behaviors, because they never, ever get punished. Not only do they not get punished. They get a bailout.</u>

    I wonder how the guys and gals on Wall Street would behave if they knew that in mid-2011, a 2009 conviction in China of a well-respected woman entrepreneur, one of the wealthiest women in China, on charges of "illegal fundraising" was upheld by their courts. Her sentence is execution. Compared with what Lloyd Blankfein and his fellow lords on Wall Street pulled off that lost millions of Americans their life savings, jobs, and houses, what this woman did was like jaywalking. A bailout, they got a bailout with the money of these very same taxpayers. The bailouts allowed them to continue to receive their tens of millions of dollars in pay and bonuses. Yet, and this is just another one of those if I did not read it and confirm it I would not believe it facts, a Goldman Sachs computer programmer went to work for another investment bank and took with him some of Goldman's computer code for something called "high frequency trading," and in 2011 got eight years in jail, for stealing computer code relevant to a very small part of the investment banking business. In unbelievable contrast, Lloyd Blankfein and others like him destroyed the financial system, wiped out peoples savings, cost millions their jobs, and nothing happened to them other than record setting bonuses a year later.

XI. THE GRAND CHARADE:

U.S. IS #1

World War II ended with a bang that decisively catapulted the United States into the position of the worlds leading country. Our country's "military industrial complex" produced an atomic bomb before either Germany or Japan. History will I am sure do nothing but applaud the research and development as well as the general industrial and organizational capabilities of the United States for accomplishing this feat. The world would have gone on to be a very different place, harshly different if it were not for the United States.

Russia, at the end of World War II would certainly like to have shared the lead of the world but was in second place. However, a few years later they too created a very big bang, possibly some spies on the U.S.'s nuclear secrets played a role, but even if that were not true it would have happened a few years later anyway. Russia's accomplishment was of no value for any war currently in progress other than the cold one, but certainly gave notice that anyone thinking of starting another hot one had better not forget Russia. The next big step-up in Russia's world image was the launching in 1957 of the first vehicle into outer space. Sputnik let everyone know that they could not just counterpunch the United States in technological achievement but beat us to the punch as well.

As the decades went on, the U.S. and Russia typically played out their quest for world dominance through nonnuclear spats in other countries. Eventually, through some skilled political maneuverings, supported by the superior economic and technological strength of the United States, the old USSR threw their hands up and said in the words of one of the greatest fighters of all time, Roberto Duran, *"no mas."* Several of its member countries left the Soviet Union and for the most part, communism was abandoned as their only economic system and each one of the countries marched off into the future with this or that blend of economic systems.

Japan after World War II ceased to be a concern as a military threat. In the subsequent years they went about making tremendous gains in their own industrial base and economy. In some areas they were certainly at the cutting edge of technology, and combined with what back then was a low-cost labor force, made some tremendous economic strides. It was these strides that eventually led them to bring the vaunted automotive industry of the United States to its knees.

After WWII, for the better part of forty years, the United States was certainly the dominant super-power of the world. On the two counts of economic size and strength as well as technological prowess we were certainly number one. Occasionally Russia would do this or that which got everyone's attention. However, as came out once the Soviet Union fell apart, it seems that the United States and the rest of the world had seriously overestimated Russia's capabilities in both its technological and economic strength. When push finally came to shove they waved the white flag and the Berlin wall came tumbling down along with communism as a viable stand-alone economic system. Cynics might point out that the overestimate of Russia's military might was a charade played by the U.S. military suppliers to keep those contracts coming.

Although the above is a very brief account of the world since World War II, what should be clear is that as goes a country's technological prowess, so goes its economy and its status amongst the other countries of the world. In fact, even if one looks back further in history, in general, technology has always been what fueled the United States' ability to control its destiny.

When the first settlers landed at Plymouth Rock, and then over the next two centuries began their expansion to the north, south, and west of the original colonies, they did so through superior technologies. In this case applying these technologies to weapons. Our ability to kill our enemies far surpassed the ability of them, usually indigenous peoples to kill us. Once this was made perfectly clear, they had no choice but give up their lands and sign treaties or they would be killed off before they could kill us off. Eventually the United States expanded just about all the way to the Pacific, but there were still some lands held by Mexico. So same deal, give us Texas, New Mexico, Arizona, and California or we will kill all of you before you can kill all of us.

I appreciate this may seem a somewhat eccentric view of the world, but as far as the bottom line, this is in fact what happened. I view it with some humor that Mexico is now in the process of reclaiming these areas through making love not war and producing lots of babies. As Kurt Vonnegut was so fond of saying about the funkiness of how things sometimes turn out, "so it goes."

Our ability to claim our destiny as a country in the land of the Americas as well as keeping our interests protected throughout the world, up until recently, has been about our ability to win wars through our superior technology transferred into weapons. And why did we have that ability, because of our vast and substantive economy. And why was our economic engine the clear and above all number 1, because of our technology. Kind of like chicken or egg, but also a true case of synergy. The armaments that slayed the real Americans and Mexicans, the armaments that won us World War II, and the armaments that did-in vast numbers of Iraqis with an amazingly low ratio of U.S. casualties were all about our technology. In the incredibly rugged and mountainous terrain of Afghanistan that significantly neuters our technology we are being held to a stalemate by folks who ride around on donkeys and motorbikes.

The lesson should be clear as a bell, as goes a country's world status as a technology leader, so goes its economy and as goes its economy so goes its ability to make the rest of the world bend to its wishes—its desires for certain outcomes in far-off and distant lands to turn out the way we wish. The true measure of who is number one.

Right now, at the end of 2011, I am sure it is not just me that is concerned about the United States and its position in the world. We seem to be losing our ability to control events outside our border, and sadly, due to governmental paralysis via an infection of partisanship, even events within our own borders. The charade that this chapter is about, is the feeling that I do get however, that an awful lot of people in this country believe, at least they talk and act that way, that the U.S. is still number one. We are not, and the situation is getting worse by the year. The following pages give the facts to document just how far we have fallen.

Competitors are there right now, capable of developing their own technologies as well as utilizing the technologies stolen from others to create economies that can fund the military resources to keep others, including the United States, from getting in their way,

With the rise of these competitors, it is likely that number one status will be achieved by no one. There will in the future be at least two and probably even more countries of equal strength both technologically and economically to keep each other from the ability of unilaterally imposing their will on the others. At no time therefore is it more imperative that the United States keeps its technological and economic engine from sputtering. It is now true more than ever that economic strength comes from technological strength.

Yes it is true, but there is a little more to the story than just being a technological innovator. The rest of the story is what you do with that technology and how you convert it into economic prosperity and a better quality of life for the citizens of the United States. Nothing demonstrates that all is not well in this conversion process from technological innovation into a strong economy better than the state of health care in our country.

During the deficit ceiling debate in the summer of 2011, I was just stunned to hear politician after politician calling the health care system of the United States the number one in the world. A charade, the fact is that we spend about twice as much as any other developed country on our health care and it is darn hard to find just one measure of health care provided to our citizens upon which we rank number one. Fact, a study in 2008 found that 45% of Americans think we are number one in health care. For what it is worth, when only Republicans are polled it is 68%, Democrats 38% and Independents are 40%. In the chapter about controlling health-care costs, a description is given of how the leaders of other developed countries speak of the U.S. health-care system as an abomination and under no circumstance will their country mimic the U.S.

A 2007 report to Congress by the Congressional Research Service, says that the United States spends $6,102 per person for health care, a figure more than two times the average of the OECD (Organization for Economic and Development Countries) countries. On another measure, our health care expenditures are 15.3% of our economy compared with 8.9% the average for these countries. Switzerland was in second place at 11.5%. What do we get for all this money, a higher than average mortality rate and a shorter than average life expectancy. The only measure upon which the United States was at the top is in waiting times for voluntary hospital procedures but not in waiting time for doctor's appointments. When the study takes out the increase in spending due to an aging population as well as the general economic growth of a country, we are number one in a measure of "excess" health care inflation. This excess is nothing other than a company deciding to raise its price and the willingness of the government or private insurance willing to pay the price.

Don't' kid yourself, we do not, I say not, get more bang for the buck as all the politicians who call us #1 in healthcare would lead you to believe. Some of the bad news from this OECD study, out of 30 countries we rank 24th in deaths from respiratory diseases. Amongst 26 countries that reported on measures of deaths from medical errors, the United States is the third highest. Infant deaths, the same, third highest, only Turkey and Mexico beat us. When how infant mortality is measured is taken into account, comparing apples to apples, eight countries use very similar measures, amongst those eight we have the highest proportion of infant deaths. We spend twice as much for our health care per person yet we rank at best, only eighth in infant mortality. How can that be?

So in spite of our spending ridiculously more than any other country for our health care we are not even close to being number one. The same is true for our educational system, once the envy of the world. The point I wish to make is that since as goes technology so goes our economy and as goes our economy so goes our status in the world. It must be understood that education and the development of technology are one and the same. Therefore there is nothing, not one thing more essential to our maintaining our status as #1 or at least tied for #1 than our educational system.

Technology, the driver of tomorrow's economy is all about science. Cars, airplanes, rockets, pilotless drones, computers, satellite communication, cell phones, and the whole variety of both preventions and cures for disease are the heart and soul of a twenty-first century top-ranked country. A country is doomed to second rank status if it does not have an educational system based upon science that teaches its young people not just about the sciences such as physics, chemistry, and biology, but teaches them how to think scientifically, logically, that will allow for the efficient progress of its financial, service, and social systems as well.

No education then no science. No science then no technology. No technology then no economy. No economy then no military. Boom.

Our future rests with our being able to turn out the young adults who will for a small few be the innovators and developers of not just the technologies but also the companies that based upon these technologies fuel our economic growth. Equally importantly is an educational system that turns out people qualified to work in these companies. People who can interact with technology.

It is something that is not much discussed by politicians but that is right at the heart of one of our unemployment problems. In the 1980s, if a person lost their job working a drill press, not a very big change to learn the skills needed to work a lathe for another company. However, if one lost a job working a drill press in 2011, the chances are that the available openings for running similar metal-working equipment are few and far between. Instead, the openings most probably required some computer skills and familiarity with one or another basic operating systems. To change from running a lathe to running a computer that runs ten lathes at once is a big jump, especially if one had not grown-up interacting with a monitor, mouse, and keyboard.

In spite of the severe unemployment, many job openings go unfilled with employers bemoaning the ability to find technically qualified job applicants. A recent Bureau of Labor Statistics study found three million job openings going unfilled. A study by the Adult Commission on National Literacy shows that 90 million adults have literacy skills that are so bad they could not be provided with postsecondary education or job training. According to a Wells Fargo/Gallup Small Business Index Survey, 42% of businesses could not fill job openings, reporting that it was "hard to find qualified employees for positions available."

The cause for concern, and one of the many fact-based arguments for calling our being #1 a charade are the results comparing our educational system with those of other countries. In head to head comparison of high school students in science, reading, and math, the United States is not even in the top ten. The United States ranks 14th in reading, seventeenth in science, and 25th in math. At the top are Shanghai and Hong Kong, with the rest of the top ten filled with other Asian, Scandinavian, and European countries. In 1995 we were second worldwide in college graduation rates, now we are also not even in the top ten, ranking 13th. If one looks at the percentage of adults, ages 25-34 with the equivalent of an associates degree or higher, the United States ranks 12th in the world, a measure that once upon a time we were in fact number 1.

Just looking within the United States only about 30% of high school graduates could be considered proficient in science and only 3% qualified as ready for advanced courses in college. In looking at the college entrance exams, less than 25% of high school graduates scored high enough to expect they would be able to pass freshman courses in math, English, and science. Twenty-eight percent scored so poorly that they could not be expected to pass even one of these courses. YET WE ARE NUMBER ONE, YES ALL YOU JINGOISTIC BELIEVERS OF WHAT POLITICIANS TELL YOU. WE SPEND MORE PER PUPIL ON EDUCATION THAN ANY OTHER COUNTRY. YET WE ARE OUT OF THE TOP TEN IN RESULTS. WE ARE NUMBER ONE IN OUR ABILITY TO WASTE MONEY ON EDUCATION. WE SPEND MORE THAN ANY OTHER COUNTRY ON HEALTH CARE BUT ARE OUT OF THE TOP TEN IN MOST MEASURES OF OUR CITIZENS HEALTH. WE ARE NUMBER ONE IN OUR ABILITY TO WASTE MONEY ON HEALTH CARE.

Speaking of politicians, there is not one that when running for office does not promise increasing money spent on education along with reforming the system. President Bush made a serious effort to combine making funds available with putting measures in place to test for productivity, the effectiveness of the money being spent. His "No Child Left Behind" program was going to actually demand some accountability if you got federal money to spend. So, what did the educational establishment do, the teachers and principals were the ones doing the cheating to make sure the students produced good test scores. At least in Atlanta that is what they did and could make a pretty good guess that as the old saying goes, "all they did wrong was get caught."

It began a decade ago, allegations that teachers and principals in the Atlanta school system were conspiring to inflate the grades of their students on the standardized tests used to measure performance. In July of 2011, a Governor's report on the matter was announced. Cheating was found to occur in 44 of 56 elementary and middle schools where performance was examined. Evidence sufficient to name the names of 178 teachers and 38 of their principals who were found to have altered answers on tests as a way of inflating the student's performance. There were many more indications of cheating, but the evidence was not thought compelling enough to release names.

The extent of this cheating was grotesque. Teachers stood by and watched as students took the test and would point to the correct answer if the student needed help. Poor performing students were seated next to high-performing students to facilitate cheating. Teachers held what became known as "erasure parties" where they sat and went over every test and erased where the wrong answer-circle was filled in and put a pencil mark in the right circle. During the decade that this went on, the Atlanta public school system received awards for teaching and school administration. Atlanta's superintendent of schools in 2009 received the national Superintendent of the Year award for Atlanta's progress. Oh, and by the way, during her stay she received $600,000 in performance related bonuses. Pennsylvania, New Jersey and Connecticut are now in the beginning stages of their own investigations that are showing similar patterns of cheating. In a competitive world, for limited rewards, once one school system cheats to inflate their scores, others have little choice (see the "Nice Guys Finish Last" section of the "Charadelettes" chapter).

Writing this chapter is painful. In 1966 I was a tourist in Russia at the height of the cold war. Seeing it first-hand changed me profoundly. Ugh. When my plane landed in Helsinki, just walking off the plane and seeing the expression on people's faces brought a certain sigh of relief. It was not just the blond babes, but smiles, lots of content people just walking here and there with a pleasant expression on their face.

I am a huge fan of the United States. It is the individual that is important. No country allows for an individual to make of his life what he wants more so than does the United States. A trip to Russia was all it took to cement those feelings about the U.S.A. My own story with its ups and downs, the experiences I have had while chasing the gold-ring in three different careers, could only have happened here. As one commentator once said, "in the United States you get to become what you ought to." Everyday you get to wake up in a well ordered society, where relatively speaking laws are obeyed and a person can plot out a long term plan to achieve their goals and if they have it within them to perform, they stand a good chance of getting there or at least very close. Regardless of from where you start, great advancement in whatever way you want is possible.

In that sense having to chronicle the demise of this country is painful. Never was the often repeated comment in these chapters about how so many topics of this book have turned out to be the gifts that keep on giving been more true than in this chapter. The evening of just finishing this chapter up to the point about the Atlanta school system, came the announcement of the downgrade of the U.S. credit rating. It is unimaginable that this could happen. Yes, Standard and Poors is the same credit agency that gave AAA ratings to all those bottom of the barrel mortgage backed securities, missed Lehman Brothers and AIGs demise, and made a 2 trillion dollar mistake in its calculation of the U.S.'s finances (by the way it said it was not "material," see the chapter on Wall Street for a discussion of that word). Nevertheless, how discouraging and further proof that we ain't what some still think we are and most importantly what the b.s.ing politicians tell us we are.

In a global economy, where many country's economies are in part vulnerable to their interactions with other countries, disputes will happen. Whether these disputes are about access to each other's natural resources, import and export tariffs, territorial disputes over resources under the ocean, or the host of other such conflicts, serious conflicts inevitably occur. A countries clout in settling these disputes is hopefully related just to their economic strength that allows them to drive a favorable bargain, but in the worst case can finally come down to their military strength . As the United States economy has begun to falter, our clout to settle such purely economic disputes has certainly dwindled. Our unique military power is still clearly #1. However, the size and strength of a country's military is simply a matter of their ability to spend money to pay the troops and buy the weapons. It was thus that the Soviet Union threw in the towel in response to their economic stumbles precluding them from competing with us in the arm race.

In this context, there are four countries, known as the BRIC, Brazil, Russia, India, and China that are considered the four major countries on the fast track to economic top-tier status and thus inevitably a similar military status if they choose to spend the money to become so. Realistically, the corruption and other internal disorganizations of Brazil, Russia, and India make their number one status well over the horizon if they ever make it. However, China is in some ways there already, and in all the others that make a country a threat both economically and militarily, they are near the finish line and on the fast-track to reaching the goal.

China released a long-term economic plan, "National Medium-and Long-Term Plan for the Development of Science and Technology (2006-2020)" with a single focus, innovation, that intends to make China a global leader in technology, both innovation and manufacturing by 2020. To quote a few scary lines, "enhancing original innovation through co-innovation and re-innovation based on the assimilation of imported technologies." As to the "co-innovation and re-innovation" parts it is now standard Chinese policy that for any company asking for rights to import its products into China or establish a manufacturing facility, a major *quid pro quo* is an agreement to disclose the technology within the product to China's engineers.

They are very serious; zealous might be a better word. In just the past decade, China has grown from the world's seventh largest economy to being 3rd in 2007 and passed Japan for number two spot in 2010. In terms of the number one spot, from the humorous such as beer production, to the more industrially critical such as coal, and to the cutting edge of technology, wind power, the United States has already lost its number one spot to China.

Sergio Marchionne the head of Fiat which now also owns Chrysler, has sounded the alarm about the automobile industry. In referring to China, he describes their current automotive production, "produce almost entirely for the enormous domestic market, but their future plans for the export market are significant…[Western auto makers] cannot afford to be unprepared for the ascent of China…need to continue to work to make our industrial base more competitive, because the day of reckoning is inevitably coming."

As the Johnny Cash song says, "I hear that train a comin'." It is China "acomin' round the bend." The threat to the United States from China is not just economic where they win the global battle for customers and thus shrink our economy, but perhaps even more serious is the implications upon the military balance of power for their someday passing us as the #1 economic empire. Whoever wins the economic war also wins the military war. A country must have a large GDP to support spending on the military. As grows China's economy so will it grow a world-class, "we are number 1," military. It launched its first ever aircraft carrier in August of 2011.

Even though the guns have yet to fire, the war is definitely on. The war today with China is another version of a cold war. It is on and going heavy in the marketplace for what are called rare-earth minerals. They are called "rare" not because there is not much of them across the globe, but because from a mining standpoint, a lot of earth must be mined for a small quantity to be extracted. They are a crucial part of high-tech components, from the rechargeable batteries in hybrid cars to missile guidance systems. If it is a high tech electronic device, it contains a rare earth mineral crucial to its function.

Currently China holds 97% of the world's stockpile of rare-earth minerals used in manufacturing. For the first time, China is now considering these minerals as falling under their export quota regulations. They have used such market manipulation in the past. Several countries including the United States use to mine these elements, but in the 1990s China launched a trade war and by flooding the markets with product, they lowered the price and caused most other countries to close their operations. Only Japan and South Korea have any stockpiles of these minerals

Congress in their own magical way of doing things has recognized our vulnerability to China's control of this market yet right now there are two competing bills about what to do about it. One recognizes the situation as an emergency and wants to begin building a strategic reserve, just as we have with oil. The other bill wants a study of the situation before an action is taken. What planet are these people living on? Is the Yankees versus the Red Sox mentality the only concern or do these people have the country's best interest in mind?

Our first line of military defense against China is the island nation of Taiwan, a heavily militarized island thanks to weapons sales from us at very favorable terms. In its most recent annual report to Congress on Chinese military capabilities, the Pentagon focused on Chinas growth in ballistic and cruise missile capabilities that would be used primarily against Taiwan. This growing shift in the balance of power between China and Taiwan led to the Obama administration approving in 2010 a $6.4 billion sale of arms to Taiwan. In any meeting between the two country's diplomats, the rapid growth of China's military and the U.S's arming of Taiwan are always somewhere on the agenda. It is almost as though both China and the U.S. view the inevitable, a clash that must someday come whether it is for access to natural resources, dominance of the

Pacific countries, or the other list of problems that history has shown us will inevitably occur between two economic competitors.

In the initial stages of preparing an outline for this book, I certainly felt that the United States education system and some other issues related to our rearing of the next generation had to be a subject. I initially intended the variety of charades involving our educational system and "theories" of modern child rearing deserved a chapter unto themselves. However, the more I thought about it, I realized that the real importance of what is going on with the next generation of adults is that they are the ones that will keep the U.S. competitive in the global marketplace and keep the U.S. able to provide its citizens with a quality of life second to none. This chapter, about the United States losing its role as world leader is the appropriate place for a discussion of the massive charade going on in our raising of the next generation.

Earlier in the chapter I presented some evidence that something is broken in our educational system. It is inevitable that we will lose our competitive edge since the young people we are educating do not score even in the top ten of countries much less near the top. There is another component in addition to education that will determine how well prepared the next generation will be to ensure that the United States keeps pace in a global economy. It does not involve an objective measure of test scores but instead is about the "warm and fuzzies." How well prepared psychologically will the next generation be to handle the challenges of global competitiveness?

Today's educational system is far different than it was when the generation that made us number 1 was educated. Similarly the way children are raised is far different today than it was. Insight into the mindset, education, and emotional toughness of the generation that will be staring at each other through a gunsight is provided by a Chinese woman who is a professor at Yale Law School and wrote a book, *Battle Hymn of the Tiger Mother* published in early 2011. The book is a lightning rod for every issue currently debated about what has happened to the educational system and parenting that made the United States what it was and is creating what it will become. Here are some quotes from an essay she wrote in the *Wall Street Journal*, 1/8/11, that reflects the ideas in her book.

"There are tons of studies out there showing marked and quantifiable differences between Chinese and Westerners when it comes to parenting. In one study of 50 Western American mothers and 48 Chinese immigrant mothers, almost 70% of the Western mothers said either that 'stressing academic success is not good for children' or that 'parents need to foster the idea that learning is fun.' By contrast, roughly 0% of the Chinese mothers felt the same way."

"Other studies indicate that compared to Western parents, Chinese parents spend approximately 10 times as long everyday drilling academic activities with their children. By contrast, Western kids are more likely to participate in sports teams."

"When I was extremely disrespectful to my mother, my father angrily called me 'garbage' in our native Hokkien dialect....I felt terrible and deeply ashamed...But it did not damage my self-esteem or anything like that....As an adult, I once did the same thing to Sophia (her daughter), calling her garbage...When I mentioned that I had done this at a dinner party, I was immediately ostracized."

"Chinese mothers can say to their daughters, 'Hey fatty—lose some weight.' By contrast, Western parents have to tiptoe around the issue."

"Western parents are extremely anxious about their children's self-esteem. They worry about how their children will feel if they fail at something, and they constantly try to reassure their children about how good they are notwithstanding a mediocre performance on a test or at a recital. In other words, Western parents are concerned about their children's psyches." " 'Oh no, not this' I said rolling my eyes. 'Everyone is special in their special own way,' I mimicked sarcastically. 'Even losers are special in their own special way.'"

Ms. Chua sums up in the concluding paragraph of the essay, "Western parents try to respect their children's individuality, encouraging them to pursue their true passions, supporting their choices and providing positive reinforcement and a nurturing environment. By contrast, the Chinese believe that the best way to protect their children is by preparing them for the future, letting them see what they're capable of, and arming them with skills, work habits and inner confidence that no one can ever take away."

Now let us take a look at some of the details of the facts summarized earlier in this chapter. The top five countries in 15 year olds reading abilities are Shanghai, China; South Korea; Finland; Hong Kong, China; and Singapore, the United States is 17th. In math abilities, Shanghai China; Singapore; Hong Kong, China; South Korea; and Taiwan, China; with the United States coming in 31st. In science, Shanghai, China; Finland; Hong Kong, China; Singapore; and Japan; with the United States 23.

It should be obvious that the United States is on a very different track from many countries. Education is no longer a top priority. I say this because putting all the bulls__t aside, if it were we would take the steps to change the miserable performance of our students. It is not hard, it just takes the will to confront and punish failure instead of rewarding losers and providing them with a giant book of excuses to choose from as bogus explanations for their failures.

In China, children attend school 41 more days a year than they do in the United States and it is not only about Asia. France for example, the core high school curriculum such as math, science, geography, literature and writing comprises two and half times as many hours as it does in the U.S. A recent study by the Kaiser Family Foundation found that American children spend 53 hours per week using "entertainment media" and only 39 hours in school. As reported in *The Economist*, 1/1/11, a Mr. Smith who runs a multi-level marketing company in China ran afoul of the authorities when he tried to set up interviews with students as potential employees, the article states, "Mr Smith's firm had crossed an invisible line. 'I think it's a Confucian thing' he muses. Chinese people place an immense value on education, and abhor anything that might distract students from their books. Mr. Smith's firm now steers clear of students."

It is clear that our educational system is broken. We set one standard of performance for an educational system with a tremendous diversity of students. We spend enormous resources as if every student can learn trigonometry, write creatively, and possesses the same aptitude for abstract thinking. Not everyone can become an Einstein if only their parents built their self-esteem, fed them a nutritious breakfast, became involved with their homework, and they had a great teacher. Once upon a time, without even bothering with such things, our educational system was doing just fine. What changed, the evidence is clear, the student body changed.

Simply throwing more and more money into the educational system has made little progress. Indeed in the beginning of the big push to raise performance there probably were some serious deficiencies that did not allow any one individual to perform to the height of their potential, but it did not take long to fix that problem. In recent years very little improvement in performance has occurred even with an increase in both government and private funds. Time to stop and reevaluate. Borrowing a terrific phrase from the Marines recruitment advertisement, "Be all that you can be," perhaps a variation explicates one of the problems with our "affirmative action" driven education system as well as pointing out just how well targeted is the message, "Be all that you can be instead of being forced to become what you can't."

What I find amazing is the number of reports done by groups with some relationship to the Congress describing the gap between the education and training of this country's youth and the skills needed by our country's employers. Along with some of the studies previously cited in this Chapter is one by the Senate's own Small Business Entrepreneurship Committee which describes how the directors of the Small Business Administration's regional offices again and again point to the problem of finding qualified workers as to why there are so many unfilled job openings in a time of high employment. With their own study teams finding just how pointless is all this money being spent trying to get people to do what they simply cannot, you would think Congress would realize what a charade it all is. Certainly it isn't that they are spending the money for the sake of appealing to a voting bloc, nah, they wouldn't do that.

IBM has gotten fed-up with their inability to hire enough properly educated and vocationally trained people. Funded by IBM, New York City will open what is being called a P-tech school. It is a six year high school located in an underprivileged neighborhood focused on a traditional high-school core curriculum along with training specific for a career with computers. Graduates get an automatic job interview at IBM. Rashid David, the principle of the new school describes the program as having, "the power to change generations," and refers to the graduates "have serious job skills and will be first in line for job opportunities."

It is not just IBM that has become so fed up with our educational system that they have stepped in to create a school to do it right. The National Association of Manufacturers, driven by its members frustration in not finding sufficiently skilled employees is collaborating with the Gates Foundation to work with community colleges to turn out graduates with the skills needed to fill these job openings. It was a similar program in South Carolina that convinced BMW to open a manufacturing plant in that state. In fact, BMW is involved in designing the curriculum at a local community college. The Chicago Manufacturing Renaissance Council created a school, Austin Polytechnical Academy in a poor neighborhood to give high school students skills needed for manufacturing jobs.

Why is our educational system condemning some students to four years of hell as they try to master subjects they simply cannot master no matter how nutritious a breakfast they eat? Is it any wonder that most end up dropping out and getting in trouble? Why has it taken industry to step in and create its own schools to turn these folks into productive citizens?

I will tell you why, and it is a dirty little secret that will now be revealed, you heard it here first folks. *Science* magazine is one of the most prestigious scientific publications in the world. It is the publication of the American Association for the Advancement of Science. It might be thought of as the *Scientific American* for scientists where only the best papers on the most interesting of subjects get published. In addition to publishing scientific papers, its front section has book reviews, updates on the comings and goings in the world of science, and a lead editorial.

In the June 24, 2011 issue, the Editorial, "Education Is Not a Race" was by the Dean of the Stanford University School of Education. Here are a few quotes from her discussion of the concept of using standards to measure educational effectiveness: "generating debilitating anxiety and encouraging a culture of cheating, this competition takes the joy out of learning." "offer ample opportunities for students to get extra help; make sure that at least one adult is paying attention to every student's emotional needs…survey students regularly on the sources of their stress." "if students have multiple opportunities to earn a good grade (by rewriting papers or retaking tests)"

I simply could not believe that in the same neighborhood as Stanford University is Sand Hill Road, the street that is the "mecca" of venture capital in the United States. As I read the Dean's Editorial I wondered if these principles of attending to "debilitating anxiety," "blaming the system and not the person who cheats," and focusing on "emotional needs" had been applied to the innovation and economic development of our new high-tech companies that have made us the envy of the world, where we are truly still number #1, would any of that happened? Can you imagine running a company and having the CEO relate to the employees in that fashion? How about a new position, CENO, chief emotional needs officer? This is the Dean, the head of Stanford's education department espousing the philosophies that have destroyed our educational system. Any wonder we are not in the top ten in any measure of High School education amongst the developed countries of the world. The Ivory Tower of the University is now more detached from ground level than ever.

Hah, I should not be so harsh, since she provided me with a perfect segue into a major issue that has taken over the attitudes in our country not just in education but in regards to raising the next generation of folks who will create our country's destiny. Emotion. Animals are very emotional, they fight for dominance, fight over food resources, the males fight for the right to have sex with the females, they fight over territories and on and on. These are animals driven by their instincts, they have no choice about acting this way, stimulus followed by response, it is in their nature.

Our human emotional experiences are simply the expression of the instinctual drives we have inherited from our animal ancestors. As we humans have used our intellects and our abilities to control our emotional responses for the sake of the greater good, we have been able gradually over the centuries come to live harmoniously in larger and larger groups. Families merged into tribes, tribes into cities, cities into states, and states into countries. If we had not learned how to suppress our emotions we could never have had the energy and time to grow abundant crops, raise large numbers of animals for food, and develop commerce to support growing populations, we would still be living like animals. There can be no question that the success of any one individual in making their way through life, as well as to be able to live together in groups, is putting our emotional responses in second place to the acts required to achieve our goals.

In dramatic contrast to this unambiguous relationship between the need to learn to control our emotions as we grow from childhood to adulthood in order to achieve our goals, is the "zeitgeist" of our current culture. The academic educational establishment has been pushing into the educational system a shift of focus to the recognition and celebration of the individual's emotional experience. It is the centerpiece of the Dean's Editorial. It is the centerpiece of the self-esteem movement. It is a recipe for disaster.

This new wave of putting children's emotions at the head of the line is a common thread through so much of our twenty-first century culture. I see the dramatic rise of drug abuse amongst our youth, both legal in the form of antidepressants and antianxiety drugs, as well as the illegal drugs as an attempt by the immature person to quell their storms of emotions. No wonder since they are actually encouraged to let these emotions flourish for which they are ill-prepared to cope. Fueled by the University-level academic community as so perfectly shown by the Stanford Deans comments, our K-12 schools are encouraged to help students give expression to their emotions and educational programs are planned to minimize the challenges to their emotional sensitivities. They never have to learn to cope with emotions, to repress them and get on with the job at hand. Competition is seen as evil.

The central core of a young person's education is to prepare them for their responsibilities of adulthood. Adulthood where they will need to provide for themselves and their families. An adulthood where they will have to time and time again suppress their own emotional feelings for the sake of accomplishing their goals which requires that they interact productively with other people. The celebration of emotions is counterproductive to accomplishment.

Okay, I expect a lot of you out there are getting irritated by my "America bashing." Well, hell, don't take it from me, instead how about from someone who represents all that is AMERICA, a former rodeo champion bull rider. It seems that these days on the world stage we are not even number 1 in bull riding. In fact, in the past few years the Brazilians have taken over the top 5 places in America's own rankings of professional bull riders. One of our best is Dustin Elliot. He says the reason Americans have fallen behind is, "The secret is dedication. We're Americans, we're lazy, that's the bottom line—we sleep in. I hate going to the gym its boring." A bull rider for Christ's sake, not some Ph.D. like me saying it. I mean John Wayne, Clint Eastwood and all that real 'Merican tough guy cowboy stuff.

I would like to make the case that we are not only failing to educate students for the competitive world they will face as adults in terms of a core curriculum but we are doing them a severe disservice by also not preparing them for the psychological challenges they will face in the future. In the business world there are no "do-overs," nor are there "grief counselors" after you are fired. In fact, we are actually harming our young people by encouraging them to get in touch with their feelings and to give full expression to their emotions.

In fact, flooding the schools with "grief counselors" as seems the standard routine after a "bad" event may actually be taking those who are just fine in handling such trauma and teaching them the expectation to get all weirded out after such an event. It was following such an event at a high school that one of the networks interviewed a student who complained that a grief counselor would not leave him alone. He described that what happened was sad, but that he wasn't "too upset or anything," but she just would not believe him. A psychiatrist, Charles Nemeroff who studies people's responses to trauma commented on the findings after the Japanese earthquake and tsunami that about 50% made it through fine without support groups thanks to their genetics, and that in fact too much help can actually hurt.

In a business meeting, conflict often occurs and is in fact essential to any productive meeting where decisions must be made. If everyone expressed their feelings, can you imagine? Yet that is the psychological lifestyle with which our modern educational establishment is infecting our next generation. The manufacturers of antianxiety medications are loving it. In fact we should be teaching our children coping skills for minimizing the impact of the emotional traumas they are sure to meet when they leave the relatively stress free world of childhood for the dramatically more stressful world of adulthood. As Freud pointed out, a little emotional repression, through the process of sublimation, can go a long way to fueling some mighty grand achievements. The psychic energy generated by interpersonal conflict in a business meeting is the source of drive that makes us creative and work to finding just the right solution. Better that route than just fuming and having a meltdown.

The word "diversity" will be present in any speech given by any educator, practicing or academic, as well as politician looking for votes within one of our ethnic minorities. They will tout the importance of opening our education system so that anyone from any background can find success. Yet this is really one of if not the biggest charades of all in our educational system. What they mean when they say diversity is to limit the word to mean ethnicity and/or skin color and that is all. They shut the door on comprehensive diversity. Diversity of talents, abilities, and potential. Nope that diversity I guess does not exist.

I have still not given up the dream of replacing Mickey Mantle as the next great Yankee centerfielder. In second place for me is to become a Formula One World Champion racing driver. I was ready to commit myself to 24 hours a day, for as many days or years it would take. I would have signed up for that commitment at any age. Yet certain realities have intruded. In the case of being a baseball player I was afflicted in my early twenties with a form of arthritis that in retrospect was probably presaged by the variety of joint injuries going as far back as my little league days. As far as racing driver I am severely vulnerable to motion sickness. It was in my mid-sixties that just because I was willing to part with the money I actually had an opportunity to drive a Formula One car. After two laps I had to come in, trying to control a rocket ship accelerating from 60-120 mph in 2.5 seconds much less rounding a curve well over a hundred m.p.h. with tires on the edge of sliding off the track and while ready to puke meant it was time to let reality intrude.

Now, no one would argue that the arthritis and motion sickness were physical causes that meant I could never realize my dreams. No different from the guy 5' 10" wanting to become the next great Laker center. No matter how nutritious a breakfast, parental support, hours of practice, it just ain't going to happen. Our brain is what learns. All my life I have enjoyed music and been very visual. My parents valued such things far more than baseball or racecar driving. As a child I was given every opportunity to learn painting and play a musical instrument.

The results were was pathetic. Even late in life I have tried banjo and harmonica, but it was again simply pathetic. My brain just does not have the talent for such an activity. It also probably did not have the athletics talents of eye-hand coordination etc. to become either a great ball player or race car driver, although....

Diversity means more than skin color and ethnicity. It is not true that as so many love to say that want you to buy their book, DVD, or vote for them: "You can become anything you want to be." It is a charade. Our brain is what learns. It is just as much a part of our body's physical characteristics as is my arthritis and motion sickness or the growth hormone that made the guy dreaming of becoming an NBA center only 5' 10". We have different brains that have different abilities to learn different things. When our educational system fully accepts the true meaning of diversity as in talents, skills, abilities, and potential we can cut our education spending in half and produce better results instead of wasting our time and money trying to get everyone to match one set of standards. Much less save those who cannot pass a set of tests for only certain abilities years of torment from failure that is truly no fault of their own short of getting a brain transplant. In some cases, trigonomentry just ain't going to happen. We have been hard at it for forty years, why won't we just accept what the facts tell us?

The rapid increase in the self-medication of our young people through "recreational" drugs as well as the prescribed medications such as antianxiety and antidepressant pills is all we need to know to realize that something is terribly wrong with the way we are raising our children, over and above book learning. Our young people are emotionally disturbed and deal with it by using drugs to mellow themselves out. The finger of blame must point to the shift that occurred in the last twenty years or so to the way we have taught our young people to cope with the emotions that naturally occur in responses to the comings and goings of success and failure in their lives.

Once upon a time, as the child grew, they were taught not to give vent to every emotion they felt. One cannot get along in a lawful society if a person acted out upon every anger they ever felt toward another person. Making one's way from childhood to adulthood, especially in any venue that requires interaction with another human being, is dependent on suppressing one's emotions.

Yet, today that training is not just absent, the current pressure coming out of the educational and psychology establishment is just the opposite. For today's educational establishment emotions are to be encouraged and catered to, a sure recipe for anxiety and depression. It is a far more subtle aspect of the decline of the United States than a number on a test, but equally as destructive.

So here we are, the first decade of the twenty-first century has passed. The United States thanks to Russia's decline was for a while alone at the top, the clear number 1. Admired and respected by many other countries. Yet today, it is a very fragile position. The evidence of our decline is all around us, from our debt-rating being lowered for the first time in our country's history, to our obvious educational failure, and our inability to do anything about a health care system that has run amok in outrageous costs for second-rate care.

Of the BRIC countries that are competing to join us at the top or relegate us to second place, it is China that poses the most realistic threat. It is currently an economic threat but will by the inexorability of the process be a military threat as well. After all that has gone on through two great World Wars and one great Cold War, one would hope that military conflict would be a thing of a past. However, with five countries competing for a zero sum game of economic growth and its inevitable competition for market share and natural resources across national boundaries, it is unrealistic to think that weapons will never be fired in the support of economic conquest.

Our ability to win this struggle is primarily dependent upon our ability to develop one generation after another of future citizens that are up to the task. Currently it is clear that our education system is not up to the task. A top priority for our future. However, if our current political climate remains, it is hard to be optimistic, some games of charades go on for so long, the people playing them forget and think it is a true reality. There are things that would have to be said and decisions that would have to be made that could only happen if the charades come to halt.

It was coming across a chart by the International Monetary Fund ranking the world's 33 "advanced economies" on nine different factors into three categories, best, worst, and worst of the worst that seeing these rankings made me truly feel sick to my stomach. The United States ranked worst of the worst on three categories, worst on two, and amongst the best on three. Not number one on anything. Just thinking about where we once were and where we now are is profoundly disturbing.

The World Economic Forum in Fall of 2011 released a ranking of the world's most competitive economies based upon economic data and a survey of 15,000 business executives. We were placed fifth, behind Switzerland, Singapore,

Sweden and Finland with a commentary of "escalating weaknesses." We have the people, the money, the everything that if it were being managed appropriately we should be #1 on almost everything. Something truly truly wrong is going on. It is especially tragic when one hears so many politicians telling their all-to-believing listeners how great we are. Wake up folks!

After writing this chapter, I came across an article, 8/27/11, in *The Economist* magazine, "Mexico's Economy." I was bit startled. The article was about why Mexico's economy has been stagnant for the past decade and had an eerie similarity to much of what this book described as responsible for the stagnation of the United States

Before the emergence of the BRIC countries, evidently economists had Mexico pegged as the next great economic miracle, yet it never happened. Mexico's population is richer than any of the BRIC countries except for Russia and better educated, more industrialized, and more business-friendly than Brazil. In describing what happened to keep Mexico from realizing the growth that was expected a decade ago, the lawlessness as evidenced by the drug-cartel problem was front and center as well as the fact that a small group of extraordinarily wealthy business owners also own the politicians. Of course no such thing exists in America, at least not on the face of it unless you take into account the endemic corruption that we call lobbying and campaign contributions. President Eisenhower did warn the country about the emergence of a controlling "military industrial complex."

To quote the end of the article about Mexico: "The price of political deadlock is rising. A failure to raise taxes…Lack of reform risks condemning Mexico to stagnate with America. As politicians start campaigning for next years presidential election, they should ignore the business lobbyists…they can surely be persuaded to back it."

Prior to writing these last three paragraphs, the last words of this chapter were, "Wake up folks!" Could it be that decades down the road *The Economist* could have a nostalgic article about the once great country, the United States and why it stagnated as the BRIC countries outdid us that would also end with the same message to us.

XII. THE ACADEMY AWARDS OF CHARADES

CHARADES

1, Richard Nixon: "I am not a crook"

2, Bill Clinton: "I did not have sex with that woman"

3, Hillary Clinton: paraphrase after the Monica Lewinsky story broke: "I was shocked to learn that my husband would ever have an affair"

4, All the politicians who spoke so vehemently against the stimulus packages but then held ceremonies with their local constituents as they handed over the stimulus checks.

5, Dr. Drew Pinsky: For showing all those young aspiring celebrities that addiction is a sure-fire path to stardom. Look up "narcissism" and "egomaniac" in your Freud, Dr.Drew.

6, Entertainment producers who ban showing smoking in their productions, yet celebrate and portray as stars morbidly obese people, such as the star of the movie, Precious.

7, United States military for lying to Pat Tillman's family and to the American people about the real reason for his death, friendly fire.

8, Oklahoma with a plaque of the Ten Commandments on its Capitol grounds ranks 10th in the country for watching porn.

9, The United States Government soon after the bank-rescue following the financial meltdown ended up owning 27% of Citibank. At a shareholders meeting, a proposal was put up for a vote that would have brought greater transparency to Citi's holdings of CDO-derivatives, one of the financial instruments at the center of the meltdown. The United States government voted its shares against bringing transparency.

10, Lindsey Graham, a conservative Congressman wants to change the Constitution so children of immigrants born in the U.S. do not automatically get citizenship. Yet historically, conservatives have been the leaders against changing the Constitution based on temporal issues, the concept of a "living" Constitution.

11, The reality TV shows about adventurers risking life and limb and facing starvation even though they are accompanied by a producer, soundman, and cameraman who help set-up these shots.

12, All that fine-print on the bottom of your TV screens during commercials, especially the ones for medications, that are so small they are impossible to read. They are not there by accident, but by law, yet no one in charge of such things seems to care they cannot be read.

14, House Representative Joe Walsh during the debt ceiling debate, "I won't place one more dollar of debt on the backs of my kids." Eight months earlier his ex-wife had filed suit against him for $117, 347 in back child support.

16, Major League Baseball for calling their championship series the World Series while excluding teams from many countries that stand a chance of beating the Major League's best.

17, The Congressional hearings on the use of steroids when questioning Roger Clemens split in the character of their questions, supportive or antagonistic, exactly along party lines. On political issues maybe one makes the case of partisanship because after all the two parties represent two different approaches to government. But on the use of steroids in baseball? It is hard to be optimistic.

ANTI-CHARADE AWARDS

1, Pill Tillman: Gave up multimillions of dollars of an NFL career to serve his country, much less also giving up his life.

2, Joseph de Maistre who described the greatest charade of all when he said: "Every nation has the government it deserves, later paraphrased as: "In a Democracy, the people get the government they deserve." Quit bitching people the government is you.

3, On October 14, 2010, Joe Kernan one of the terrific anchors on CNBC said knowingly on-air to the other anchors, "You think I believe what I read on the teleprompter." Possibly referring to the just released SEC investigation of itself that concluded politics did not influence its investigation of Goldman Sachs.

4, Allen Simpson and Erskine Bowles who took on the job of putting together a bipartisan package of cutting government spending and reorganizing our tax code to increase revenue. A major undertaking that took 6 months and ended with a report on December 1, 2010. The great deficit reduction debacle that ended with the Standard Poors' downgrade of August 2011 occurred as if Simpson and Bowles never existed.

5, William Black, a lawyer with years of academic and government service was put in charge of prosecutions in the Savings and Loan meltdown of the late 1980s. He brought about 1000 criminal prosecutions involving illegal acts that caused the meltdown. The head of it all, Charles Keating, went to jail for 4 and 1/2 Years. So far no, zero, zip criminal prosecutions have been brought over the financial meltdown of 2008 that made the Savings and Loan failures look like small change.

6, Little League for holding a true World Series

XIII. WILL IT EVER STOP?

OUR FUTURE HANGS

IN THE BALANCE

In this last chapter, I would like to remind you of some of the most egregious and destructive charades described in the previous chapters and add a few new highlights to them. Things are going seriously wrong in the United States. What I find most disturbing is that what is really going on is hidden by this comprehensive game of charades being played by Wall Street, the media, and politicians on the American people. Since many of these institutions have a mutual self-interest in keeping these charades alive-and-well it is hard for me to be optimistic for the future. Hopefully by exposing these games for what they really are, awareness will bring a refusal to play-along from the American public when they make investment decisions, decide what news to follow, and go to the ballot box.

The 2008 meltdown, a cataclysm for this country was caused by a regulatory failure on Wall Street. To fix things, the Dodd-Frank bill was enacted amidst great media fanfare and soliloquies from the actors in that great theater of Congressional hearings Dodd Frank is now all but neutered and the same bets by investment banks on the same types of very risky securities will continue to happen. A GRAND CHARADE AMONGST GRAND CHARADES! As proof, now that final language is being written, at the end this chapter is a series of headlines and quotes from articles in the Wall Street Journal.

The War on Drugs is certainly a war typical of the ones America seems to fight these days. Relative to the number of local folks who are killed in the countries in which these wars are fought, very few Americans have died. In addition, a lot of money has been spent. Perhaps the greatest charade of our War on Drugs is that when a drunk kills someone with their car or a murderer uses a gun, the United States looks for responsibility to the consumer of the alcohol and driver of the car as well as the person who pulled the trigger as the criminal. The maker of the booze, car, and gun are never considered culpable. Yet in the WOD, it seems that the United States main effort is to hold the producers and distributors of the drugs culpable and not the users. Imagine if everyone who smoked marijuana in the United States was brought to trial?

Another part of the WOD charade is that the violence south of the border is really just between the criminal gangs so "it couldn't happen to nicer guys and the law-abiding citizens are unaffected." Maybe in the beginning, but these days, as in August of 2011, a small casino got caught in the crossfire. A casino mostly used by middle aged ladies playing bingo. Over 50 of them were killed, mostly by being burned to death in a drug-gang related episode.

Monterrey is Mexico's center of industry, its richest city. In July of 2011 over twenty people were killed in a bar that was laced with machine gun fire since at times drug deals took place in the bar. As described in a Los Angeles Times article, July 10, 2011, "The drug violence has turned it into something more like a Wild West outpost, with gun battles in the street, brazen kidnappings and frequent slayings of police officers..." All because we will not hold the consumers of marijuana in the United States liable for their actions or God forbid, legalize what everyone does anyway.

The War on Drugs is also another example of one of these "whack-a-mole" games. First we worked out on the drug producers in Peru and Bolivia then they moved to Columbia, after Columbia to Mexico. Now that they are being harassed in Mexico, guess where they have now gone. The chickens ladies and gentlemen are coming home to roost with the cartel's marijuana plantations and their methamphetamine labs now in the United States.

Without a doubt, next to Washington the most powerful institution in the United States is the media. They determine what we know. Not just the facts but what we care about. Short of what we see and hear with our own eyes and ears, all that occupies our minds is put there by the media. As described in the chapter about the media, in keeping with their critical role in our lives, one would hope the media would accept their responsibility, especially in the news, to provide us with a reasonably fair and accurate view of the events occurring around the world. I am sure we would all agree that over the past few decades, the news has drifted more and more towards entertainment, leading to the coining of the new term, "nonfiction entertainment."

The founder of this trend recently passed away. Some lines from his obituary in the February 10th, 2010 Wall Street Journal are illuminating: "Frank Magid helped re-imagine television news as a form of entertainment...introduced flashy, fast-paced local news read from teleprompters by coifed anchor teams who bantered with their fellow broadcasters... 'happy talk'...increased audience and advertising revenue...profit centers rivaling prime-time programming. Walter Cronkite is quoted, "Any real newsman knows that sort of stuff is balderdash" " Magid claimed he was only giving the people what they wanted...Charles Kuralt told of traveling the country and watching local news, 'My overwhelming impression is of hair.'"

Of course people have the ability to change the channel or turn off the TV. However, there comes a time when we go into the voting booth and place a vote that determines the future of our country. A vote based upon information we obtain from the media. It would be nice if the electorate were informed by the media on something other than an "if it bleeds it leads" basis.

In terms of just outright pure charade with no redeeming features is the "Student Athlete." The relevant chapter describes it in some detail. It has become clear from exposé after exposé that the major sports teams at athletic powerhouses such as Ohio State and USC in terms of violating the NCAA's rules are simply criminal enterprises. One recent episode at the University of Miami sums it all up.

The former Ponzi scheme operator, Nevin Shapiro, is now serving a 20 year sentence. Mr. Shapiro for a decade prior to wearing striped pajamas had been an avid booster of Miami's football team. It seems he was not getting the kind of attention he thought he deserved so now in a cage, he is singing like a canary. Cars, hookers, booze, payments to family members and just the usual college booster stuff we have come to expect goes on in major college sports. Mr. Shapiro is the poster boy for the charade of "student athlete." Hard for the school to say "never happened" when the guy who did it is doing the singing. The NCAA investigation is still ongoing. Miami may be only the second team to receive the NCAA's harshest penalty known as the "death sentence." So far, much of Miami's starting team have received suspensions from a few games to the whole season, and many have received individual fines related to the amount of money they received from Mr. Shapiro.

The only comprehensive answer is a minor league system that has been so productive for baseball but in the case of football and basketball it would consist of teams still branded with the University name but owned by NFL or NBA teams. It frees athletes to be athletes and students to be students. No more athlete being followed around by paid "minders" to make sure they attend class. One could even imagine athletes who wanted to pick up a few credits as a hedge for their future given free tuition. SMU could be a farm team of the Dallas Cowboys or Miami a farm team of the Miami Dolphins. A true win win for everyone, the players, the schools and the NFL.

On the theme of scoundrels, how about those fine fellows on Wall Street. Yes sir young man, you seem like a fine candidate for the job of investment banker, but first to show us you have the right stuff, sell your mother on the street. The chapter about Wall Street describes the seemingly species-typical trait of investment bankers to care about no one other than themselves and to push the law some time to its limits and sometimes over the limits in the pursuit of filling their own bank account. Mind you this is done through earning commissions while convincing investors to put their money in deals in which they are told they cannot lose. How about those mortgage back securities? Slam Dunk!

One specific aspect of the investment banking business, the role of the stock analyst, really does show just what a charade the whole damn institution is. Recall that when the tech-bubble burst in 1999, everyone in government and the media threw up their hands in shock when it came out that the stock analysts who write the research reports on individual companies are really not at all analysts, but really just shills for the companies that are clients of the investment bank for which they work.

Truly pathetic was the shock displayed on CNBC by their talking heads who would prominently feature these analysts on their show. They knew what these folks are up to but said nothing. Well how about people investing their kid's college money based upon these analysts promoting garbage companies on the financial news shows. Shocked I tell you, shocked, as these hundred-dollar stocks plummeted to a few bucks a share. Ratings up, advertising revenue up, job well done by one and all. Well kid, how about that night school?

A recently highly publicized IPO was for LinkedIn. The research analysts working for the banks that managed the IPO all came out with glowing reports for the stock issued at $45/share. These reports were not just the *quid pro quo* for LinkedIn choosing them for the IPO but also in the hope of earning future investment banking business. For example, Bank of America's analyst valued the stock a strong buy with a target price of $92/share. UBS came out with the number of $90/share. Yet analysts not affiliated with the IPO rated the stock at best a "hold" and for most a "sell." Morningstar, a gold standard of stock research not related to an investment bank gave a sell rating to the stock and said the company's business "doesn't justify the lofty valuation." An article in the Wall Street Journal commented, "Some of the valuation rationales are pretzel-like twists of logic. Remind anyone of 1999?"

A web site with an interesting perspective one never ever sees in the mainstream media [who would come on the shows if the talking heads challenged them to stop the con and tell the truth?], but one that does base its conclusions on the hard facts is www.guerillastocktrading.com. In an article in August of 2011 it made a list of some gems about Wall Street's stock analysts, here are a few:

"In August 2001, the acting director of the SEC testified before Congress that nearly all major Wall Street firms were guilty of lying to small traders and investors like you and I."

"A year later, the attorney general of New York Elliot Spitzer said that institutions engaged in secret operations that were "an outrageous betrayal of [investors trust] and a shocking abuse of the system, perverted to produce greater revenues for the firm."

"Before the 1990s most stock analysts made their money via a flat salary. In the 1990s that changed to most of their compensation coming from bonuses directly linked to their ability to promote, and sell, a corporate client's stock."

"Not one major firm on Wall Street tied its analysts compensation to their actual track record in picking stocks. Analysts could be wrong once, wrong twice, wrong a hundred times, and they'd still earn huge bonuses, as long as they continued to recommend and sell the shares of their corporate clients."

And last but not least is one that should make any private investor's blood run cold or an employee with their 401K plan in their employer's stock:

"In 2001, well before the Enron collapse, Chung Wu, an analyst at UBS Paine Webber, sent an e-mail to Enron employees warning them that holding the company's stock—then worth almost $37 a share—could cost them "a fortune." The e-mail enraged Enron executives, who complained to UBS Paine Webber. Chung Wu was fired. UBS PaineWebber quickly issued a new buy recommendation [on Enron], and the matter was secretly covered up. Three months later, Enron shares were selling for less than 25 cents."

Any more questions about what to do with your retirement plan, or money saved for your kids education? How about that Wall Street? How about CNBC cheering all this along to keep "John Q. Public" tuned in? A mutuality of self-interest and a grand charade, you betcha!

On the subject of pure naked selfish greed off the backs of others, now is a great time for a brief review of one of the most critical issues in our debate over how to control the costs of medicine. In the chapter about health care costs, it focused on several issues, one of which was the interaction between how much a medicine costs and how effective it was in comparison with other medications.

In that chapter, mention was made of a drug called Avastin, known to be effective for specific types of cancer and not effective for others. A group of citizens with breast cancer egged on by the company making Avastin, along with the company's lobbyists pushed for "fast-track" approvals of Avastin for breast cancer.

It became more politics than medical science. Avastin was in fact tested and it failed dismally. It was far less effective, if effective at all compared with the standard of care, Taxol, which is also by the way far cheaper. Moreover, Avastin caused several deaths from one of its side-effects. The FDA advisory panel voted 12-1 against approval for breast cancer. Avastin costs about $90,000 for one year of treatment. Due to lobbying efforts and Medicare's legislated inability to use a comparison of one drug against another for effectiveness, doctors interested in earning those kickbacks from drug companies will still be prescribing it and Medicare will continue to pay $90,000 per year for a course of treatment.

In an interview, 10/9/11, on CBS, Jeff Immelt President of GE and head of President Obama's job creation counsel, in commenting on a role for government in fostering innovation, said, "All of health care innovation has come out of NIH [National Institutes of Health, the source of taxpayer funded medical research]." So much for the argument used by drug companies to justify their extraordinarily high profit margins that they need these profits because of the costs of their research into new drugs. In fact, drug companies spend more on marketing and sales than they do on research and development thanks to taxpayer dollars paying for most of the real research.

So far, the only thing debated by the politicians on controlling health-care costs is shifting who pays, from the government programs to private insurers or vice versa. Then throw in the companies providing medical insurance to their employees, individuals who buy their own insurance and different levels of copays. The combinations are many, yet they do not address the real issues as previously described in the chapter on health care costs, the rampant run-away costs of all those charges that go into the costs of healthcare. The current debate is simply shifting around who pays the bill.

The main government source of payments for health care, Medicare, seems to have no interest in policing fraud. Recently, spurred by fraud exposed by others, a major investigation by the Senate's Finance Committee showed that the three largest billers to Medicare shifted how they provide services specifically to bilk Medicare out of as much money as possible. The panel's report concluded "examples of for-profit companies defrauding" the program at taxpayer's expense. Showing their outrage, the chairman of the committee, Max Baucus said, "the gaming of Medicare by these companies represents serious abuse of the home-health program." and Senator Grassley, "The federal government needs to fix the policy that lets Medicare money flow down the drain."

Perhaps we should elevate these senate reports to the same function as the theater of senate hearings. Since nothing substantive ever comes from them, their main purpose seems to be providing a structure for fatuous sound-bite pronouncement. Nothing has been done to the billion dollar corporations who pay bills for the reelection campaigns. However, lest the small guy make a mistake, as in the fellow from Goldman Sachs who got 8 years for stealing some computer code in contrast to the senior management who defrauded investors out of billions and have yet to be charged with anything. Believe it or not, the owner of a relatively small company providing mental health services just got fifty years for defrauding Medicare out of 205 million dollars.

Bribery, graft, and corruption, no sirreee, not in the good ol' U.S. of A. That only happens in all those other dirtbag countries, " you know Vern, where the people s__t in the streets." I betcha the folk who say things like that have countries like Pakistan in mind. Yep they know how to do it. In fact, their Washington lobbyists have been hard at work in Washington. The firm of Locke Lord Strategies is paid $75,000 a months to keep Pakistan's best interests in the minds of our Congressman. One of their partners says he is on the hill everyday talking to Congressman promoting their interests. Pakistan has paid their firm over $2,000,000 since 2008. Currently these daily trips are focused on convincing Congress that Pakistan really truly, scouts honor, had no idea that Bin Laden had been living just a few miles from their main military headquarters. Yup, seamless, bribery, graft and corruption just like back home morphing into lobbying right here in the good ol' U.S. of A.

Congress is just great, really every American no matter how rich or poor, their elected representatives are in Washington to look out for them. It seems almost trivial compared with Dodd-Frank or the War on Terror, but the issue of swimming pool drains shows just how blind is the eye of our lawmakers to how rich or poor are their constituents. Swimming pool drains have been known to be dangerous to small children who have drowned when caught in their suction. Complaints have been lodged for a decade or more. Yet it was not until the child of a hedge-fund megamillionaire and the granddaughter of a former Secretary of State were killed that the lobbyists for the swimming pool industry were defeated and a law put in place to mandate the use of child-safe drain covers.

Hey, how about all those "sound bites" about this or that scoundrel being found guilty by the SEC or other regulatory agencies and ordered to pay fines, our representatives hard at work punishing those who act in something other than our own best interests. Yup, you betcha, just another charade. For example, The Commodity Futures Trading Commission (CFTC) and the SEC since late 2005 have levied $12.3 billion in fines but only less than $8 billion was ever paid. In an attempt to better their record, these unpaid claims have been sent to the Treasury Department for collection, so far on SEC claims, $3million has been collected of $1.3 billion owed and for the CFTC claims, $1million out of $812 million has been collected. Budget crisis, what budget crisis?

The following is not a joke, while typing these paragraphs, a postal worker came to the door with a letter for me to sign that I received it. I owed $394.00 to the I.R.S. and since they had previously sent me a letter and I did not pay-up, I had ten days to pay or they were going to come and seize my property. This has its origins in my accountant having sent in the wrong form for some matter and I thought she had it all squared away two months ago. I just got off the phone with the I.R.S. and they said it was a mistake, to ignore the letter. I made a note of her name and her employee I.D. number. I wonder if I can find a lobbyist on Google.

Charities, goodness doing the research for that Chapter really was depressing. A recent book by Alex Perry, *Lifeblood,* describes his chronicling of philanthropist Raymond Chambers' work alongside the United Nations in trying to defeat the plague of malaria in sub-Saharan Africa through the distribution of hundreds of millions of fine-mesh bed-nets. Although Mr. Chambers and the United Nations tout this program as making a significant dent in malaria for the cost of only $10.00 per net, the author runs his own numbers and comes up with a figure around $3,500.00. per net per person. All this for a true 20% reduction in deaths. In the places where they work, that much money is a multiple of the peoples annual income.

Describing the high-profile charity of Oxfam, Mr. Perry says they use an "endless stream of speeches and press releases…I found it hard not to conclude that the aid world, or part of it, sees crisis as opportunities" in large part to provide themselves with a luxurious life-style while jetting around the world hyping up crises needed to raise money to support mostly themselves. Along the way some good is done but rarely anywhere near the results claimed.

As the last chapter of the book, let me end it by perhaps the most pernicious of all the charades, the "sound bite" charades used by politicians to trick Americans into thinking they are working on our behalf. There is no better example than the Dodd-Frank bill. The financial calamity of 2008 was the greatest shock to the U.S., economically or otherwise since the great depression. After the depression, Congress in 1933 passed the Glass-Steagall act to create the boundaries for just how much risk banks can take with their depositor's money. Since that is exactly what banks did with their depositor's money, take extraordinary risks, that caused the meltdown of 2008, how could that have happened? What happened is that in 1999 Congress under intense lobbying pressure from banks, repealed Glass-Steagall. Only our best interests in mind, yes indeedy.

After the 2008 calamity, Congress passed another bill to make sure it never happened again, the Dodd-Frank bill. Lobbyists decided not to wait 66 years before having it repealed, they went to work immediately before the final language of the bill could be written. A law professor decided to look into just who the peoples representatives really represent as the Dodd-Frank bill was being written. The professor found that in terms of face-to-face meetings with government officials involved in writing the bill, the score was 350 for people from the financial industry and 20 for just plain folk. Kinda makes the Pakistan's of the world look like amateur hour. Here is a chronological list of headlines from the *Wall Street Journal* and for some a quote from the underlying article about what happens to a bill after the politicians have given their sound bites for the peoples consumption:

2/24/10: <u>Attempt to Curb Risky Trading Hits Senate Wall</u>, "it [Dodd-Frank bill] has won support from several former Treasury secretaries but triggered a violent reaction on Wall Street."

6/24/10: <u>Negotiators Ease Finance Rules</u>, "Democrats are also considering exempting smaller payday lenders and check cashers from the new consumer-product agency's scrutiny." Recall that pool drain example about the little guy without a lobbyist working on their behalf. Who needs protection more than the folk who use payday lenders?

4/21/11: <u>Wall Street, Banks Press to Shape Dodd-Frank Rules</u>, "The documents show financial industry lobbyists are spending time with regulators…to roll back certain provisions, especially new limits on debit-card fees. The industry is working to influence…including sweeping ones for the nearly $583 trillion derivatives market." Recall from the chapter on Wall Street, it was the very risky derivatives market that used the mortgage backed securities as their basis that blew the whole thing up.

4/30/11: <u>Treasury Carves Rule Exemption</u>:

5/3/11: <u>Rule Over The Abuse Of IPOs Delayed</u>:

6/26/11: <u>Collateral Rules Criticized:</u> "Some law makers and financial firms are resisting rules…Dodd Frank law that could require banks to set aside more collateral when they make certain trades in the derivatives market."

7/30/11: <u>Financial Regulators Face Test Ahead of Deadline:</u> The Financial Stability Oversight Council created by Dodd Frank, warned in a report this week that money funds remain vulnerable and could exacerbate financial shocks.

8/22/11: <u>Taking a Bite Out of 'Volcker', Draft Proposal of Namesake Rule Would Allow Banks to Make Bets Using Their Own Capital:</u> "In effect, that opens the door for banks to make all manner of bets on the market." "If you can do portfolio hedging, that gives you a license to do pretty much anything."

Dylan Ratigan, a talking head of MSNBC said on 8/9/11: "Thousands of lobbyists have descended on Washington, Dodd-Frank will be a shell." Same issue another perspective, Texas Congressman Lloyd Doggett referring to why it is so hard for Congress to pass effective legislation of Wall Street: "We can't write a law that their lawyers can't get around." Write a rule, lawyers find a way around, change rule, lawyers find a way around it, "whack-a-mole."

The Epilogue that follows this chapter is named that for lack of a better name, but is pretty important to the theme of the book and for you the reader not to get the wrong impression of my "political" views. Yes, I have been critical of the country, at times it was even painful to have to put on paper what I have, but facts are facts. So if you have made it this far, I hope you will read the Epilogue so you will not dismiss this material by labeling me a Yankee or Red Sox fan.

XIV. EPILOGUE

There are two main philosophies that have allowed our country to become as great in so many ways as it has become. The primary one is the concept of a meritocracy and the secondary one is the concept of free-market capitalism.

A meritocracy is another way of stating the Darwinian principle of the survival of the fittest. In a meritocracy, those with the greatest inborn talents (this includes self-discipline) and learned skills will win the competition for whichever goal it is that they and others aspire. This means that the singers with talents for music and the self-discipline to learn and practice the skills needed to become a successful entertainer will be the stars who make big-bucks and whose music we get to enjoy. Similarly, entrepreneurs with inborn independent spirit, intellect, and self-discipline to acquire the skills needed to build a successful business will become very very rich and we will enjoy the quality of life provided by the products their companies develop. Great stuff. The taxes on the profits made by these companies as well as their employees income provides a safety net for the less fortunate.

Free market capitalism is really just another form of the Darwinian survival of the fittest. Economic prosperity brings the greatest good for the greatest number of people. Economic prosperity comes from companies being allowed, through providing goods that customers want, to make profits. These profits provide for additional economic expansion and just as described above the tax revenues generated provide a safety net for the less fortunate, national defense and infrastructure, etc. Companies with a business model that does not allow for self-sustaining profits should be allowed to fail.

However, that being said, we currently provide a quasi-socialist form of free market capitalism to certain industries in need of government support, for example ranching where the government provides functionally free feed for their cattle by grazing rights on public land, oil and gas drilling tax breaks, and utilities such as water, sewers, electricity, and natural gas where the government insures that almost all Americans have these services available at a reasonable price and of a reasonable quality. So far, in specific industries this variation on free-market capitalism seems to work well.

Two other products are so necessary to our citizens quality of life as well as to the future of our country that they too should be delivered with a certain standard of quality and at a reasonable price, just as for water and electricity.

They are health care and education. As described previously, the government tries to do this but fails miserably.

There is a danger in the philosophies of the meritocracy and free market capitalism. History has shown unambiguously that given free reign, businesses will take advantage of their customers. In some cases such as those described in previous chapters, oil drilling, coal mining, gas transmission, pharmaceutical industry, and investing, companies left to their own pursuit of maximizing profits will kill their customers and employees and defraud them of their life savings. Therefore, the public needs protection from the meritocracy and free market capitalism run amok.

We have laws of personal conduct that make certain actions by those unwilling to control themselves such as robbery and murder illegal. The same must also be true within the concept of free enterprise and a meritocracy. Just as there are those who try to make their way as traditional criminals so too are there those will try to make their way in business with practices that kill and maim both physically and economically.

If this were not true there would in fact be no need for regulatory control of business by the government. Most, if not all existing regulations came into being for one and only one reason, abuse by business, whether it is practices that led to the depression or pharmaceutical companies that made and sold drugs that did far more harm than good. So all you "anti-regulatory" folks out there, get real. Business abuse precedes regulation. Businesses have no one but themselves to blame. In fall of 2011, a judge in Montana awarded $43 million in penalties to families who had a member die from working in a mine where the company knew the asbestos dust was lethal. About 400 people lost their lives. How about airplanes? How about regulations governing the training of pilots and airworthiness standards?

The economic meltdown of 2008 was directly caused by a general antiregulatory posture of the Washington administration in place at the time and the removal by the previous administration of the Glass-Steagall bank regulations. Glass-Steagall was created in response to abuses that led to the depression, they were removed and business was at it again and not quite another depression, but very very close. If business did not full-well deserve them through their own actions, regulations would not exist. Get real folks.

Our culture has deteriorated. In the lyrics of popular songs the police are demeaned and the language is about threats of physical violence in general and most troubling about abuse against women in particular. The games that young people play on their electronic devices and even in real life are about violence and mayhem. From movies to television, violence is celebrated along with the characters who participate in it. Heroes fire off assault rifles and kill by the tens as if there are no consequences. Bad guys are at times celebrated for similar acts. Sexual violence is also celebrated. All of this occurs in prime time.

In general we are a free-market capitalist meritocracy. Capitalists have a right to throw anything they want out into the marketplace. If it sticks, meaning people buy it in sufficient quantities to make it profitable, then the marketplace has spoken. Television viewers have the right to vote with the channel selector. The sponsors who make shows profitable will notice your vote. Movie goers vote at the ticket office. If shows and movies are not watched, they will go away and if violent games not purchased they will have a similar fate. Just as the saying goes about in a democracy the public gets the government they deserve, it is also true that in free market capitalism a country gets the social culture it deserves. So no moaning and groaning, the culture is you.

It is education that has me most troubled for the future of our country. Our educational system has abandoned the meritocracy. As long as all have access to an equal education providing them with the opportunity to become whatever their inborn talents and learned skills allows them to become that is all that is needed. However, today the push is to remove a sense of competition, everyone gets a trophy. Nothing could be more destructive for our ability to survive in a year-by-year intensely more competitive global economy.

The bottom line: If we become mediocre as a country it will be because our educational system, the training ground for adults, has come to accept mediocrity as just fine as long as everyone still gets a trophy. There is little more that needs to be said.

www.ingramcontent.com/pod-product-compliance
Lightning Source LLC
Chambersburg PA
CBHW071453040426
42444CB00008B/1319